SOCIAL POLICY REVIEW 1988–9

Edited by **Maria Brenton**

Lecturer in Social Policy,
University of Wales, College of Cardiff

and

Clare Ungerson

Senior Lecturer in Social Policy,
University of Kent at Canterbury

Longman

Published by Longman Group UK Limited
6th Floor, Westgate House, The High, Harlow, Essex, CM20 1YR

First published 1989

British Library Cataloguing in Publication Data
Social policy review — [No. 1] —
1. Great Britain. Social policies
361.6′1′0941

ISBN 0-582-04617-3

ISBN 0-582-04617-3

Typeset by Kerrypress Ltd, Luton
Printed and bound in Great Britain by
Biddles Ltd, Guildford and King's Lynn

Contents

Contributors

Sally Baldwin	Director, Social Policy Research Unit, University of York.
Graham Bowpitt	Lecturer in Social Studies, Department of Social Studies, Trent Polytechnic.
Andrew Dilnot	Director, Personal Sector Research Programme, Institute for Fiscal Studies.
Peter Kemp	Lecturer in Housing, Salford Centre for Housing Studies.
Mark Kleinman	Research Associate, Department of Land Economy, University of Cambridge.
Michael Levi	Reader in Criminology, University of Wales, College of Cardiff.
John McIlroy	Staff Tutor in Industrial Relations, University of Manchester.
Alan Maynard	Professor of Economics and Director of the Centre for Health Economics, University of York.
Stewart Miller	Lecturer in Social Policy, University of Kent.
Gillian Parker	Research Fellow, Social Policy Research Unit, University of York.
Roland Petchey	Senior Lecturer, Department of Applied Social Studies, Sheffield Polytechnic.
Christine Whitehead	Senior Lecturer in Economics, London School of Economics.
Brian Wilcox	Chief Education Adviser, Sheffield Local Education Authority.

1 Introduction

Maria Brenton and
Clare Ungerson

In the final paragraph of our introduction to last year's *Year Book of Social Policy, 1987-8* we made two predictions for 1988–9. We said, with foreknowledge, that this year the Year Book would change its name to the *Social Policy Review*, and, secondly, with only a little hesitation and of course far more importantly, that the year 1988 would mark a 'watershed' in the development of British social policy. So it has proved. This year has seen the introduction of wide-ranging and radical reforming legislation in two of the most important arms of social policy: the Education Reform Act and the 1988 Housing Act. At the same time, the government set up a review of the National Health Service which threatened at its inception to be as radical an undoing of the post-war design for the service as the initial design was in itself a radical departure from what had gone before. The legislation to make the 'community charge' or 'poll tax' the new basis for accountable local government spending was put in place by the Local Government Finance Act 1988. Nigel Lawson's March budget – widely hailed as one of the most important for at least a decade –achieved a central aim of Conservative economic policy in reducing personal taxation in preference to increased expenditure on the social services. At the same time, he set in motion the necessary procedures for radically reforming the taxation of marriage. Finally the report on the services for community care, known as the 'Griffiths report' after its committee's chairman, was published, although, as we go to press, a government response is still awaited.

There was therefore no difficulty in deciding which were the important issues for the *Social Policy Review 1988–9*. The major social services of education, housing, health, and personal social services, had to be covered. Only social security could be omitted since the major social security reforms are already in place and have been discussed at length in two previous *Year Books* (1986–7, 1987–8). In this *Social Policy Review*, we can identify two key areas of linkage between our various contributors – the role of local government, and market philosophy. The familiar themes surrounding government preference for the market as a mechanism for allocating resources, constantly reiterated in political rhetoric and increasingly demonstrated in policy enactments, are of course those which connect competition, efficiency and financial discipline with consumer choice and accountability. A related and equally dominant preoccupation of government at the present time is the limitation of the powers and functions of local authorities, and the form of local government in the future has been fundamentally challenged by measures passed in 1988. This is not to suggest that what has occurred constitutes a break with past policy – on the contrary, the quickening of legislative activity and policy developments this year represents the continuity and growing self confidence of an administration whose aim to restructure the welfare state has been endorsed to its satisfaction by a third term of office.

Some of 1988's policy developments reflect both aims – to redefine the power of local authorities and to assert market superiority. For example, the Education Reform Act embodies an attempt to diminish the power of local authorities over secondary education and maximise central control over key areas of the curriculum and finance so as to attune the education system more to the demands of the economy. It also seeks to introduce elements of consumer power and competition into the local educational process. At the same time, part II of the Act seeks to insert the disciplines of the market into higher education. In this volume, Brian Wilcox discusses these themes in relation to secondary schools and John McIlroy examines the situation in the universities.

Two articles particularly concentrate on the theme of local government and the dimunition of that institution's power. Stewart Miller in his paper on citizenship and the community charge examines the way in which all local electors irrespective of income will be forced to feel the direct impact of local government spending decisions. Accountability here is to be harnessed to central government's designs under the guise of enhancing local democracy and promoting good financial housekeeping. Peter Kemp, in his article on the 1988 Housing Act, describes the new powers of central government in so far as they apply to the wholesale transfer of council housing out of the local authority domain into the quasi or actual privately rented sector. Once again, just as with the Education Reform Act, central government hopes to mobilise consumer power to counteract the supposed waywardness of local authorities and, at the same time, encourage the transfer to the market of a major social service – council housing – which for at least the past fifty years has been taken for granted as part of Britain's collectively provided social service enterprise.

At the same time as this squeezing of local authority autonomy by, on the one hand, consumer power and, on the other, central control, there has been one important countervailing voice – namely the Griffiths report. That report suggests that the entire responsibility for community care services should be shifted to local authorities with central government providing block grants on the basis of agreed plans drawn up at local level. The report re-uses the traditional argument for local autonomy – namely that only locally based institutions fully understand local needs. Perhaps for this reason the government apparently delayed the publication of the report until the day after budget day and, in early October 1988, has yet to respond to Griffiths' proposals. Baldwin and Parker, in their paper on the report, consider some of the inherent difficulties and contradictions built into the report – in particular the question of developing consumer 'choice' in a service that is predominantly run by professionals and intended to be allocated on the basis of 'need'.

Similar ideas on consumer choice are contained in the debate on health care. In his paper on primary health care – an issue which has received a lot of attention this year – Roland Petchey examines the White Paper *Promoting better health,* and offers an overview of recent policy trends in this field. He assesses a range of proposals concerning choice for consumers, the promotion of competition among general practitioners and the linking of remuneration to performance. In a paper on the 'crisis' in the National Health Service, Alan Maynard examines the financial health of the health care system in the context of a renewed ideological debate on its funding. In his opinion the outcome of the government's review of the NHS is 'likely to be modest'. Amid the clamour of such bodies as the Centre for Policy Studies and the Adam Smith Institute for the introduction of market mechanisms into the health service he feels there is a growing recognition among politicians that there are no easy solutions to its problems. The notion of 'efficiency' is not an attribute of either a market or a non-market system, in Maynard's view, and he expands at some length on the utility of the QUALY or 'quality adjusted life year' as a criterion of efficiency for health care. Again, the debate between those who support or oppose a market approach lies in conflicting perceptions of demand as determined by consumers or by professionals.

Within the context of discussion of the insertion of market principles into the administration and allocation of social services, it is interesting to read Whitehead and Kleinman's critique of the new legislation contained within the Housing Act, 1988 which will largely de-regulate the privately rented sector and allow for rents to rise to market levels. The ostensible aim of this policy is to increase the supply of privately rented accommodation but Whitehead and Kleinman argue that it will do no such thing. The market is already distorted by another government policy – namely, tax relief on mortgage interest – which exaggerates the demand for owner-occupation but which the present government clearly believes is not a form of subsidy but rather an encouragement of the market principle. Moreover, Whitehead and Kleinman suggest that the only way in which effective demand for private renting can be increased, and hence supply, is through large increases in housing benefit through the social security system. The only other possibility of expansion of supply is through the new Business Expansion Scheme which provides very generous tax reliefs for those willing to invest in the cheaper end of the privately rented sector. Clearly, as Whitehead and Kleinman show, the 'market' is not as simple as at first appears.

Other major changes in the tax system were announced by the Chancellor of the Exchequer in his 1988 Budget, in particular the taxation of marriage. Andrew Dilnot argues in his paper that the Chancellor has unravelled some of the assumptions about wives' dependency on their husbands but, at the same time, has failed to tackle one of the most unusual features of the British tax system – namely the generous treatment of two-earner couples in contrast to the rather less than generous treatment of single earner couples, particularly those with children. Despite the claim by the Chancellor that he had introduced a radical reform of personal taxation in response to widespread criticism of the existing system, Dilnot's paper suggests that the major problems of distribution of allowances between individuals in different marital circumstances have not been adequately tackled.

The last two papers depart from these general themes in their respective treatments of two important institutions in British society – the police and the Church of England. Firstly, reflecting a preoccupation exhibited consistently by government ministers and the ranks of the Conservative Party faithful, Mike Levi, in a paper on 'Policing developments in the 1980s', reviews the changes generated by successive Acts of Parliament – from the Police and Criminal Evidence Act 1984 to the Criminal Justice Act 1988 – and, against this background, traces the steady expansion of the powers of the police amid a public debate on police-public relations and accountability. In tapping populist sentiment concerning crime, discipline and order and the moral authority of the family, ministers have always been assured of a high degree of consensus and support from 'the Tory Party at prayer', but as Bowpitt illustrates in our final paper, the basis for those assumptions has become less certain in recent years. The Church of England, predominantly middle class, with a unique constitutional position as the Established Church, has become in small but significant ways, a growing source of critical opposition to government policies and has caused dismay and discomfort in official circles. Graham Bowpitt traces the evolution of liberal attitudes among anglicans which have become increasingly at variance with the church's traditional espousal of the established order, finding in liberation and feminist theology and evangelical renewal, grassroots influences which have stimulated a new critical awareness among church leaders of the worsening position of the British poor.

Finally, despite our previous comment that the changes being introduced in 1988 are all of a piece with developments since 1979, it is also important not to under-estimate the real changes that are now taking place in the structure of the British 'welfare state' (a term which in itself seems increasingly irrelevant and of historic use only). Until 1988 it was possible to argue that the cloth of collectivism was being snipped away at the edges, and an altered coat would emerge to fit more straitened circumstances. But there seems little doubt now that the very fabric is being changed, and the new coat – if coat at all – will emerge looking almost entirely different. It will, of course, be the task of future *Social Policy Reviews* to consider how far this is, in fact, the case. The responsibility for doing that will no longer fall to Maria Brenton who has co-edited the *Year Book* and now the *Review* for the past five years and has decided to stand down. Ours has been a very agreeable co-editorship, and we both regret that – like all good things apparently – it must come to an end.

2 The great reform of the universities

John McIlroy

Introduction

The 1987 Education Bill received the royal assent in July 1988. It was one of the most intensely debated and bitterly contested pieces of legislation since 1979. Strenuously opposed by the educational establishment and the opposition parties, the Bill introduced in November 1987 split the Conservatives. Liberals, such as Edward Heath, urged the government to retreat over its key proposals and the radical right, led by Norman Tebbit, asserted that the legislation did not go far enough and would quickly require extension and reinforcement.

The furore was hardly surprising. The scope of the legislation was far greater than that of the landmark 1944 Education Act and its impact upon every corner of the education system potentially more far-reaching. Public attention and critical scrutiny was initially focused on the Bill's provisions for remoulding the school system, particularly the proposals for a national curriculum and state-maintained schools. But if the first political exchanges scarcely touched on the changes scheduled for higher education in part II of the Bill, there was a growing awareness of the legislation's revolutionary intentions towards this area. And it was soon being argued that, 'universities have been singled out for particular damnation' (Young, 1987). Predictably, commentators of the centre and left saw the measures as recasting higher education institutions as 'agents of the government' (Griffiths, 1987, p2) and as a 'menacing shadow over the universities' (Young, 1987). Perhaps more surprising was the view from the right that, 'the advantages hoped for from this revolution will most likely prove illusory, the harm wrought by it very real' (Kedourie, 1988, p2). And the scathing verdict from prominent partisans of Thatcherism that 'If the British government really believes in the freedom of the individual and the beneficence of the market it will withdraw part II of the Great Education Reform Bill' (Rogaly, 1988).

This small storm and the consequent intensive debates in the House of Lords did some justice to the reach of the Bill's provisions and the important restructuring of higher education they would entail. The 1988 Act did not, however, represent sudden innovation. It was, rather, the culmination of past tendencies, long maturing but appearing since 1979 in sharper form. And the debate surrounding the legislation was the continuation, albeit in a more intense and focused form, of past controversies. In a powerful sense, the Act crystallised and set the seal of legitimacy on processes which were already far advanced. Before examining the details of what is involved in the legislation it is essential to scrutinise its background and context.

Thatcherism and the universities

The system that the incoming Thatcher administration inherited was one which, despite dramatic expansion in the post war period, was still characterised by elitism, liberalism and laissez-faire. Previous governments had acquiesced in a high degree of university autonomy. The allocation of state funds was delegated to the academic-dominated University Grants Committee which acted as a buffer between the state and individual institutions. The block grant system gave individual universities wide discretion as to exactly how these funds should be disbursed. Minimum state intervention underpinned self-validation of university academic standards through the system of monitoring of provision by external examiners, drawn from other universities, and research councils which were also under academic control. University self-government was tempered only by largely cosmetic lay representation on university councils. The university system operated on the basis of a rough parity of esteem between institutions. Whilst this was modified by history, resources and specialisation, exhibited at its highest in the Oxbridge – Redbrick split, there was relative uniformity of curriculum which strongly reflected the arts and humanities as well as the sciences. Universities urged the unity of teaching and research, operated in a strong ethos of academic freedom and sought to blend the critical pursuit of pure knowledge and the development of the individual with a preparation for life skills.

Home students were financed through mandatory awards, subject to a means test, for all admitted with two A-levels. Student numbers had increased from 90,000 in 1956, to 297,000 in 1980 (Gosden, 1983). But only 22 % of the majority entrant age group were in higher education in Britain, compared with 28 % in France, 39 % in Japan and 43 % in the USA (National Economic Development Council, 1982). The elitist UK spent more of its national product on higher education than most of its European competitors but recruited smaller numbers of students at a higher cost (Blackstone, 1983). The post-war expansion had left the working class largely excluded from the universities (Edwards, 1982). An authoritative study published in 1980 concluded

> Our evidence holds no comfort for those who believe that class differences in educational attainment reflect a fair distribution of opportunities to those with the intellectual ability or cultural capacity to profit therefrom. Wastage of talent continues and was massive over most of the period with which we are concerned (Halsey et al, 1980, p200).

The system was, however, in the throes of modification. As early as 1945, the UGC had amended its terms of reference to include the objective of ensuring that universities met 'national needs'. By the 1960s, it was demanding from universities 'a further deliberate and determined effort to gear a large part of their output to the economic and industrial needs of the nation' (UGC, 1974, p107). There were increasing pressures from the state for higher education which was more vocational and science-related, which took a human capital approach and which catered less for individual development and far more for the manpower demands of the economy (Council for Scientific Policy, 1968; Committee on Manpower Resources, 1968).

By the late seventies, commentators noted that

> The ideological challenge to the university ideal is based on the idea that education is fundamentally an economic resource which should be employed in a way which maximises its contribution to the development of Britain as an industrial nation...(Tapper and Salter, 1978, p15).

The utilitarian approach, complemented from the mid-seventies as economic problems intensified, by a searching for savings from higher education reached a new peak under the Callaghan administration which called for a reappraisal of the whole educational system on these lines (Centre for Contemporary Cultural Studies, 1981). The universities were particularly vulnerable to pressure from the state as by 1979 around 80 % of their income came from government funds, a 30 % increase on 1945 (Carswell, 1985). And there were tendencies towards a more *dirigiste* approach from both state and UGC (Farrant, 1987). Nonetheless, intervention remained limited as pre-Thatcher governments sought to change higher education largely through developments *outside* the universities, such as the establishment of the thirty polytechnics, intended to counter the established institutions' inadequate response to vocationalism and manpower needs, and the creation of the Open University, intended to modify their elitism. However, the assimilation of new institutions to existing patterns was much commented upon (Annan, 1987).

Despite this, the case for the industrialisation of the ivory towers was often overstated. British universities had long had intimate links with industry whilst OECD reports showed that, by 1980, in higher education as a whole 'Britain has a markedly lower proportion of students studying arts and a higher proportion studying science and technology than other leading competitors and comparable European countries' (Sanderson, 1987, p134).

From 1979, pressures to relate the universities more directly to economic need and erode their traditional rationale and autonomy were intensified. Conservative policies have been informed by both economic and political considerations. Initial cutbacks in state funding were motivated by general considerations as to the allegedly debilitating role of public expenditure. These were stiffened by an anti-intellectualism and philistinism which saw much of what went on in universities as unproductive or positively dangerous, an abuse of privilege rooted in lack of accountability to state or society. Scrutiny of government rhetoric on the need for improved 'standards' and greater 'efficiency' usually disclosed little more than ministerial maximising of popular stereotypes in which leftist teachers undermined enterprise values and critical sociologists produced disaffected students in an ambience more related to a holiday camp than a cockpit of useful intellectual production. Ministers' views on the need to 'remove finance from the people who wrote about ancient Egyptian scripts and the prenuptial habits of the Upper Volta Valley' (Tebbit, 1983, p1) were, however, given intellectual justification by writers who detected an indifference to industry as intrinsic in modern English culture and educational philosophy related to the specific formation of British capitalism and divisions within it (Wiener, 1981; Barnett, 1986).

The Conservatives were hostile to manpower planning by the state, and to a degree, dubious about the role education could play in economic revitalisation: 'there was growing scepticism about the economic utility of investment in higher education' (Jackson, 1988, p112). If higher education was to contribute it would have to survive the tests of the market. Public expenditure cuts were not only desirable for wider economic and social reasons: they would force universities into the market. State regulation of higher education was inefficient. It produced featherbedding and restrictive practices. Producers and consumers must be brought together more directly and more effectively with a pared down role for the state as broker. The allocation of higher education by market processes would maximise the economic utility of the product and stimulate its optimal distribution. Whether, and to what degree, universities could contribute to economic regeneration would be discovered by injecting market forces, at least to a far greater extent than had previously obtained. The 'hidden hand' would gradually replace the 'nanny state'. This process required political stimulation. As one Minister observed, 'UGC money is easy money...You have to apply pressure on the higher education institutions by holding down their block funding to seek alternative sources of support' (Jackson, 1988, p110). The major alternative source of support was industry and industrially oriented bodies such as the MSC. The pursuit of such funding would produce a shift to vocationalism, science and technology and introduce more competition, more efficiency and more differentiation into the university system.

Previous governments had relied on exhortation and outflanking pressures, such as the creation of the polytechnics. This had failed to break the logjam. Now was the time to go for the jugular, for only financial pressure could create, 'the first real incentive to go out and raise external income' (Jackson, 1988, p110). If a certain agnosticism was still discernible in the early eighties, the replacement of Sir Keith Joseph as Secretary of State by Kenneth Baker led to a more powerful assertion that universities could play a role in economic renovation through the replacement of the culture of state-dependence by the culture of market entrepreneurialism. Short term contraction would be facilitated by the fall in the birthrate which had taken place in the sixties and seventies. Initial straitened circumstances would produce a shake-up, a shake out of deadwood and dead attitudes and a new orientation towards the imperatives of Thatcher's Britain:

> We have to rebuild a successful economy in Britain, we have got to restore profits. With restored profits we shall once again have a corporate sector and individuals who have the money to invest in higher education, to donate to higher education,to promote alternative sources of funding (Jackson, 1988, p115).

Conservative policy 1979-1986

The first steps in what appeared to be essentially a strategy of state withdrawal in favour of a new market model of higher education were the removal of subsidies to overseas students in 1980 and the announcement of a further 8.5 % cut in the global sum allocated to universities over the period 1981–1984. Overall, universities were facing a fall of some 13–15 % in their total grant. However, the results of this exercise were, from the government's point of view, very mixed ones. The cuts were administered by the UGC according to traditional criteria, rather than the canons of the new conservatism. The technological universities, such as Aston, Bradford and Salford, suffered more than their traditional counterparts. The cut administered to Salford was around 30 % whilst Cambridge escaped with a loss of under 5 %. The 4,400 staff who initially accepted redundancy under the ancillary premature retirement scheme came more than proportionally from the science and technology areas. And the cutbacks led to a fall in the numbers of engineering students (National Audit Office, 1985).

On the one hand, the response of universities such as Salford in entering the market to restore their losses strengthened the Conservative view on the efficiency of cutbacks (Ashworth, 1985). On the other hand, the role of the UGC raised doubts as to whether the industrialisation of the universities could be achieved with this body as change-agent and the state as back-seat driver. Suspicion of the UGC grew, as did a preference for earmarking funds and channelling them for specific purposes through a variety of other agencies.

Emboldened by its 1983 election success, the government deployed a further battery of pressures on the universities. The insistent emphasis on greater efficiency produced the Jarrett Committee, established to report to the Committee of Vice Chancellors and Principals and the UGC on the effectiveness of management systems in the universities. The committee's report recommended that vice-chancellors should be recognised as chief executives; that planning and resources committees should oversee budget delegation to financial centres within the university; that department heads should be appointed, rather than emerge through rotation and should have a strong management role; and that universities should become more cost conscious, adopt new accounting systems and develop up-to-date marketing techniques. Performance indicators should be created to measure progress and new systems of staff appraisal and development should be negotiated. Greater accountability would be achieved by more lay representation particularly industrial personnel on university bodies. The report was clearly attempting to assimilate traditionally democratic academic institutions to a more authoritarian business model (CVCP, 1985).

The Green Paper *The development of higher education into the 1990s* codified many of the government's preoccupations. The emphasis on standards and selectivity was reaffirmed. Competition between institutions could produce clearer rankings and a reallocation of funding, so that in the paper's view 'it is not improbable that some institutions of higher education will need to be closed'. 'Higher education', its first paragraph declared 'must contribute more effectively to the improvement of the performance of the economy'. Universities must not only produce more scientists and technologists, they must also stimulate 'the entrepreneurial spirit'; 'develop the talent of entrepreneurs'; create 'positive attitudes to work'; ensure that students are not only 'able' and 'skilled' but 'well motivated'. Academics must 'be concerned with attitudes to the world outside higher education and, in particular, industry and commerce and beware of anti-business snobbery'. In handling students and curriculum, staff were exhorted to remember that 'of special importance are the innovators and entrepreneurs who will create new jobs and those who achieve vocational qualifications for which there is a market need'. Academics should be rewarded for adaptation to the new ethos and, indeed, encouraged to establish their own consultancies and businesses. The new interpenetration between capital and academia should be recognised by captains of industry playing a greater role on university bodies, sponsoring academic appointments, advising on curriculum and becoming involved in teaching (DES, 1985).

A minor theme in the Green Paper and in other government pronouncements was the need for universities to liberalise access and develop continuing education. Once again, this was related strongly to the economic ideology and one again, what appeared lacking was any willing of the financial resources required to make any significant progress in these areas (DES, 1985).

The government's impatience with the slightest dissent from the view that universities' essential mission was to serve capital was illustrated by a number of well politicised inquiries into slenderly based allegations of bias in social science teaching and research (Social Science Research Council, 1983; Scruton and Cox, 1984). The government, permanently impressed by the hazards of the early retirement lottery as exhibited in the 1981 exercise, periodically raised the removal of the system of tenure which was increasingly seen as a barrier to stronger management, redundancy and greater flexibility of labour. The uses of demoralisation as a change-agent were reflected in the fall in the real value of students' financial support and staff salaries (Association of University Teachers, 1985). And by 1986, a number of universities, most notably Aberdeen, Cardiff and Hull, were experiencing acute financial pressure.

The lessons drawn from the 1981 cuts also led to the appointment of a committee headed by Lord Croham, chair of the Guinness Peat group and former head of the home civil service, to look at the UGC's ability to make policy and effectively distribute resources. The committee's report confirmed the principle that government should play no part in distributing grant to individual universities. It recognised that the UGC had to be seen as 'an arm of government' with industry as its major client. But it insisted that any reformed body should be 'visibly its own creature enjoying the confidence of the government, the universities and the community at large' (*Review of the U.G.C* 1987, p4.2, 4.3). To meet this tall order, Croham recommended that there should be a smaller streamlined committee with a director general and half of its members drawn from outside the universities. This revamped body should continue to award block grants on a three year cycle with more selectivity between institutions and with money earmarked within the grant for specific purposes. An element of decentralisation and greater lay involvement should be secured by the establishment of a UK Education Committee with 10–15 members appointed to advise the secretary of state on national goals and reforms.

The UGC itself had gone a long way towards accepting the bases of government philosophy, even if it did not endorse the specifics of the strategy. Even before the cuts were underway the chair of the UGC was musing on the 'excision of feeble limbs' and forecasting a 'greater degree of direct intervention by the UGC in the affairs of individual universities than has been customary or necessary in the past' (Parkes, 1980). The committee accepted that universities should play 'an essential role in promoting economic prosperity' and forge closer links with industry although they attempted to place this objective in a wide context of individual development and cultural renewal (UGC, 1984). The UGC and CVCP felt with justification that if they were to contribute to change on the lines desired by the state then far more pump-priming was required. They were, therefore, opposed to the cut-backs but not to the changes the cut-backs were intended to induce. Their supplicatory relation to the government appeared to be 'thy will be done, give us only thy daily bread with which to do it'.

The university hierarchies adapted to all aspects of the government offensive with a rush of working parties on appraisal, performance indicators, academic standards, the external examiner situation and continuing education. The UGC was increasingly perceived within the universities as, in Croham's words, 'not outside the machinery of government but part of it' *Review of the UGC* 1987, p2). This view was strengthened by the UGC's involvement in the selectivity exercises so close to the government's heart. From 1987, 15 % of UGC grant was to be distributed on the basis of UGC ranking of research performance on a four point scale from 'outstanding' to 'below average'. This exercise attracted a mass of criticism as impressionistic and unscientific (Bentham, 1987; Gillett, 1987). A series of reviews on particular subject areas were commissioned. The first on earth sciences suggested a division of universities into three tiers, those with research departments, those with main subject teaching departments and those with service teaching departments (UGC, 1987a). Further reviews on philosophy, sociology and social policy and administration were announced. A report from the research councils stimulated fears of the development of a three tier system where some universities would maintain a high level of research, others would teach but maintain research in some departments, and still others would be essentially teaching institutions (Advisory Board For Research Councils, 1987).

The 1987 White Paper

By the 1987 election universities were slowly changing under the impact of government pressures. They had suffered a funding cut of more than 10 % and were scheduled to face a similar reduction by the early 1990s. The number of full time undergraduates had fallen from 253,400 in 1981–2 to 246,400 in 1986–7. With intensifying competition for places, the percentage of applicants fell from 54 % to 44 %, although there had been growth in the polytechnics (UGC, 1987b). The unit of resource had been protected at the cost of falling numbers and the effect was 'to channel students away from relatively well resourced universities with highly qualified staff to polytechnics somewhat less well endowed' (Sanderson, 1987, p17).

There had been an increase in the percentage of students in engineering and science, compared with arts and social studies but the switch was limited, partially due to the fact that, in a situation were resources were squeezed, it cost twice as much to produce a physics graduate as it did to produce a social science graduate. Despite increasing subventions from industry more than 60 % of universities' funds still came from the UGC and around 80 % from public sources (UGC, 1986). Similarly, in other areas where the government required change, such as continuing education, rhetoric had far outweighed action.

In this situation, the government appreciated that the task of reform was likely to be more longscale and arduous than perhaps it had first assumed. As in other areas, policy became more interventionist as barriers to privatisation disclosed themselves. Given that university dependence on the state was likely to continue for the conceivable future, there was a need to utilise it to limit autonomy and manipulate the structures of dependence to change behaviour. Given that the professed change of attitudes within the universities smacked more of a succumbing to *realpolitik* than of Pauline Conversion and, the government suspected, was infused with a strong element of political stratagem, there was a perceived need for the state to continue to supervise the management change in a market direction. The 1981 exercise had underlined the limitations of arms length reliance on academic managers who in their heart of hearts were, at least, lukewarm about government strategies.

The 1987 white paper, therefore, smacked more of centralised planning of the universities than previous pronouncements. It was also interesting for its rehabilitation, or writing up, of a number of previously neglected themes. It commenced rather like its 1983 predecessor with the assertion that

> Higher education should serve the economy more effectively; pursue basic scientific research and scholarship in the arts and humanities; have closer links with industry and commerce; and promote enterprise...above all there is an urgent need in the interests of the nation as a whole and, therefore, of universities, polytechnics and colleges themselves for higher education to take increasing account of the economic requirements of the country... The government and its central funding agencies will do all they can to encourage and reward approaches to higher education institutions which bring them closer to the world of business *(Higher education: meeting the challenge,*1987, IV, 1).

But the government now argued with an apparent change of emphasis that matters could not be left to the market

> In a period when student numbers could decline sharply for demographic reasons the government considers student demand alone to be an insufficient basis for the planning of higher education. A major determinant must also be the demands for highly qualified manpower stimulated in part by the success of the Government's own economic and social policies *(Higher education: meeting the challenge*, 1987, p2.10).

These sentiments, echoed in the 1987 Conservative election manifesto, 'we must meet the nation's demand for highly qualified manpower to compete in international markets', herald a return to manpower planning, previously regarded in the 1960s and 1970s as discredited and as incompatible with a market approach. The government now pledged itself to a more interventionist stance and even stated that if graduate output fails to synchronise with 'the economy's needs' then 'the government will consider whether the *planning framework* should be adjusted' *(Higher education: meeting the challenge*, 1987, p2.13, our emphasis). The planning framework was to be established by the DES and firm state control over the process exercised through a more pliant Universities Funding Council which, in the wake of the Croham Report, would replace the UGC. More detailed central control would be exercised via important changes in funding, involving a shift from block grant to detailed contracts by which universities would deliver specified services to government. The polytechnics, in a further move towards state control, would be removed from local authority patronage and supervised by a Polytechnic and Colleges Funding Council.

Within this prescription for more, not less, state intervention, the White Paper announced government plans for an increase of 5 % in student numbers, from 693,000 student places in higher education in 1985, to 726,000 in 1990. A decrease is projected thereafter to 691,000 by 1996 in accordance with falling numbers of 18 year olds, before a further increase to 723,000 in the year 2000. This represents a 14 % increase on earlier projections but the projected expansion is firmly tied to the demands of employers, more efficiency in the universities and a widening of access.

This latter issue is taken more seriously than in previous pronouncements and is confronted in sober and understanding fashion. It will be necessary, the government feels:

> to accommodate students with a wider range of academic and practical experience than before, many of whom will not have the traditional qualifications for entry. Not only will entry requirements and procedures have to be changed; institutions of higher education will have to adapt their teaching methods and the design of courses to accommodate new types of students... . (The government) believes increased participation in higher education need not be at the expense of academic excellence, indeed the stimulus of change should help to sharpen awareness of the different types of achievement that properly form part of the output of higher education *(Higher education: meeting the challenge*, 1987, p2.15)

To these ends, the White Paper emphasised the importance of vocational qualifications and access courses, as well as A-levels, as routes into higher education. It also emphasised again the importance of continuing education. But as with the burning question of student support – the real value of student grants has declined 17 % in real terms since 1979 – there is a vacuum when it comes to the question of more resources to stimulate these developments.

In May 1987, the government published a series of consultative papers dealing in more detail with key aspects of the higher education reforms. In the wake of their election success the Education Reform Bill was unveiled in November.

The Great Education Reform Bill

Government policy had, thus, through the 1980s moved towards more state planning and more state control. The Bill as published appeared to justify the views of academics that it would 'sound the death knell of university autonomy' (Moodie, 1987, p338), a perception reinforced by experienced commentators: 'the universities will not be crying wolf when they say it is the end of autonomy' (Crequer, 1987).

The UGC would be replaced by a Universities Funding Council of 15 members. Of these 6–9 would have experience of higher education, the other members contributing industrial, commercial or financial expertise. The Secretary of State would be given powers to 'attach such conditions as he may determine' to the funds the UFC would distribute to the universities. The UFC itself would then be able to attach 'such terms and conditions as they think fit' to the funds they channelled to individual universities. If a university failed to comply with such terms and conditions it could be made to repay to the UFC the funds it had received – with interest. The Bill further provided that the UFC 'shall comply with any directions given to it by the Secretary of State' but there was no mention of any duty on the council to advise the government on the needs of the universities. Its powers to advise would be dependent on the government. Moreover, there would be an open authority to impose by delegated legislation 'such additional powers as the Secretary of State thinks fit'. Similar provisions were applied to the new Polytechnic and Colleges Funding Council (clauses 92, 94).

Commissioners would be appointed to change the statutes of individual universities which enshrined lecturers' rights to tenure. Whereas in the past most universities had only been empowered to dismiss for 'good cause' – a limited category of severe misconduct or grave dereliction of duty – dismissal could now be justified on grounds of financial exigency. Provision was also made for dismissal for redundancy, in terms of the statutory definitions contained in the Employment Protection (Consolidation Act) 1978. These provisions, when law, would apply not only to those taking up employment after the bill had received the royal assent, but to all academics whose appointment was made or who accepted a new contract, after 20th November 1987. Thus, staff changing jobs within universities which involved a new contract of employment, in some cases by accepting transfer or promotion, would lose tenure. Further concern was occasioned by a DES statement that the legislation would enable a university to replace a senior academic with a junior academic on grounds of cost, a practice outside the statutory definition of redundancy (clauses 131, 132, 174).

The Bill created a system by which the government could dictate policy to the universities in order to subordinate the academic to the manpower demands of the economy 'stimulated in part by the success of the government's own economic and social policies'. Apart from its enhanced industrial component, a carefully selected UFC – and the government took pains as to the selection of personnel – was not, in itself, likely to dissent from policy imperatives. However the new structures would render any opposition – in the likely event of its emergence – impotent, through 'a system of centralised control wholly at variance with the British tradition' (Beloff, 1987).

The Secretary of State, Kenneth Baker, argued that the powers given to him in the Bill would not be used without weight being given to the arguments of the UFC and the universities. The power to give directions was only there as 'a last resort' (Baker, 1987). The under secretary claimed that similar unrestricted powers to give directions to the research councils were to be found in the Science and Technology Act but they had never been used. Critics of the Bill, in their turn, inquired as to why so much trouble was being taken to introduce such unprecedented powers in the face of such united and fervent opposition if there was no intention of using them. They went on to claim that in the case of the research councils the powers were often referred to by the DES to secure acquiescence in Ministerial imperatives (Kingman, 1988). Faced with an unprecedented array of controls, universities were being asked to rely on the government's good faith 'The bill in sum does what Conservatives have usually said should not be done. It places total power in the hands of a minister and asks us to trust him to keep fundamental freedoms unimpaired' (Young, 1987).

Government suggestions as to the detail of the terms and conditions the government would in future attach to university finance also caused alarm. The UFC, it appeared, would move decisively from the 'block grant without strings', non-interventionist pattern of regulation. It would 'make money available on contract to universities...monitor performance in accordance with contracts...enquire into the extent and quality of teaching and research in the universities and plan for their development...' (DES, 1987a, p3). The new system of contracting would involve:

(a) a greater precision in the specification of what is expected of institutions in return for public funding, leading to,
(b) closer links between funding and institutions' performance in delivering specified provision backed up by,
(c) periodic re-negotiation of contracts taking account of institutions' relative performance (DES, 1987b, p3,4).

Three alternative or interacting forms of contract were presented for discussion. In the first form, there would be one comprehensive contract between the UFC and each university covering all the institution's teaching and research over a rolling three year period. The second 'two tier' contract would cover, at the first level, all 'core' teaching and research carried on in an institution and, at the second level, supplementary contracts dealing with new research innovations in syllabus or the creation of new student places. The third style of contract would break a university's work down into congeries of arrangements between the UFC and the institution, laying down terms and conditions for different faculties, departments, or even courses. All of these contracts would be detailed and specific, require close monitoring to be inbuilt and entail statutory penalties for non-compliance or ineffective performance:

> The funding bodies will need at an early stage to enter into a dialogue with instructions about what measures of performance it might be serviceable and feasible to collect and also how these indicators might be used to assess institutions' delivery of provision contracted with public funds (DES, 1987b, p10).

This system, it was pointed out, was alien to legal ideas of contract, given the absence of free argument, as against imposition; the monopoly position of one party; its preponderant power; and its ability to directly inflict financial penalties on the other party. It would enable the government to intensify competition between universities and determine in broad terms, and in the image of government policy, what was taught and researched, although with what level of exactitude, given the UFC's lack of detailed expertise, was open to question. The contracting system in itself would curtail academic freedom (Griffiths, 1987). The removal of tenure would further facilitate a minimising of opposition and lubricate changes required, indeed already underway, in the mergers of institutions, closure of departments and transfer of staff occasioned by the cut-backs and UGC reviews. The new contract system would require universities to move further in the direction of flexibility models of employment with a 'core' of permanent workers and 'periphery' of unprotected part-time and short contract workers, taken on and laid off according to the rise and fall of the institutions' fortunes in the new contracts market. Already, according to the CVCP, only a quarter of UGC funded new appointments in 1985–6 involved tenured contracts (Williams, 1988). The changes could also further weaken academic freedom. Whilst ministers stated and restated their commitment to academic freedom they refused until the end to embody specific support for it in the legislation.

The nature of the UFC as an instrument of government, its sweeping powers, the proposed contract system, the removal of tenure all added up to a qualitative change in the standing of universities:

> one consequent convincing scenario sees universities gradually but remorselessly robbed of their autonomy. They incrementally mirror the requirements of the state, their staff become more pliant and conformist, their teaching and research becomes increasingly orthodox

> and conventional, reflecting the concerns and demands of government, civil servants and employers (McIlroy and Spencer, 1988).

The universities' financial dependence on the state, their conservative conception of politics and their elitist relationship to society ruled out any largescale opposition to the Bill. Outside their own limited constituency they possessed little active support. Nonetheless, that constituency which, in keeping with past traditions, was strongest in the House of Lords was mobilised. The CVCP acted to some degree as a pressure group shaking off their passive collaboration in government policies. But only to some degree. A tremendous amount of effort went into the campaign against the Bill and, in the case of the Association of University Teachers, opposition was related both to its philosophy and its detail. But the case-against put by the leadership of the universities was well demarcated and limited. Their judgment was that tenure, for example, could not be defended – even if they wished to defend it. The more forthright judgment of Kenneth Baker was that:

> Vice-Chancellors have made it clear separately, independently and collectively that they welcome the end of tenure. They have been rather more fulsome about that in our private discussions than in their public utterances. They welcome the end of tenure because they want a greater degree of managerial control for the reorganisation of their departments... Some but not all want a definition of academic freedom (Baker, 1988, p172).

Given the nature of this opposition – and, of course, the government's majority, the changes as the Bill progressed through Parliament were small if important ones. In March 1988, with the Bill approaching its report stage in the Commons, Kenneth Baker made a number of concessions on the powers of the Secretary of State and the new funding councils. The UFC was now given a statutory right to advise the government on the needs of the universities. The Secretary of State's power to impose additional functions on the UFC was specifically limited. It was made clear that the Secretary of State could not make conditions directly applicable to individual universities and that any directions to the UFC by the government would have to be made by orders laid before both Houses of Parliament. The UFC would not be able to control any funds universities raised from private sources, whilst it would only be entitled to demand repayment of specific sums channelled via the UGC to which conditions had been attached. Moreover, the academic members of the UFC would now have to be practising academics 'engaged in the provision of higher education'. And Mr Baker also agreed that amendments would be introduced in the Lords laying a duty on the Commissioners to establish new appeals procedures for staff facing dismissal.

In the Lords, the peers voted to include in the legislation a statement proposed by Lord Jenkins of Hillhead on academic freedom. This declared that in revising university statutes the commissioners had to ensure that academics would still possess 'freedom within the law to question and test received wisdom, and to put forward new ideas and controversial and unpopular opinions, without placing themselves in jeopardy of losing their jobs or privileges'. Another amendment from Lord Wedderburn was passed which excluded the dismissal of senior academics and their replacement by junior and cheaper staff from the definition of redundancy. A further successful amendment affected the contract system. It replaced the power given to the UFC to make 'payments' to the universities 'subject to such terms and conditions as it thinks fit' with a narrower power to make 'grants specifying particular obligations and subject to general guidance'. However the government saw this amendment as endangering the introduction of a contract system and the original provision was restored when the Bill returned to the Commons, although the clause continued to refer to 'grants' rather than 'payments'. Finally, when the Bill returned to the Lords in July the government agreed to write in a commitment for the UFC to consult with universities and relevant bodies such as the CVCP, before imposing terms and conditions on their funding.

The future of the universities

Initiatives in higher education demonstrate the pragmatic and evolutionary nature of contemporary Conservative politics. State policy towards the universities in the 1980s has been characterised by an uneasy, and at times contradictory oscillation between market and manpower planning approaches. Initial scepticism and suspicion about the role of the universities – what do we *do* with them? – has been replaced by a powerful insistence on their economic role. The emphasis on direct market mechanisms as the optimal means of providing a service to industry has been accompanied by the creation of greater centralisation and subordination to the state and a rehabilitation of manpower planning. The rigours of the Bill were refined as it passed through Parliament. The potential accretion of power to the state still involved in the legislation is undeniable. Whether such centralisation is a temporary grudging expedient, essential to ensure greater resort to market relationships, or whether it represents a more permanent increment to state control remains to be seen. Certainly in the shorter term, the exact nature of the new settlement in higher education will depend to a large extent on how the legal skeleton is fleshed out and how the powers accorded to government and UFC are utilised.

For example, a hard version of the contract system could constitute a powerful means of external supervision and control of academic activities. A softer version of earmarking, of the type that operated between 1943 and 1952, would be far less onerous. A key question will be what percentage of UFC finance will be earmarked in this fashion and what proportion will continue to be passed on to the universities as core funding, on a similar basis to the old block grant system. Moreover, what - admittedly small scale - experience there is of similar control systems, such as those applied in the past to university adult education, demonstrates the difficulties external agencies face in realising finegrained control and the inutility in practice of many formal performance indicators (McIlroy, 1989).

In similar fashion, critics sympathetic to the government have pointed out that universities are not commercial enterprises geared to the delivery of commodities, nor should they be. Moreover, planning cannot second-guess an ever-changing market and dynamic technology nor guarantee, short of direction of labour, that graduates will slot into their intended economic roles. A far greater degree of autonomy than the Act permits must go with universities relating more sensitively to the market both through closer relations with private enterprise and subsidies switching from producers to consumers through a system of student vouchers (Kedourie, 1988; Rogaly, 1988).

However, scrutiny of the possible limitations of recent policy should not blind us to the real degree of change the legislation embodies. For example, we already have a substantial body of evidence on the problems the removal of tenure will entail from the recent workings of the short term contract system and historical case studies (Fieldhouse, 1985). A key factor will be the extent to which the shake-up it involves secures legitimacy amongst second level managers in the universities and consequently gradually changes ideology and behaviour.

Such acceptance is unlikely to stem from the power of its intellectual underpinning. The programme of reform all too often proceeds from a critique which lacks any sustaining evidence and fails to demonstrate how its proposals would improve matters. The efficacy of the market is asserted not argued. All the evidence suggests that turning education over to the market will freeze or extend existing divisions and inequalities. It it difficult to see how it will increase access. The central problem is the premium market relationships place on financial considerations and the manner in which these will often conflict with educational and social considerations. If universities are to devote themselves to a far greater extent to overseas students, industrial management, applied science and technology vocational training there will be an educational and social – and indeed an economic opportunity cost. Through forcing rationalisation and even closures, competition may produce less, not more, choice. Charges of inefficiency and lack of quality are plagued by differences over objectives. But even in terms of the state's obsession with economic criteria, what little research there is provides little sustenance for the government case: 'When output is measured by degrees and diplomas the universities' performance in respect of output relative to input was much better than that of the British economy public sector and private sector, as a whole' (Marris, 1984, p114). Rather than being to blame for economic problems, education is being unfairly blamed for problems which arise in the sphere of production (Lodge, 1986).

Whilst the evidence appears to show that the education system contributes in general fashion to economic development, the specific contribution higher education can and should make to the creation of economic regeneration is contentious (George and Wilding, 1984; Morris, 1985). The insistence on direct and specific links between education and industry and the incessant harping on the role of education in providing specific skills and knowledge which dominate government thinking are highly problematic, given the complex relationships between pure and applied knowledge. Moreover, in contrast with Conservative philosophy, there is a swing in the USA, Japan and Scandinavia to the view that: 'In a rapidly changing society the best education is general rather than specific, giving students the capacity to learn the "thinking skills", the intellectual flexibility that will enable them to adjust to economic changes and technological advances' (Grubb, 1987, p14).

It is questionable to what extent we can predict the likely benefits of research or teaching, measure them according to economic criteria or even know what the costs will be.

> In its very nature, fundamental research has built-in unpredictability; it may eventually turn out to have a commercial pay-off or it may not. A strictly utilitarian approach runs the risk of sanctifying current orthodoxy, of promoting safe ventures at the expense of speculative but potentially worthwhile activity. It also pre-supposes the funding managers who decide – and *de facto* impose – national priorities are more adept at picking winners than anybody else (Becker and Kogan, 1987, p10).

Even within the government's framework, it is difficult to see how the policy of increasing selectivity and stratification can stimulate progress. Or how many of its objectives – increased access is, again, an excellent example – can be attained with less rather than more resources (Becker and Kogan, 1987). The CVCP are presently predicting a loss of 5,000 more university staff by 1991, the number of teaching posts having fallen 12 % since 1981 (*Times Higher Education Supplement*, 1988).

The available evidence discloses a widespread indifference in British industry to basic training, let alone wider education and research. Whilst this position is open to change, it seems that where employers are prepared to purchase education and research they tend to look to immediate relevance and pay off (Constable and McCormick, 1987; Handy, 1987). Moreover, the view that in terms of institutional autonomy and academic freedom industry will serve as a liberator from the state is a naïve and self serving one.

All of this points to the need for a greater degree of autonomy and freedom for the universities than the Education Act is prepared to allow. If partisan and contentious conceptions of economic needs are not to determine the teaching, research and organisation of higher education, then it seems vital that universities rearticulate their essential purpose in terms of the creation and development of social knowledge by an independent intelligentsia, with a strong social awareness and keen social responsibilities. This necessitates that critical freethinking, the development of the individual, the transmission of culture, must be woven together with the generation of economically useful knowledge, not subordinated to it. In this perspective, universities exist not simply to serve the needs of the controllers of the economy and state but a whole range of subordinate groups whose interests compete and conflict with those of the powerholders. This will require an attempt to organically develop greater accountability, through blending with some sublety the interests of teachers, students and community representatives, rather than driving through a shotgun marriage between the university hierarchy and the captains of industry. The present government strategy is hostile to such purposes. In as much as they oppose it, the universities are defending not simply vested interest but a wider social interest.

A major problem is that all too many critiques of the Great Education Reform Bill stop at a defence at the 1979 status quo, asserting that, in the past, universities have had an excellent record in 'serving the nation'. This view is wide of the mark, for, in the past, universities have clearly *not* served all sections of the nation. A recent survey states that in the 1980s:

> ...students entering university are drawn overwhelmingly from the higher occupational groups of this society. The relative chances of young people from different backgrounds gaining access have changed only slightly and then in favour of those groups already well off (Williamson, 1986, p73–4).

There is a continuing exclusion of black students (Little and Robbins, 1981) and the UK has a smaller percentage of women amongst university entrants than any comparable country (OECD, 1983). There has been limited progress in adult and continuing provision and it, too, fails to involve working class students (McIlroy and Spencer, 1988). Despite the emphasis on increased access only around 10 % of university entrants are admitted on non-A-level criteria (Fulton, 1988). Under 5 % of undergraduates study for part-time degrees compared with 45 % in the USA and 40 % in Canada (Tight, 1988).

Perhaps there is a need to now defend the liberal university. But the liberal university was itself severely lacking. A reform of British universities is long overdue. And the Conservative prospectus hits many obvious targets. The debilitating division between the two cultures of humanities and the sciences is alive and kicking. The curriculum of higher education is far too narrow. There is a compelling case for broadening it, so that scientists study some arts and social science and all students study some science. Increasing access to educationally deprived groups is an urgent problem. It would be futile and counterproductive to deny that there is deadwood in the universities or that we need to align higher education more closely with the world of work, render it more accountable to society and liberalise entry to it; or that critics of present policies need to examine alternatives to the projected central control of funds by studying seriously the current spate of proposals for voucher systems.

But there remains a world of difference between a critical vocationalism and enterprise studies; between striving to blend academic freedom, institutional autonomy and social accountability and a *diktat* which weakens the former without strengthening the latter; and between a redrawing of the binary line within the university system to produce more fragmentation and elitism and the erosion of the binary line between universities and polytechnics to produce a more efficient and equal higher education. There is a case for change and an itinerary for reform. But the present government is travelling in the wrong direction.

References

Advisory Board For The Research Councils (1987) *A strategy for the science base*. London, ABRC.

Annan, N (1987) The reform of higher education in 1986 *History of Education* **16**(3):217–26.

Ashworth, J (1985) What price an ivory tower? *Higher Education Review* 17(2):31–43.

AUT (1985) *Universities and higher education: the case for expansion*. London, AUT.

Baker, K (1987) Speech to CVCP, 30 October (press release).

Baker, K (1988) *Hansard* Standing Committee J 25 February, London, HMSO.

Barnett, C (1986) *The audit of war*. Macmillan.

Becker, T (ed) (1987) *British higher education*. Allen and Unwin.

Becker, T and Kogan, M (1987) *Calling Britain's universities to account*. London, Education Reform Group.

Beloff, Lord (1987) *The Times*, 2 December.

Bentham, G (1987) An evaluation of the UGC's research ratings of the research in British university geography departments. *Area* 19(2):147-54.

Blackstone, T (1983) Access to higher education in Britain. In

Phillipson, N (ed), *Universities, Society and the Future* University of Edinburgh Press.

Carswell, J (1985) *Government and the universities in Britain: programme and performance 1960-80*. Cambridge University Press.

Centre for Contemporary Cultural Studies (1981) *Unpopular education schooling and social democracy in England since 1944*. Hutchinson.

Committee on Manpower Resources for Science and Technology (1968) *The flow of scientists, engineers and technologists: report of the Working Group on Manpower for Scientific Growth*. HMSO.

CVCP (1985) *Report of the Steering Committee for Efficiency Studies in Universities*. London, CVCP (Jarratt Report).

Constable, J and McCormick, R (1987) *The making of the British manager*. British Institute of Management.

Council For Scientific Policy (1968) *Enquiry into the flow of candidates in science and technology into higher education*. HMSO.

Crequer, N (1987) Putting a price on knowledge. *The Independent* 21 May.

DES (1985) *The development of higher education into the 1990s*. Cmnd 9524, HMSO.

DES (1987a) *Changes in structure and national planning for higher education: Universities Funding Council*. London, DES.

DES (1987b) *Changes in structure and national planning for higher education: contracts between the funding bodies and higher education institutions*. London, DES.

Edwards, E (1982) *Higher education for everyone*. Spokesman Books.

Farrant, J (1987) Central control of the university sector. In Becher, T (ed) *British Higher Education*. Allen and Unwin.

Fieldhouse, R (1985) *Adult education in the cold war*. University of Leeds Studies in Adult and Continuing Education.

Fulton, O (1988) Elite survivals: entry standards and procedures for higher education admission. *Studies in Higher Education*. 13(1):15-25.

George, V and Wilding, P (1984) *The impact of social policy*. Routledge and Kegan Paul.

Gillett, R (1987) Serious anomalies in the UGC comparative evaluation of the research performance of psychology departments. *Bulletin of the British Psychological Society*. 40:213-20.

Gosden, P (1983) *The educational system since 1944*. Martin Robertson.

Griffiths, J (1987) *The attack on higher education*. Manchester, Council For Academic Freedom and Democracy.

Grubb, W Norton (1987) Blinding faith in the new orthodoxy. *Times Higher Education Supplement,* 26 June.

Halsey, A, Heath, A and Ridge, J (eds) (1980) *Origins and destinations: family, class and education in modern Britain.* Oxford University Press.

Handy, C (1987) *The making of managers.* British Institute of Management.

Higher education: meeting the challenge. (1987) HMSO (White Paper).

Jackson, R (1988) Higher education in Britain. *Higher Education Quarterly.* 42(2): 111–18.

Kedourie, E (1988) *Diamonds into glass: the government and the universities.* London, Centre of Policy Studies.

Kingman, Sir John (1988) Newsnight, TV Programme, 6 January.

Little, A and Robbins, D (1981) Race bias. In Piper Warren D (ed) *Is higher education fair?* London, Society For Research into Higher Education.

Lodge, P (1986) Education. In Wilding, P (ed) *In defence of the welfare state.* Manchester University Press.

McIlroy, J and Spencer, B (1988) *University adult education in crisis.* University of Leeds Studies in Adult and Continuing Education.

McIlroy, J (1989) The funding of adult and continuing education in Britain. *International Journal of Lifelong Education.* 8(1).

Marris, R (1984) The great university miracle. *Times Higher Education Supplement.* 6 April.

Moodie, G (1987) Le roi est mort: vive le quoi? Croham and the death of the UGC. *Higher Education Quarterly* 14(4):329–43.

Morris, D (ed) (1985) *The economic system in the UK.* Oxford University Press.

National Audit Office (1985) *Redundancy compensation payments to university staff.* HMSO

National Economic Development Council (1982) *Education and Industry.* NEDC.

OECD (1983) *Policies for higher education in the 1980s.* Paris, OECD.

Parkes, Sir E (1980) Quoted in *Times Higher Education Supplement.* 14 November.

Phillipson, N (Ed) 1983) *Universities, society and the future.* University of Edinburgh Press.

Piper, D Warren (ed) (1981) *Is higher education fair?* London, SRHE.

Review of the University Grants Committee (1987) Cmnd 81. HMSO (Croham Report).

Rogaly, J (1988) Whitehall pays – and Whitehall calls the tune. *Financial Times* 5 February.

Sanderson, M (1987) *Education opportunity and social change in Britain.* Faber and Faber.

Scruton, R and Cox, C (1984) *Peace studies.* London, Institute for European Defence and Strategic Studies.

SSRC (1983) *An investigation into certain matters arising from the Rothschild Report on the Social Science Research Council.* London, SSRC.

Tapper, T and Salter, B (1978) *Education and the political order: changing patterns of class control.* Macmillan.

Tebbit, N (1983) Quoted in Wolpe, A and Donald, J (eds) *Is there anyone here from education?* Pluto Press.

Tight, M (1988) The value of higher education: part-time or full time...? *Studies in Higher Education* 12(2):169–85.

Times Higher Education Supplement (1988) Leadership risked as UGC predicts 5,000 job losses. 12 February.

UGC (1974) *University Development 1967–72.* HMSO.

UGC (1984) *A strategy for higher education into the 1990s.* UGC.

UGC (1986) *University statistics 1985–6.* Universities Statistical Record.

UGC (1987a) *Strengthening university earth sciences.* (Oxburgh Report) UGC

UGC (1987b) *University statistics 1986–7).* Universities Statistical Record.

Wiener, M (1981) *English culture and the decline of the industrial spirit 1850–1980.* Cambridge University Press.

Wilding, P (ed) (1986) *In defence of the welfare state.* Manchester University Press.

Williams, E (1988) Tenure's grip loosened. *Times Higher Education Supplement* 11 March.

Williamson, B (1986) Who has access? In Finch, J and Rustin, M (eds) *A degree of choice? Higher education and the right to learn.* Penguin Books.

Wolpe, A and Donald, J (eds) (1983) *Is there anyone here from education?* Pluto Press.

Young, H (1987) The menacing shadow over the universities. *Guardian,* 8 December.

3 The Education Reform Act (1988): implications for schools and local education authorities

Brian Wilcox

Introduction

The Education Reform Act (HMSO, 1988b) represents the most substantial and complex piece of educational legislation since the Butler Act of 1944. It is far reaching it its implications and designed to change profoundly both the government and practice of education. The Act consists of 238 sections and 13 schedules. Exactly half the number of sections (119) are devoted to matters pertaining to schools. Those remaining are concerned with: higher and further education (42); the special case of the Inner London Education Authority (35); and miscellaneous and general provisions (42). This chapter deals principally with the schools related aspects of the Act. Higher education matters are the subject of a separate contribution in this volume by John McIlroy.

The major changes which the Act is designed to effect in the case of schools can be summarised briefly as follows:

- the introduction of a national curriculum and an associated programme of testing and assessment;
- and end to the artificial limits on parents' first choice of school;
- the right of schools to opt out of local authority control and receive direct government funding;
- the establishment of city colleges;
- the delegation of school budgets to the governors of secondary schools and larger primaries.

The intention to produce a radical reform of the education system was clearly expressed in the Conservative Party's manifesto prior to the General Election of 11 June 1987. After the Party's electoral victory events moved swiftly with the publication of a series of consultation documents in July and August. The Government sought responses to these documents within the following two months. The protestations of teachers and others about the unreasonableness of requiring responses so swiftly, and at a time which coincided with the main holiday period, were to no avail. The Government persisted with its schedule and the Secretary of State, Mr Kenneth Baker, was able to introduce the Education Reform Bill into the Commons on 20 November 1987.

In the event however some 20,000 responses were received by the Department of Education and Science (DES). Whilst the responses were not published by the DES an analysis of them was produced independently, in a remarkably short period of time, as a book by the political journalist Julian Haviland early in 1988 (Haviland, 1988). Haviland's account confirms the general picture, apparent from the many articles and comments which appeared in the educational press, of massive reservations about the Government's proposals. It seems unlikely that the Government took much note of this unprecedented opposition, for the Bill included few substantive changes that were not consistent with the views outlined in the consultation documents.

Initially Mr Baker was inclined to refer to his forthcoming Bill as the Great Education Reform Bill – the implication being that history would come to rank the Bill alongside the previous reforming Acts of 1918 and 1944. However, as Simon (1988) reminds us, these Acts were consensus measures which were widely supported and passed after at least two years of consultation. Perhaps it was the recognition that his Bill did not satisfy these two democratic criteria, or possibly the emergence of a somewhat belated sense of humility, that explains the subsequent dropping of the word 'great' in the title of the Bill. On the other hand it may have been an attempt to shake off the risible acronym of GERBIL which had quickly provided a universal shorthand for the Great Education Reform Bill!

In its passage through approximately 370 hours of parliamentary debate the Bill expanded its initial 147 sections to 238 and 113 concessions were made by the Government to the Bill as a whole. As far as the school aspects are concerned most of the changes were at the margins. Thus the Act which finally became law on 29 July 1988 contained all of the fundamental points which had been foreshadowed in the consultation documents.

Before turning to consider the main changes and implications for schools and local education authorities (LEAs) it will be useful to understand the Government's espoused aims for reforming the educational system. These are clear from Mr Baker's speech on the Bill in the Commons on 1 December 1987.

> We need to inject a new vitality into . . . (the education) system. It has become producer-dominated. It has not proved sensitive to the demands for change that have become ever more urgent over the past ten years. This Bill will create a new framework, which will raise standards, extend choice and produce a better educated Britain . . . That means freeing schools and colleges to deliver the standards that parents and employers want . . . In a word it means choice. The purpose of the Bill is to secure delegation and widen choice . . . I am glad to see the growing consensus for many of the measures in this Bill. The opinion polls clearly show its popularity with the people who count – the parents. That applies, above all, to the national curriculum, which is the bedrock of our reform proposals . . . The proposal (for open enrolment) is a natural extension of our concern to maximise parental choice . . . Our proposals (for opting out) . . . will widen choice for many parents in the State-maintained sector for whom all too often the only choice is take it or leave it. This wider choice will help to improve standards in all schools as we introduce a competitive spirit into the provision of education – and at no extra cost to the consumer . . . I would sum up the (Bill) . . . in three words – standards, freedom and choice (quoted in Haviland, 1988, pp 2–4).

The intention here is to produce a consumer oriented education system driven by the twin engines of choice and competition. The assumption is that these, together with the tighter control over pupils' learning which the national curriculum represents, will lead to an improvement in educational standards and achievements.

The implications of the Act for schools and LEAs

The national curriculum and programmes of assessment

The legislation here applies only to maintained and grant maintained schools. Thus the concept of a national curriculum is substantially vitiated by the exclusion from its requirements of independent schools on the one hand and the new city technology colleges (CTCs) and city colleges for the technology of the arts (CCTAs) on the other.

The curriculum for all pupils of compulsory school age (i.e. 5–16 years) will consist of the core subjects of mathematics, English, and science (and Welsh for schools in Wales which are Welsh speaking) together with the foundation subjects: history, geography, technology, music, art, physical education, and (for pupils 11-16 years) a modern language. In addition religious education is defined as part of the basic curriculum. Religious education and the daily act of worship are to be 'wholly or mainly of a broadly Christian character' although non-Christians can have a separate assembly under certain conditions and subject to the approval of standing advisory councils on religious education to be set up by the Act. These will advise LEAs on matters connected with religious education and worship.

Although the Act does not specify the amount of time to be spent on different subjects the Government's intention is that all schools will teach core and foundation subjects and religious education to pupils 5-14 years 'for a reasonable amount of time' from September 1989 (Baker, 1988b). Programmes of study, attainment targets and arrangements for assessment and testing will be introduced by orders for the core and foundation subjects. At the time of writing subject working groups established by the Secretary of State in science and mathematics (DES,1988c; 1988d) have already reported and submitted their proposals. The working group for English has also been established and its report is awaited. The reports of subject working groups will be available for wide consultation. The results of this will inform the National Curriculum Council (NCC) - established under the Act - so that it can make clear recommendations to the Secretary of State. It is envisaged that programmes and targets for mathematics, science and English for five year olds, and mathematics and science for twelve year olds will be implemented in schools in September 1989. Working groups in the other subjects will be established in due course and their programmes and targets introduced into schools in a phased manner over several years (DES, 1988e).

The introduction of a national curriculum can be seen as the logical outcome of attempts by previous governments (both Labour and Conservative) over the last twelve or so years to achieve both a broad consensus about the curriculum (perceived as having an unacceptable degree of diversity) and clear accountability for its provision. Indeed the collective failure on the part of schools and LEAs to secure these requirements on a voluntary basis has probably helped to precipitate direct intervention by the Government.

When the national curriculum proposals were published in the first of the consultation documents (DES, 1987) they met with widespread dismay. They seemed to hark back to a rigid subject based curriculum reminiscent of the 1904 Regulations, and were totally out of keeping with the flexible and imaginative integrated curriculum approaches pioneered by primary schools and increasingly by secondaries. To some extent these early anxieties have been dispelled as it has become clear that the Act specifies neither the time to be spent on subjects nor the way in which they should be taught. The Secretary of State and his senior officials have sought to give reassurance on two basic points. Firstly that a national curriculum is not a threat to an integrated approach. Secondly that the national curriculum is not the whole of the curriculum and 'LEAs and schools will continue to need their own well-thought-out and coherent policies for the curriculum and its delivery, as the 1986 Act requires' (Baker 1988a). Furthermore the recommendations of the science and mathematics working parties have generally been well received by teachers and others.

Having said that however, it must be admitted that the national curriculum has a basic flaw. The ultimate purposes which the total curriculum should serve in an increasingly pluralist and secular society have been left largely unexplored. The Act specifies 'a balanced and broadly based curriculum which promotes the spiritual, moral, cultural, mental and physical development of pupils at the school and of society; and prepares such pupils for the opportunities, responsibilities and experiences of adult life'. Whilst unpacking the implications of this kind of statement cannot be accomplished within the confines of a Parliamentary Act, the fact is that the task has been largely ignored in the welter of curriculum documents produced by the DES and Her Majesty's Inspectorate (HMI) in recent years. The consequence is that we have no well formulated and broadly agreed view of the total curriculum which is capable of informing the development of individual aspects. In effect the national curriculum will be constructed bit by bit over the next few years as successive subject working parties produce their recommendations. We shall just have to wait and see whether all the bits add up to a convincing and worthy whole.

The case for a national curriculum is logically distinct from the case for a national testing programme. It is perfectly feasible to have a national curriculum without an associated test programme. For example, the Soviet Union which has perhaps the most detailed and prescriptive national curriculum has not yet found it necessary to establish a complementary state testing apparatus (Wilcox, 1988). In contrast the Government has decided to have both, in what appears to be a heavy belt and braces attempt to control the curriculum from the centre. The Government's intention to have testing of pupils at ages 7, 11, 14 and 16 years with the aggregated results publishable on a school by school basis has been met with almost total opposition. Teachers and others have expressed anxieties about such matters as: the distorting effect of crude paper and pencil tests on childrens' learning; the potential of testing to lead to 'labelling' individual children; the damaging effect on schools of the publication of 'league tables' of results.

The Act, it should be noted, uses the more general term 'assessment' rather than 'testing'. The Act does not describe the nature of the assessment arrangements – these will be specified in due course by order of the Secretary of State. He will be guided by the detailed proposals of the special Task Group on Assessment and Testing (TGAT) which he established (DES, 1988a, 1988b). TGAT has in fact produced a sophisticated assessment model which has been welcomed by Mr Baker. It has also dispelled at least some of the initial anxieties. TGAT proposes a system based on a combination of moderated teacher assessment and standardised assessment tasks. The standardised attainment tasks and the teacher assessments should use a wide range of methods (oral, written, practical) so as to minimise curriculum distortion. The assessment would be *criterion referenced*, i.e. demonstrating what pupils have achieved against attainment targets, rather than *norm referenced*, i.e. where pupils are compared against each other. The primary purpose would be *formative* so that results help decisions about the pupil's further learning needs. The results of individual children would be confidential to those who need to know. Aggregated results would be available and reported publicly, without identifying individuals, for groups of pupils or the school as a whole. The latter should only be published as part of a broader report on the work of the school.

TGAT proposes an economical model in which each subject to be assessed has a small number of *profile components*. Where possible, one or more components should have more general application across the curriculum. Each profile component will comprise a cluster of attainment targets having some homogeneity in relation to the skills, knowledge and understanding which the subject promotes. Each profile would consist of up to ten *levels* which would define the sequence of progression over the age range 7–16 years. For age 7 years, only the first three levels would be used: level 1 for a pupil needing additional help, 2 for satisfactory attainment, and 3 for advanced performance calling for special treatment to maintain good progress. At age 16 years levels 7–10 would broadly correspond to the higher GCSE grades.

The TGAT model has already provided the basis for the assessment proposals which have been submitted to the Secretary of State by the subject working groups on science and mathematics. The translation of these into practical reality presupposes both a substantial training operation – potentially for all teachers – and a research and development programme to produce the range of assessment tasks required. Both of these tasks pose formidable challenges. However, even if all goes according to plan, the first fully reported results of assessment will not be before 1991/92 and that only for mathematics, science and English for 7 year olds.

Reported results for the remaining age groups in the other subjects are unlikely to be available before the middle to late 1990s. This is a relatively long time-scale both in political and educational terms and must raise the question of whether or not the programme will be overtaken by the next reform!

The immediate prospects however may suggest an almost Prussian style curriculum in which the Secretary of State has powers to define and amend programmes as he deems fit. This enlargement of his power has been a cause of much concern. His response has been to draw attention to the checks and balances to which he is subject, e.g. his obligation to consult the National Councils established under the Act, i.e. the NCC and the SEAC (School Examinations and Assessment Council).

Until now headteachers and their staff, compared to their peers in other countries, had perhaps the greatest degree of autonomy in determining the nature of the curriculum. The Act would seem to move them decisively towards the more prescribed curriculum context which characterises some other countries. Furthermore the situation ahead may turn out to be an even more assessment driven one than is the case now. The formidable curriculum and assessment apparatus which is proposed will be given two further guarantees of its realisation. Local advisory services and inspectorates are to be charged with the task of monitoring and evaluating its implementation. Secondly, parents will be able to refer any grievances about the curriculum experienced by their children to the new LEA complaints machinery.

Open enrolment, opting out and city technology colleges

Central to the Government's educational policy is a commitment to increasing parental choice and encouraging competition between schools in the recruitment of pupils. The Act sets out effectively three mechanisms for achieving this.

First, the LEAs and the governing bodies of voluntary-aided schools lose their power of setting a ceiling on pupil admission limits. The Secretary of State now acquires that power. The intention is to ensure that schools do not set admission limits below their physical capacity in an attempt to restrict access to more popular schools. The 1980 Act went some way towards increasing parents' choice of school and reducing the restrictive efforts of a few local authorities to protect unpopular schools. Under the new Act every school will be required to accept pupils up to its 'standard number' defined in terms of the number admitted in 1979 as determined by the 1980 Act. A school governing body which considers that it has the room to take in more pupils may apply to the LEA to have its admission limit raised. Recourse to the Secretary of State is allowed if the LEA refuses such an application. Proposals by an LEA or the governing body of a voluntary aided school to reduce the standard number must be published and be open to any objections made by ten or more local electors, by the governing body of any school affected by the proposals and by any LEA concerned.

This section of the original Bill was amended in one significant regard in the case of voluntary aided schools. These schools had been concerned that open enrolment would threaten their distinctive religious character. The Act therefore allows the governors to make arrangements with the LEA concerning admissions so that the character of the school is preserved.

The effect of open enrolment will be to make it very much more difficult to plan rationally the distribution of school places across a whole LEA. This will be particularly exacerbated in a context of falling rolls and the concomitant reorganisation of post primary education in which many LEAs are currently involved. In the case of individual schools, increasing admissions to the 1979 situation – when schools were largely full – may lead to unacceptable levels of overcrowding. This is because many schools have used the space released by falling rolls to design appropriate learning environments to cope with the multitude of curriculum initiatives which have emerged since 1979. In addition some fear open enrolment will reinforce the tendency in some areas for schools to be segregated on a racial or social class basis.

The second mechanism for enhancing parental choice which the Act allows is the opting out of schools from local authority control. The governing bodies of any county and voluntary schools with more than 300 pupils can apply to become a grant-maintained (GM) school. The procedure is initiated by two meetings of the governors, no fewer than 28 days and not more than 42 days apart, deciding to pursue an application for opting out. A secret postal ballot of all parents of registered pupils at the school must then be called. Alternatively a ballot may be called for by at least 20 % of parents. If 50 % or more of registered parents vote then a simple majority will be sufficient to determine whether an application is made to the Secretary of State. If, however, less than 50 % of parents vote then the governing body must arrange a second ballot within 14 days of the result of the first ballot being declared. Irrespective of the number who vote in the second ballot a simple majority will decide whether or not an application is to be pursued. This somewhat unusual voting procedure was the outcome of amendments made as a result of wide-spread dissatisfaction with the voting arrangements proposed in the Bill.

The original proposal had been to determine the issue by a simple majority vote of registered parents.

If the vote is in favour of opting out then the governors must publish detailed plans within six months. Objections to those proposals may be lodged within two months by local electors, the LEA or the trustees of the school concerned and the governors of any other schools affected. The Secretary of State decides whether a proposal to become a GM school is accepted or not. Where a school is being considered for closure or reorganisation the Secretary of State will decide whether to allow it to opt out *before* taking any decision on the LEA's plan.

Initially voluntary schools were concerned that opting out might lead to a change in their religious character. An amendment to the original Bill has met this anxiety by providing the protection of requiring that any subsequent proposal to change the character of the school would need the approval of its trustees.

A GM school will take over its former premises from the LEA which will then cease to maintain them. The LEA will however retain responsibility for certain services and benefits, e.g. welfare, transport provision. GM schools will receive from the DES a 100 % capital expenditure grant and revenue funding equivalent to that received from the LEA. GM schools will not be allowed to 'opt in' to LEA control. The Government has also made clear that it does not expect a GM school to change its status (e.g. from a comprehensive to a grammar school) for at least five years after opting out.

It is not yet clear what proportion of schools will avail themselves of the opportunity for opting out, eligibility for which comes into force from September 1989. Certainly the Government has been keen to press ahead and within a month of the Bill receiving the Royal Assent a privately funded Grant Maintained Schools Trust (GMST) had been established which immediately distributed a glossy brochure on opting out to every secondary headteacher. The director of the Trust has been quoted as saying that he expected that between five and ten schools would have grant maintained status by September 1989 (Hughill, 1988). Some interest in opting out is likely to be seen in some LEAs where reorganisation plans threaten the continuation of popular sixth forms. This seems to have been initially the case in the Harrogate area of North Yorkshire (Sutcliffe, 1988). Subsequently however it seems that the LEA had been at pains to reassure the community that the sixth forms were safe and, as a result, the desire to opt out had apparently died the death. Whether this attempt to be receptive to local opinion at the expense of rational planning will be characteristic of other parts of the country remains to be seen.

Much will depend on the balance of financial advantage which may accrue to GM schools. The director of the GMST has confirmed the point that GM schools will be funded on the basis of the level of spending within the LEA from which a school has opted out (Weston, 1988). Nevertheless the Act does give the Secretary of State the power to provide 'special purpose grants' to such schools as he thinks appropriate. He therefore has a potential financial inducement to stimulate opting out if the natural rate of that happening proves disappointing. It may also be the case that the desire for increased autonomy – the rationale which underpins opting out – may be more related to the wish for greater freedom on how to spend the budget than to be independent of the LEA which provides it. If that is so then that will be better met by the arrangements for delegated budgets than by opting out.

The third means of enhancing parental choice is provided by the city colleges. These colleges, designated either as city technology colleges (CTCs) or city colleges for the technology of the arts (CCTAs), are independent although the education which they will provide will be free. Their purpose is to extend the range of choice of schools available in the inner cities. They will provide a broad curriculum for pupils aged 11 to 18 years of different abilities who are drawn, wholly or mainly, from the area in which the school is situated. In the case of CTCs there will be a special emphasis on science and technology. CCTAs will emphasise technology in its applications to the performing and creative arts. The colleges will be funded directly by the DES and industrial and commercial sponsors. The latter will have their investments protected for at least seven years and will not suffer financially if the colleges should be discontinued during that period.

The first CTC opened its doors in September 1988, in premises formerly occupied by Kingshurst school in Solihull. The school has received financial sponsorship from Hanlon Plc and Lucas Industries. Apart from this the college will be funded on a level similar to other LEA schools of its size. The fears that the establishment of CTCs would have an adverse effect on recruitment levels to other schools nearby seem to be justified from early evidence in Solihull (Blackburne, 1988). In addition it has been claimed that Kingshurst was effectively creaming off the better pupils. The Labour Shadow Education Secretary, Jack Straw, has asked the House of Commons Public Accounts Committee to investigate the funding of CTCs. It now appears, despite earlier statements to the contrary, that CTCs are to receive substantial sums of public money. According to Mr Straw, £90 million of taxpayers' money has been earmarked to pay up to 85 % of capital costs of colleges without Parliamentary approval (ibid). Further colleges are likely to be established over the next few years and the Director of the CTC Trust is reported to have set herself the task of 'getting 20 CTCs up and running' (ibid).

Local financial management

The Act sets out the provisions by which LEAs will determine the financing of maintained schools and the delegation to school governing bodies of responsibility for important aspects of financial management and the appointment of staff. The broad framework of provision required by the Act is explicated in greater detail in a circular to LEAs issued at the end of August 1988, although a draft had been distributed some months earlier.

The circular (DES, 1988f) requires LEAs to submit schemes of financial delegation to the Secretary of State for his approval by September 1989. The intention is that schemes will be implemented fully in all secondary schools and primary schools with more than 200 pupils in April 1993 at the latest (1994 in the case of inner London LEAs). Schemes may however be extended to smaller schools and special schools if the LEA and the Secretary of State agree.

The items of expenditure delegated must include the bulk of school expenditure including staffing, books and equipment, and day to day delegation together with specific government grants (education support grants, LEA training grants, Section II grants etc.) and the cost of central administration services, local advisers and inspectors, home to school transport. In addition LEAs may propose to retain central provision for a limited number of other items. The requirement is that the total cost of all items retained centrally will not exceed 10 % (reducing to 7 % in three years) of the LEAs' general schools budget.

After the LEA's aggregated budget has been fixed by deducting the accepted items from the total resources available the LEA is required to determine a 'formula' of its own choosing for allocating funds to schools. The formula must inter alia take account of the number and ages of pupils and may include other factors affecting the needs of individual schools.

Financial delegation draws on the successful experience of a small number of LEAs who have already, on their own initiative, moved their financial arrangements in this kind of direction. Financial delegation represents a key aspect of the Government's policy for improving the quality of learning and teaching in schools. The DES circular has been greatly influenced by the special report on financial delegation which the Government commissioned from the management consultants Coopers and Lybrand (HMSO, 1988a). This report emphasises that the changes proposed are more than purely financial. They represent nothing less than the adoption of a new culture and philosophy for the organisation of education at the school level. To emphasise the general shift towards a management approach the report uses the term 'local management of schools' (LMS). Under LMS governors will control the running of the school and will have freedom to deploy resources according to its own educational needs and priorities. They will have responsibilities for determining the selection and appointment of staff and will be able to recommend dismissals. LEAs will effectively be removed from the detailed control of most school activities. That control will be replaced with a clearer responsibility for setting objectives and managing the system as a whole.

Although LMS is supported by the teachers associations and many educationists, it is not without its opponents. Jackson Hall, a former chief education officer, has mounted a devastating critique of the influential Coopers and Lybrand report. Whilst the report has been generally acclaimed as providing a rigorous rationale for LMS, Hall (1988) has highlighted the many reservations and disclaimers which pervade the document. Some of the main ones include: the fact that not one of the LEA pioneers of LMS yet has a fully operational system; the improbability that LMS will lead to overall savings; the difficulty of ensuring objectivity and the need to accept some rough justice (a safety net will be needed and some schools will lose out); and doubts about whether the governors and some headteachers will be willing and able to undertake their new responsibilities. He concludes bleakly by noting that a high proportion of schools will be given formula funding in a situation inevitably cramped by restrictions on local government expenditure . . .' the thrust of average costs will tighten the straitjacket on . . . schools, especially those disadvantaged to begin with. In short, LMS it what it is in its nature to be – a motor of differentiation and inequality' (ibid).

A stinging attack on LMS has also been made by David Muffett, chair of Hereford and Worcestershire education committee, all the more significant since he is a staunch Conservative (Muffett, 1988). He cites schools with identical numbers of pupils and teachers whose salary costs differed by £9,000 and for which there were substantional unavoidable variations on other costs arising largely from the nature of the premises which the schools occupy. In his view formula funding will lead to injustices at school level and cruel dilemmas for schools facing a deficit. Put bluntly if schools cannot afford their teachers are they to sack some? He, like Jackson Hall, fears that LMS will encourage the larger schools to opt out since this will compel LEAs to release 'their share' of central resources.

Implications of the Education Reform Act (1988) for the government of education

As we have seen, for Mr Baker, the Education Reform Act is centrally concerned with standards, freedom and choice. Behind these words lie two broad notions which capture much of the educational philosophy of the New Right which the Government has progressively appropriated. These are 'accountability' and 'education as a market commodity'. Standards are associated with the former concept and freedom and choice with the latter.

Concern about the standards of the public education system, e.g. the alleged failures of comprehensive schools and child centred learning, had been expressed with increasing political effect since the publication of the so-called Black Papers in the late 1960s and early 1970s (cf Cox and Dyson, 1969a, 1969b). It was in fact a Labour Government, under Prime Minister Jim Callaghan, which first attempted to address such concerns seriously by initiating what was grandly called the Great Debate in 1976/77. In the years which followed, governments of both political hues sought to achieve a greater consensus on the aims, objectives and content of the school curriculum. It was however to be the three Conservative Governments elected since 1979 which would establish a mechanism for ensuring that schools achieved a greater degree of curriculum commonality and one more in line with national priorities. The mechanism was 'categorical funding' (Harland, 1987). In brief this involves LEAs bidding for special grants from the DES and other government departments (most notably the Manpower Services Commission, now retitled the Employment Department/Training) in order to develop, under specific contractual arrangements, aspects of the curriculum identified as national priorities. Even before the advent of the 1988 Act previous government policy had already achieved a remarkable degree of curriculum consensus, particularly in secondary schools, throughout the country. The imposition of a national curriculum represents, then, a natural culmination of this process.

The national curriculum is designed to provide parents and others with a clear indication of what it is that children will learn in their years of compulsory schooling. It will also, through the attainment targets to be determined for each subject area, define the standards which are to be reached. The intention is that the achievement of these standards will be assessed and the results communicated to parents and others who need to know. In addition aggregated results will be published so that the standards of individual schools can be compared one with another. Thus it is argued will the accountability of teachers and schools be made visible to the parents. Parents will therefore have more information on schools and a better basis on which to choose one for their children.

Choice however is only real if parents have a range of schools of different types from which to choose. The hidden aim of the Act is to break what the Government sees as an LEA monopoly and to provide that choice. Thus parents who formerly only had schools in the maintained sectors from which to choose will in future be able to consider GM schools and CTCs. A major aim of the Act is to introduce competition into the public provision of education.

The Government's values 'articulate beliefs about educational achievement which assert that a system which is accountable and responsive to the choices of individual consumers of the service will improve in quality as a necessary consequence. As in other forms of market exchange, the products which thrive can only do so because they have the support of the consumers. Those products which fail the test of the market place go out of business' (Ranson, 1988 p8).

There are two basic assumptions in the Government's thinking here which should be questioned. The first is whether or not education can properly be regarded as a product. Much of the dominant vocabulary of education at the present time reinforces this view. Thus we speak of learning being 'delivered' as though it were a commodity like newspapers or the morning milk. Such a notion stands in sharp contrast to an older tradition which sees education as a complex process involving the realisation of human potential – a process which inevitably has something of the mysterious and unpredictable about it. The tendency to view education in product terms pre-dates the present Government for it has emerged strongly over the last decade or more as the imperative of vocational relevance and its associated instrumentalism have been brought to bear on the educational debate.

The second assumption is that competition between schools – regarded as functioning in an educational market – necessarily results in an improvement in quality. The opposite however may be the case. Thus if market forces overfill some schools, something of their former distinctive quality may be lost. If those same forces empty some other schools the consequences for their pupils, teachers and local communities may be dire indeed. Often it will be the more disadvantaged parents and pupils that will suffer – facing, as they may, longer distances to travel.

The desirability or otherwise of applying market principles to education is an issue common throughout the western world. A survey of the views of organisational leaders active in the field of educational policy carried out in England and Wales, the Federal Republic of Germany and the USA in 1984–5 identified this as a significant theme (Landsberger et al. 1988). Interestingly whilst most groups supported a move towards a greater use of 'market principles' in Germany, in England and the USA more organisations were against such a move.

Market theorists tend to assume in their models the existence of true competition. This will almost certainly not be the case in the post-Education Reform Act future. As Wragg observes:

> everything will be loaded in favour of City Technology Colleges and Grant Maintained Schools, intake, finances and publicity. Already expensive glossy brochures have been produced for City Technology Colleges. There are no such Government publicity puffs for jobbing local authority schools. Indeed the Governments' propaganda machine has worked consistently against them, and they, their teachers and their achievements have been consistently belittled or ignored, and the failures in the system emphasised and exaggerated (Wragg, 1988, p17).

Moreover

> the working of the market place is not to be left entirely to the hidden hand of competitive self interest. Rather it is to be interpreted and guided by the 'public' hand of the Secretary of State who will be granted an extraordinary new range of regulatory powers . . . Schools may be 'privatised' progressively but their reproduction of culture (the curriculum) will be nationalised (or Anglicised) (Ranson, 1988, p13).

A market is also not neutral in social class terms.

> the market masks its social bias. It elides, but reproduces the inequalities which consumers bring to the market place. Under the guise of neutrality, the institution of the market actively confirms and reinforces the pre-existing social order of wealth and privilege. The market is a crude mechanism of social selection. It can provide a more effective social engineering than anything we have previously witnessed in the post-war period (ibid).

The fear is that

> the process will reinforce and self fulfil the three tier view of humanity, with three different levels of school, the fully independent, the semi-privatised and the proletarian schools. The labelling will be even more pronounced than it is in our present society (Wragg, 1988, p17).

The effects of the Act on the former distribution of powers and responsibilities between Government, the schools and the LEAs are considerable. The Secretary of State likes to talk of devolving power from the hub to the rim. In reality, although additional powers are devolved to schools for the management of budgets, this has been offset by the reduction in freedom and power to determine the curriculum. The Secretary of State has acquired a vastly inflated set of additional powers as a result of the Act (182 in total). These have largely been at the expense of the LEAs whose powers have been very substantially diminished. The overall effect has been to change irrevocably the balance of power between Government, the LEA and schools so that 'Between the emerging forces of market and hierarchy is finally suffocated the centre-piece of the 1944 legislation – the Local Education Authority, and the local government of education' (Ranson, 1988, p13). The LEAs are cast as the villains, deserving total extirpation, in the educational drama scripted by the New Right. For them the Education Reform Act is but a staging post to the total privatisation of education.

Such a view may turn out to be too bleak. Important responsibilities do remain for the LEAs. The Secretary of State has reassured the Society of Education Officers that this will in fact be the case. Whilst the Government's intention is to devolve as much responsibility as possible to the level of the individual school 'the professional contribution of chief education officers and their departments, including inspectors and advisers, will remain crucial' (Baker, 1988a). Local authorities would continue to exercise 'important responsibilities including the provision of schools and their resourcing, the inspection and quality control of schools, teacher management including appraisal, staff development and in-service training' (ibid). These roles are not insignificant ones and are at the heart of the provision of education. They require the LEA to move from a role of control to one of the management of influence.

The future of the public system of education is difficult to discern. What however can be said with confidence is that the initials of the Education Reform Act – ERA – are most appropriate, for the Act most assuredly ushers in an educational era which will be a very different one to the one which preceeded it.

References

Baker, K (1988a) Secretary of State's Speech to SEO, 22 January, Press Report, DES.

Baker, K (1988b) Heads vital to success of educational reforms, Speech of Secretary of State to NAHT, 3 June, Press Report, DES.

Blackburne, L (1988) Newcomer worries the neighbours; Consciousness raising in the inner city. 16 September: 6.

Cox, C B and Dyson, A E (eds) (1969a) *Fight for freedom: a Black Paper.* The Critical Quarterly Society.

Cox, C B and Dyson, A E (Eds) (1969b) *Black Paper Two: the crisis in education.* The Critical Quarterly Society.

DES (1987) *The national curriculum 5–6.* A consultation document.

DES (1988a) *National curriculum. Task Group on Assessment and Testing.* A report.

DES (1987b) *National Curriculum. Task Group on Assessment and Testing.* Three supplementary reports.

DES (1988c) *Mathematics for ages 5 to 16.* Proposals of the Secretary of State for Education and Science and the Secretary of State for Wales.

DES (1988d) *Science for ages 5 to 16.* Proposals of the Secretary of State for Education and Science and the Secretary of State for Wales.

DES (1988e) *Local Education Authority Training Grants Scheme: financial year 1988–90.* Appendix A, Circular 5/88

DES (1988f) *Education Reform Act: local management of schools.* Circular 7/88

Hall, J (1988) Directed to the wrong church. *Times Educational Supplement.* 5 August: 4.

Harland, J (1987) The new INSET: a transformation scene. *Journal of Educational Policy.* 2 (3): 235–44.

Haviland, J (1988) *Take care Mr Baker.* Fourth Estate.

HMSO (1988a) *Local management of schools.* A report to the DES by the management consultants Coopers and Lybrand.

HMSO (1988b) *Education Reform Act 1988.*

Hughill, B (1988) Competitive edge sharpens. *Educational Supplement.* 16 September: 1.

Landsberger, H A, Carlson, J R and Campbell R T (1988) Education policy in comparative perspective: similarities in the underlying issues in debate among educational elites in Britain, the Federal Republic of Germany and the USA. *Research Papers in Education* 3 (2): 103–30.

Muffett, D (1988) Soft at the centre. *Times Educational Supplement,* 19 August: 4.

Ranson, S (1988) From 1944 to 1988: education, citizenship and democracy. *Local Government Studies* 14 (1): 1–19.

Simon, B (1988) *Bending the rules: The Baker 'reform of education'.* Lawrence and Wishart.

Sutcliffe, J (1988) Opting out loses its novelty value. *Times Educational Supplement.* 16 September: 12.

Weston, C (1988) Official prompts funding confusion. *Times Educational Supplement.* 16 September: 3.

Wilcox, B (1988) No testing for Soviet citizens. *Times Educational Supplement.* 29 April: 24.

Wragg, E (1988) *Education in the Market Place.* National Union of Teachers.

4 The demunicipalisation of rented housing

Peter Kemp

Introduction

In Britain, unlike most other west European countries, non-profit or social housing is dominated by local authority provision. Elsewhere in western Europe, housing associations and co-operatives are more important than local authorities in the provision of social housing to rent (Harloe, 1987). Despite a significant expansion of the housing association sector in Britain since 1974, local councils still accounted for nine out of ten social rented houses in 1986. However, all this seems set to change, for the role of local authorities as providers of rented housing is now being seriously questioned for the first time since they became firmly established as major landlords in the early 1920s.

Having spent its first two terms of office concentrating almost exclusively in housing policy on extending individual home ownership, the Conservative administration under Mrs Thatcher has now turned its attention to the provision of rented housing. The 1987 White Paper on housing policy (Department of Environment 1987) and the Housing Act 1988 envisage a major restructuring of the market for rented housing.[1,2] The Government hopes to achieve a sharp reduction in the importance of local authorities as landlords and a correspondingly increased role for other agencies, including housing associations, co-operatives, trusts and private landlords. Local authorities are to be confined to at best an enabling role, bringing together the public and private sectors and facilitating provision by other agencies.

Taken together, these changes represent the most important recasting of housing policy since the first world war. Although the likely scale and pace of change that the new policies will achieve is at present difficult to predict, there is no doubt that a significant transformation in rented housing provision is now underway. The article by Whitehead and Kleinman examines the likely impact of deregulation in the privately rented sector, while this article examines the changes to social housing provision.

The polarisation of housing tenure

In order to understand the nature, causes and significance of the changes that are beginning to take place, it is important to be aware of the long term forces at work as well as those that arise from the immediate context. For it would be mistaken to imagine that the demunicipalisation of rented housing is simply a product of the recent resurgence of the New Right and, more particularly, of the political project often referred to as 'Thatcherism'. Although it is true that, in many respects, the 1987 White Paper and the Housing Act do bear the unmistakable stamp of the New Right political philosophy, they are also a response to the long term restructuring of the housing market and to changing attitudes towards housing tenure which pre-date 1979. It is necessary, therefore, to briefly outline these long term trends before discussing the housing policies of the Thatcher government.

Since the early years of this century, the housing market in Britain has been undergoing a process of polarisation. Owner occupation has grown from around 10 % of the stock in 1914 to 57 % in 1979 and 65 % in 1986. Over the same period renting from private landlords has fallen from 90 % to only 8 % . Local authority housing steadily expanded from almost nil in 1914 to a peak of 29 % in 1971, at which level it remained until 1979. Although sales and falling new build have reduced the relative and absolute size of the sector under the Conservatives, local councils still owned 24 % of all housing in 1986. Hence since the second world war, as the privately rented sector has declined, the housing market has become increasingly polarised between owner occupation and council housing (Hamnett, 1984). By 1986, these two tenures accounted for about nine out of every ten dwellings in England and Wales. This has meant that, for those households unable to afford to buy their own home, virtually the only alternative is renting from their local authority. As Table 4.1 shows, councils account for just over two thirds of all rented houses and for nine out of ten houses rented from social landlords.

Table 4.1 The provision of rented housing in England in 1986

Sector	*Dwellings*	
	(000s)	*(%)*
Local authority	4,609	70
Housing association	494	7
Private landlord	1,516	23
All rented housing	6,619	35

Source: Department of the Environment, *Housing and Construction Statistics*. HMSO, Table 9.3.

Accompanying this polarisation of housing tenures, however, has been a 'residualisation' of the council sector and a dominant view of owner occupation as by far the preferred tenure. Particularly over the last decade, local authority housing has been increasingly housing the poorest and most disadvantaged households in society (see Table 4.2) and much of the best stock has been sold under the right to buy policy (Forrest and Murie, 1986). Those tenants who remain in the sector are arguably stigmatised by the increasingly prevalent view that, if you are not a home owner, it is because you cannot afford to be one rather than because you prefer to rent. Certainly, since the early 1960s, governments of all parties have presented home ownership as the most attractive way of securing access to accommodation and council housing as a poor second best.

Table 4.2 Income of households in council housing in Britain

	1968 *(%)*	*1978* *(%)*	*1983* *(%)*	*1986* *(%)*
Proportion of council tenants who were among the:				
Poorest 30 % of all households	31	42	52	60
Middle 20 % of all households	23	23	23	22
Richest 50 % of all households	46	35	25	18

Source: Willmott and Murie (1988, p31); Department of Employment (1988, Table 4).

Yet it is important to stress that the role and iconography of council housing have changed over time. In particular, there has tended to be an alternation in the role that council housing has been required by central government to play within the housing market and this has partly reflected the different political philosophies of the two main parties. The Labour Party has, in general, tended to give council housing a fairly broad remit, aimed at meeting general housing needs within the community. The Conservatives, by contrast, have preferred to cast council housing in a narrower, residual role, aimed at meeting those 'special needs' (such as rehousing families from slum clearance schemes and the elderly and disabled) that the private sector was unable to meet (see Merrett, 1979).

Yet while the Conservatives have in the past been prepared to concede an important, if residual, role for council housing they have always been 'reluctant collectivists' (George and Wilding, 1976; Hamnett, 1987). On pragmatic grounds, Conservative Governments, in the absence of a private rented alternative, have used local authorities as a vehicle for providing housing to rent. Although they would have preferred to see private provision of rented housing, almost no new build has been forthcoming since 1945 and the existing stock has gradually diminished despite several attempts to reverse the decline (Kemp, 1988). It is perhaps in part because of the long term collapse of the privately rented sector that the Conservatives have promoted owner occupation quite so vigorously, for the alternative appeared to be public housing to rent. This also seems to account for the promotion of housing associations by the Conservatives since the Housing Act 1961.

However, over the past decade, council housing has undergone something of a crisis of confidence. In part, this has reflected the rise of the New Right and the 'new romanticism' about the beneficence of the market that has swept across most of the advanced industrial nations (Piven, 1987). But criticism of council housing has also come from the left (e.g. CDP, 1976). This growing disillusion has particularly focused on the way in which council housing is managed. It is often alleged that council housing management is paternalisitic, insensitive to tenant wishes and inefficient. Indeed, the Audit Commission (1986) in a recent report argued that there was a 'crisis' in the management of council housing.

However, despite some agreement about some of the problems with council housing management, the Left and the Right differ significantly in their policy prescriptions. For many on the Left, the answer is to transform the way in which council housing is managed, particularly by decentralising management to the estate or neighbourhood level and by increasing tenant involvement in the running of their homes. Although the Conservatives also view this kind of activity with favour, they do not see it as being sufficient. Instead, the answer is increasingly seen to lie in the privatisation of council housing. Underlying these two different perspectives for tackling the problems of council housing is a difference in political philosophy. Those who wish to see council housing transformed from within hold dear, generally speaking, to the social democratic or citizenship view of social policy. But those (such as the present Government) who favour transferring council housing to the private sector tend to prefer a more market oriented model of social policy (see Clapham, et al., 1989 for a fuller discussion of this).

Housing under the Conservatives, 1979 to 1986

Of course, the Conservative Government returned to office in 1979 was committed to rolling back the state and, in particular, to selling council houses to their tenants. The Housing Act 1980 gave council tenants the right to buy their home at substantial discount (depending on length of occupation) from the market value. Since 1979, a million council houses have been sold, two thirds of them under the right to buy. As a result, the local authority sector has declined relatively and absolutely (See Table 4.3) for the first time since 1919. However, since 1982 the number of right to buy sales has begun to decline. The shift to selling tenanted estates, therefore, represents a logical next step if the privatisation drive in housing is to be maintained. Thus shortly after the 1987 election, the Minister for Housing stated that the 'next great push after the right to buy should be to get rid of the state as a big landlord' (Waldegrave, 1987, p8), a view that is encapsulated in the recent Housing Act.

Table 4.3. Local authority housing in England and Wales 1976–86

Year	*New build*	*Sales*	*Total stock (000s)*	*(%)*
1976	112,028	5,313	5285	29
1977	108,483	13,020	5398	29
1978	87,799	30,045	5463	29
1979	69,734	41,740	5495	29
1980	70,824	81,480	5477	29
1981	49,407	102,730	5410	28
1982	30,176	202,050	5230	27
1983	29,923	141,460	5108	26
1984	29,185	103,180	5021	26
1985	23,478	93,145	4943	25
1986	16,089	89,890	4867	24

Source: Department of Environment, *Housing and Construction Statistics 1976–86*. HMSO, 1987.

While the 1987 White Paper does mark a new determination to extend the privatisation drive into the provision of rented housing, much of the ground-work for this new policy was in fact carried out prior to the 1987 election. For example, in retrospect, it is apparent that, in effect if not in intention, the financial framework within which local authorities operate has been changed in ways that make hiving off more feasible or more attractive than was the case in 1979. Thus Exchequer subsidies to local authority housing revenue accounts have been reduced considerably since 1979/80, so that by 1986/87 only 29 % of councils were in subsidy (Malpass and Murie, 1987). The consequent real increase in local authority rents since 1979 has not only pushed rents closer to the market level, thereby making council housing more attractive to prospective private investors. It has also reduced the relative price advantage of council housing over its competitors such as housing associations and private landlords. The poorest tenants have been protected from rent increases by housing benefit which is paid on an individual basis to tenants irrespective of who is their landlord.

The restrictions on local authority capital spending (including those on their ability to use capital receipts from sales) have resulted in the lowest peace time level of council house completions since the early 1920s. The restrictions on local authority capital spending have also prompted councils to seek alternative ways of securing investment for improvements in their stock or the provision of new build. Indeed, one of the main arguments put forward by councils hoping to hive off the whole of their stock to quasi-private trusts and other agencies is that it is a way of obviating central government spending restrictions.

The Housing and Planning Act 1986 was also a significant step towards the hiving off of tenanted estates. Many of the measures provided by this Act clarified the circumstances in which public housing could be disposed of, made it easier for private finance to be utilised, or made transfers and sales more attractive. For example, section six of the Act set out new arrangements which local authorities are required to follow for consulting tenants before disposing of tenanted properties to a private sector landlord. Section nine weakened council tenants' security of tenure by providing a new ground for possession where dwellings are to be disposed of to another landlord as part of an approved redevelopment scheme. Section ten extended local authorities' power to delegate management functions to include 'any other person' and not just co-operatives. And section 20 allowed new town housing to be disposed of to 'any person'.

In addition to these measures aimed at smoothing the way to the privatisation of council housing, the Government engaged in a sustained ideological assault on this form of provision even before the election of 1987. This campaign stressed the supposed inefficiency, paternalism and failures of local authority housing management. In January 1987, for example, the then Minister for

Housing, John Patten, argued that we should 'get rid of these monoliths' and transfer council estates to agencies 'who will be closer in touch with the needs and aspirations of individual tenants' (Patten, 1987, p23). This attempt to de-legitimise council housing has, however, continued even more strongly since the election. Patten's successor as Minister for Housing, William Waldegrave (since replaced by the Earl of Caithness), claimed to see 'no arguments for generalised new build by councils, now or in the future' (Waldegrave, 1987, p8).

This theme was continued in the 1987 White Paper, where it was claimed that in many big cities local authorities operate on such a large scale that they 'inevitably risk becoming distant and bureaucratic' (Department of Environment 1987, p2). Arguing that it is 'not healthy' for the public sector to dominate rented housing provision, the White Paper states that, at the local level:

> . . . short term political factors can override efficient and economic management of housing in the long term, leading to unrealistically low rents and wholly inadequate standards of maintenance. Local authority housing allocation methods can all too easily result in inefficiencies and bureaucracy, producing queuing and lack of choice for the tenant (Department of Environment 1987, p3).

Housing: the Government's proposals

The White Paper, *Housing: the Government's proposals* (Department of Environment 1987) outlined four main objectives for housing policy. These were to continue to encourage owner occupation, to reinvigorate what it referred to as the 'independent rented sector' (by which it meant housing provided by private landlords and housing associations), to give council tenants the right to opt for alternative landlords, and to target more effectively the use of public money. These objectives are not unrelated and an apparent sub-plot appears to be the desire to demunicipalise rented housing, partly in order to reduce the power of local authorities, particularly Labour controlled inner city councils.

Many of the proposals relating to rented housing were included in the Housing Act 1988, while others did not require primary legislation. The main changes were as follows:

1 deregulation of lettings by private landlord and housing associations;
2 changes to the financial regime for housing associations;
3 council tenants were given the right to veto proposals from

alternative landlords who want to take over the ownership of their homes;

4 housing action trusts to be set up in some rundown council estates.

The attempt to revive the privately rented sector by deregulating rents and other means is discussed in the article by Whitehead and Kleinman. Here we examine the proposals for social housing landlords.

Housing associations: the new financial framework

Future lettings by housing associations have been deregulated and are to be made on the same basis as those granted by private landlords. Previously, housing association lettings were set at rents determined by the Rent Officer. This deregulation of housing association lettings has been necessary because of two other changes that the Government wished to make for housing associations, but it also has a symbolic significance for a Government committed so strongly as that of 1987 to the market model. The two other changes were a significant reduction in housing association grant and the use of private sector finance (as opposed to borrowing via the Housing Corporation) for that part of capital costs not met by housing association grant (HAG).

These changes in the way housing associations are financed (including the way that their rents are set) are of the utmost significance for the future role and nature of the housing association sector. They will involve significantly higher rents than those they currently charge. This will mean that, for the first time since 1974 (when HAG was introduced and they began to expand as a movement), housing associations will have to consider the rent paying ability of prospective tenants before they decide to whom to grant a tenancy. This ability-to-pay scrutiny will be made all the more necessary by a further, and more significant, consequence of the changed system of housing association finance. For the implication of using private finance to fund their development programmes is that it is the associations themselves rather than, as in the past, the government, who will bear the risk. Thus in future any overruns in development costs, or increases in outgoings as a result of, say, higher interest payments will have to be met by raising rents rather than through higher grant. Housing associations, therefore, will be subject (to use the Government's phrase) to the 'disciplines of the market', and this is bound to influence their orientation and action howsoever much they may regret the fact. Despite their non-profit status, housing associations who use private loans to finance a significant proportion of their development programme will have to be more commercially aware organisations; those who do not will either cease to expand or will risk becoming insolvent.

Although much of the success of the Government's demunicipalisation strategy rests upon the ability of the housing association sector to expand sufficiently to take over a substantial slice of local authority housing, there are doubts about the financial viability of the policy. Firstly, many associations will have either not enough stock or insufficient reserves to provide the necessary security to attract private finance. Secondly, with reduced levels of HAG and, therefore, higher rents, the financial viability of the strategy will depend crucially on the availability and scope of housing benefit (as Whitehead and Klienman make clear in their article, the same is also true for the revival of renting from private landlords). Already something like two-thirds of housing association tenants are in receipt of housing benefit and this is likely to increase as rents go up in real terms. The difficulty, however, is that housing benefit has been cut on numerous occasions since the scheme was introduced in 1982–3, so that it has become less generous and goes much less far up the income scale (Kemp, 1987). There is no guarantee that housing benefit will not be cut again once expenditure has increased as a result of rent increases, thereby undermining the ability of tenants at the margin to afford housing association rents.

The net result of all this may be a bifurcation in the housing association tenantry, with homes increasingly being let to households on income support (who receive full help with their rent) and better off tenants who do not need such assistance, thus producing a partial move up market within the sector. The working poor and others at the margins of housing benefit, however, whom housing associations currently see as one of their target groups, may well find themselves effectively excluded from the sector. One way in which this unfortunate scenario could be avoided is for HAG levels to be retained at something like their existing levels (85–90 %) rather than the 50–75 % currently envisaged by the Government. That would reduce the size of the loan that associations would need to service on any development, thus keeping rents to a lower level than would otherwise be necessary.

Tenants' choice

The 1988 Housing Act also gives council tenants the right to opt for an alternative (non-council) landlord. This new policy instrument might be more accurately described as the right of prospective landlords to bid for the ownership of council properties. Thus section 92 of the Housing Act explicitly states that the purpose of Part IV (Change of landlord: secure tenants) is that of 'conferring on any person who has been approved . . . the right to acquire from a public sector landlord . . . any freehold buildings . . . occupied by qualifying tenants'. However, council tenants who have secure tenancies under the Housing Act 1980 and who are in occupation on the date the prospective landlord applies for the properties (qualifying tenants) have the right to opt out of the proposed transfer of ownership to another landlord. This new policy is called 'tenant's choice' by the Government.

Landlords who have been approved by the Housing Corporation (the quasi-governmental organisation responsible for overseeing housing associations) have the right to make a bid for council houses; the price of sale being the market value of the properties subject to tenancy and any necessary improvement works. In order for the transaction *not* to go ahead, at least 50 % of the tenants *eligible* to vote (those with a secure tenancy under the Housing Act 1980, resident at the time the bid was made) must vote against the proposal in a ballot. If the transfer is not in this way rejected, those tenants who voted 'no' remain with the council, but all those who either voted 'yes' or did not vote at all are transferred to the new landlord. Where transfers go ahead in the case of flats, the freehold of the entire block will go to the new landlord and the flats of tenants who voted 'no' in the ballot will be subleased back to the council (at the same rent as that charged to the transferred tenants) for the duration of the occupant's tenancy (Department of Environment, 1988a).

The Housing Corporation has been given a pivotal role in the transfer of council property under the 'tenant's choice' scheme. In the first place, only landlords that have been approved by the Corporation will be allowed to make a bid for tenanted council housing. Secondly, where there is more than one potential applicant landlord, the Housing Corporation will have the power to hold a 'beauty contest' in which informal consultation will be carried out to ascertain which applicant has the clearest support and should therefore be allowed to commence formal proceedings for the transfer. Thirdly, the Housing Corporation is also to be given a 'marriage broking' role, putting tenants interested in transferring in touch with potential landlords. Fourthly, 'where circumstances demand it', the Housing Corporation will be able to provide advice and other help to tenants who want to set up their own landlord or form a co-operative. Fifthly, the Housing Corporation will be empowered to advertise 'tenants' choice' and 'encourage suitable landlords to take part in the scheme' (Waldegrave, 1988a, p3).

Thus in addition to its traditional roles of supervising the work of housing associations and administering housing association grant, the Housing Corporation has a new function of facilitating the demunicipalisation of rented housing provision under the 'tenants' choice' scheme. This has led to some unease among housing associations about a possible conflict of interest between the Corporation's role of determining how much HAG each housing association will receive and 'encouraging' potential landlords (such as the associations) to take part in the scheme.

Housing action trusts

The Government has also announced proposals to set up housing action trusts (HATs) in council estates in six local authorities in England, despite opposition from the councils concerned and from many of the tenants.[3] According to the Government, the estates were chosen because they are in a state of physical disrepair, are poorly managed and suffer from a number of social and environmental problems. These HATs are to take over the ownership of the local authority housing in designated areas, carry out a renewal programme and then pass on the ownership of the properties to other individuals and organisations, either before or after the renewal has been carried out. A total of £125 million has been provided over a three year period to refurbish the 24,525 houses in the designated areas, an average of £5,000 per property.

HATs are explicitly based on the model of the urban development corporations that have been used as part of urban regeneration strategy in the inner cities (Department of Environment, 1987). During the HAT's life they will assume the landlord functions of the local authority, as well as, where it is deemed to be necessary, its planning and environmental health powers. In short, they are to be local authorities without the elected councillors. They will be set up by, and be accountable to, the Secretary of State for the Environment and will thus involve a considerable degree of centralisation of power. HATs will be set up whether or not the local authority or the tenants are in favour of the idea, and tenants will not be able to vote against the transfer of their properties to another landlord. The Secretary of State for the Environment dismissed council opposition to the imposition of HATs as 'political tomfoolery' (quoted in *Housing Associations Weekly*, 15 July 1988, p2).

Apart from being an instrument to do something about the problems of a few rundown council estates, the rationale behind HATs would appear to be fourfold. Firstly, they are a way of renewing these areas with some input from the private sector, thus minimising public spending while at the same time providing profitable opportunities for commercial organisations. Secondly, they are a way of removing from council ownership whole estates under the guise of tackling urban deprivation. In other words, they will further the objective of demunicipalising the provision of rented housing. Thirdly, and probably of most importance to the Government, they are an ideological demonstration project, a way of showing that central government and the private sector can achieve that which (by implication, Labour) local authorities cannot. Fourthly, HATs can be seen as a means of improving some of the worst estates so that they are attractive to new landlords. As the Government put it in the White Paper, 'Unless major improvements can be made in the fabric and general environment of these areas it is unlikely that policies such as the right to transfer to other landlords would be successful there' (Department of Environment 1987, p16). Thus to some extent HATs are an instrument for making even the worst estates sellable.

In combination, the setting up of HATs along with the 'tenant's choice' scheme could pave the way for a major denudation of the municipal housing stock. The likely scale and pace of change is unknown at present. The Government would prefer transfers to be made to commercial private landlords, but as Whitehead and Kleinman make clear in their article in this volume, the prospects of a major revival do not seem great. Most properties to be transferred may well go to housing associations, though it seems unlikely that they could swallow up much of the council sector within the next decade: there are currently 4.9 million council houses and only 0.5 million housing association dwellings.

Voluntary transfers

However, encouraged by the White Paper, a number of local authorities began taking steps to transfer voluntarily their entire stock to new landlords even before the Housing Bill was enacted. Examples of this include Rochford DC who are proposing to set up a new housing association for the purpose; Torbay DC which has opted for selling its stock to two existing housing associations (but which had considered a bid from Quality Street, the private landlord set up by Nationwide Anglia Building Society); Gloucester City Council which wants to sell its 6,000 houses to North Housing (the largest association in the country, with a stock of 20,000); and Ynys Mons DC in Wales which is planning to set up a private company to take over its housing.

In none of these instances has the initiative for transfer come from the tenants. Rather, it has come from councillors and from officers. In fact, there is evidence of very considerable opposition to the proposals from many of the tenants who will be affected (for example, see *Inside Housing,* 8 July 1988). Indeed, Ynys Mons DC faced such strong opposition from its tenants to its proposed privatisation that it has had to drop the plans. Significantly, these so-called 'voluntary' transfers will not necessarily involve a ballot being held, for the Government has decided that they will take place under the Housing Act 1985 (as amended by the Housing and Planning Act 1986) rather than the Housing Act 1988 and this only requires that tenants be consulted. Thus as a Government Minister has admitted 'public sector landlords can dispose of stock to another landlord provided that they have the consent of the Secretary of State, and it [is] possible that some tenants might be transferred against their will' (quoted in *Inside Housing,* 8 July 1988, p8).

The Government has recently published the criteria that it will take into account in deciding whether to grant consent to a proposed voluntary transfer of a local authority's stock. Three criteria were highlighted in the guidelines. First, the new landlord has to demonstrate a long term commitment to the low cost rented housing market. Second, where the disposal is of more than 5,000–10,000 stock, the document suggests that the Government would prefer the transfer not to be to only one purchaser. Third, and this seems to be the main concern of the Government, the landlord must be independent of the local authority.

Three aspects of independence are highlighted. First, the council's membership or shareholding in the new landlord has to be in a minority (no more than 20 %). Second, the selection of staff has to be at the discretion of the new landlord, not the council. Third, consent is unlikely to be given if it were proposed that the council provide services to the new landlord or vice versa. The exception to this is that local authorities will have to demonstrate in their application that they will be able to discharge their continuing statutory obligations (e.g. the homelessness provisions of the Housing Act 1985) and this might be done by entering into contracts with local landlords (including the purchaser of the council's stock) to provide the necessary accommodation. Significantly, it is stressed in the guidelines that 'The Government . . . considers it inconsistent with independence of the new landlord for the council to retain nomination rights, and would not expect the local authority to continue to maintain a waiting list where it disposed of its entire stock' (Department of Environment 1988b, p4).

Voluntary transfers subject to these guidelines will involve a significant retreat from the rights of citizenship. Instead of being able to turn to their local authority, households in need of accommodation will have to seek assistance from private landlords and housing associations, none of whom have a statutory duty to provide accommodation. Moreover, while councils' continuing statutory duties will be contracted out to other agencies, this is only a short step from ending them altogether. Indeed, the Department of the Environment is currently engaged in an internal review of the homelessness legislation and ministers have talked of redefining homelessness to mean rooflessness.

The future of social housing

While the Government would clearly like transfers to go ahead as quickly as possible, an important influence on the speed at which they occur will be the voting behaviour of council tenants who are balloted under the 'tenant's choice' scheme. A recent survey carried out by Gallup for the National Consumer Council has shed some light on the way the voting might shape up.[4] Gallup interviewed a representative sample of the population of Britain aged 16 years or over, stratified by region and town size, in March/April 1988 (Gallup, 1988). Council tenants in the survey were asked the following question:

> 'The Government is proposing to bring in a law allowing council tenants to vote whether they wish to remain council tenants or choose some other organisation like a housing association or building society as their new landlord. If you were asked to choose a landlord, which of the following organisations would you choose?'

Table 4.4 Council tenants' preferred landlord

	%
A housing association	7
A building society	7
A tenants co-operative	7
A private company	1
The local council	51
I would need more information before deciding	19
I don't know/I have no opinion	7
	(n=929)

Source: Gallup *Council Tenants* (1988)

As the table shows, half of the council tenants (accounting for 70 % of those who felt able to decide) said they would choose to stay with the local council. Only 1 % said they would opt for a private company, though 7 % mentioned a building society.

Relatively small percentages of tenants said they would select either a housing association or a co-operative. This survey thus suggests that while significant numbers of council tenants may opt for an alternative landlord, the majority would probably stay with their local council.

Of course, in this survey tenants were asked to consider a hypothetical rather than a real ballot. But an actual ballot of new town tenants has recently been carried out in Peterborough, where the development corporation is being wound up. The new town's housing stock is currently managed by the local council and tenants were recently asked to vote on whether to continue having their homes managed by the council (who would then take over the ownership of the properties) or be transferred to a consortium of four housing associations. On a very high turnout (84 %), the overwhelming majority (93 %) voted to be council tenants.

This was not the result that the Government was looking for and, perhaps in order to prevent a similar outcome occurring with the transfer of Telford new town's dwellings, the Government has decided that properties will be transferred to five housing associations despite considerable opposition from many of the tenants. The new town tenants will only be allowed to vote on the transfer (under the 'tenant's choice' scheme) after the dwellings have been managed by the associations for two years. Likewise, in Warrington new town, the development corporation's houses are to be transferred to four associations despite opposition from the local council and tenants. In Basildon, in a referendum held in 1987, 98 % of new town tenants (on a turn out of 71 %) voted for the local council as their new landlord. Yet the development corporation is being pressed by the Department of the Environment to transfer the houses to new or existing housing associations for a number of years before allowing tenants to choose between them and the local council. A leaked letter from the Department of the Environment to the development corporation stated that 'New town housing will be transferred in future on the same basis as tenants choice, namely they will have to be purchased at market value subject to tenancy. This may make them unattractive to local authorities when they see the new financial regime to be introduced in the Housing and Local Government Bill' in the 1988–9 session (quoted in *Housing Associations Weekly*, 27 May 1988, p4).

The details of this new financial framework have now been published in a consultation paper and involve the 'ring fencing' of housing revenue accounts, so that (from April 1990) councils will no longer be able to subsidise their rents from the general rate fund, and other measures aimed at making them more 'businesslike' (Department of the Environment, 1988c). One effect of this will be a substantial increase in rents among those local authorities who currently make transfers to the housing revenue account, and it may be that this is intended to make opting for alternative landlords under the 'tenants' choice' scheme more attractive than it otherwise would have been. For one of the main anxieties of tenants facing the prospect of being transferred to an alternative landlord is that it will involve a significant increase in rents. Indeed, the consultation paper states that, under this new financial regime, council tenants:

> . . . will be able to take better informed decisions about the alternatives the Government's housing policy is placing before them, and to decide whether to exercise the options the Government is giving them through the Right to Buy and Tenants' Choice (Department of Environment 1988c, p7).

Another main anxiety for tenants faced with a possible transfer to another landlord is that they will lose their secure tenancy and become assured tenants with significantly less security of tenure and none of the 'tenants' charter' rights (such as the right to buy, the right to exchange and the right to be kept informed about certain aspects of their tenancy), many of which were introduced by the Housing Act 1980. The National Federation of Housing Associations had campaigned unsuccessfully for a separate housing association tenancy, rather than the assured tenancy provided for in the Housing Act 1988 which also applies to private landlord lettings. Instead, however, the Government has provided a 'tenants' guarantee', which will apply to association lettings including those to tenants transferring to them from local authorities (Housing Corporation, 1988). The details of this have yet to be finalised, but three criteria that it would include have been outlined. First, houses are to be allocated to those most in need. Second, associations will be expected to offer tenants additional rights to those provided under the 1988 Act for assured tenancies. Third, rents 'must remain within the reach of those in lower-paid employment' (Waldegrave, 1988a, p2). These terms have been criticised by the Institute of Housing for their vagueness and for the fact that they are not binding. Certainly, these terms are not rights and despite the name, therefore, cannot be guaranteed. They seem unlikely to provide sufficient balm to soothe the anxieties of council or new town tenants about their prospects after a transfer.

One of the main financial obstacles to transfers is the question of the outstanding debt charges on the properties, which may be substantially more than the transfer price. Indeed, as the price will be market value subject to tenancy and any necessary improvement works, in some estates the sale price could be negative, hence the council would have to pay a 'dowry' to the new landlord instead of itself receiving a capital payment. However, the Government has announced proposals for local authority capital spending under which councils would be able to invest 25 % of their capital receipts (compared with 20 % at present) but would have to use the remaining 75 % to pay off outstanding debt (Department of Environment, 1988d). This can be interpreted as a way of easing the financial costs of estate sales for local authorities and of minimising the expenditure likely to follow from substantial capital receipts.

It is possible that local authorities will be left owning a residual dump of unattractive and unsellable housing in urban areas, housing the very disadvantaged and the homeless. Alternatively, very few council tenants may opt for an uncertain future with a landlord offering them the prospect of reduced security of tenure and higher rents. However, if there is to be a large scale demunicipalisation of rented housing, the most likely route (because tenants in these cases only have the right to be consulted rather than the individual veto they have under the 'tenants' choice' scheme) is via whole sale 'voluntary transfers'. At any rate, the Government have argued that their new policies will increase competition, reduce local authority monopoly ownership of rented housing, increase choice for tenants, and ensure increased efficiency in the housing market. Even where tenants opt to remain with their council, the very fact that they have the 'choice' to transfer, it is argued, will mean that they should get a better service than they otherwise would. This is believed to be necessary because local authorities, it is claimed (Patten, 1987; Ridley, 1987) are inefficient, insensitive, bureaucratic organisations which have taken control over people's lives and failed to respond to their wishes and aspirations. In other words, much of the justification for the very radical policies that have now been set in train is presented as the failure of local authorities as housing managers. This is contrasted with the market which, it is implied, is efficient and offers consumers choice under the spur of competition. Thus the fundamental basis of the new approach to rented housing is an explicit critique of the social democratic model and a belief in the virtues of the market (Clapham, et al., 1989).

Conclusions

The Government has made it clear that a key objective of the White Paper is 'an increase in the choice available to those who do not want or could not afford to own their own homes and in particular the breaking up of the local authority monopoly in social rented housing' (Ridley, 1988, p1). Instead of thinking of themselves as landlords, councils should hive off their stock to other agencies, either by voluntary, large scale transfers or through individual tenants opting for a new landlord. There are obvious parallels here with the opting out of schools from local authority control.

The objective of the White Paper, then, is not merely to extend privatisation in housing to the provision of rented housing. It is also specifically about *demunicipalising* rented housing and reducing the power of local authorities. There seems to be a number of reasons why this should be important to the Conservatives. First, it is part of the strategy to 'reclaim the inner cities' as Mrs Thatcher put it on election night in June 1987. According to Selbourne (1987, p34), this 'is nothing less than the belief, on the Right, that the political power (and legitimacy) of the Labour Party, and of the Left as a whole, have essentially been derived from, and rest upon, the dependency of a part of the citizenry upon the institutions which Labour has fostered. The corollary is simple, but far-reaching: dismantle the Left's institutions, and you simultaneously free the citizen and dish Labour'.

A second and related objective is to reduce the influence of local politics in the provision of rented housing or what the Secretary of State for the Environment has referred to as 'political tomfoolery'. For as Cawson (1982) has pointed out, local politics is still relatively open to competitive influences and, therefore, to working class pressures. By demunicipalising rented housing, the Government can reduce the influence of local democratic politics. Instead, rented housing provision will be subject to the 'disciplines of the market' as well as to the wishes of central government. For demunicipalisation will involve – indeed, will require – extensive state intervention and a considerable centralisation of power (directly in the case of HATs and indirectly via the Housing Corporation in the case of 'tenants' choice' and housing associations).

Thirdly, large scale local authority housing, as Waldegrave (1988b, p36) has pointed out, 'is inconsistent with the broader philosophy of this government'. This is a reference to the Government's aim of reducing dependency on the state and replacing it with an 'enterprise culture': 'it is the habit of dependence which we should seek to avoid as a primary object of policy, and surely the dangers of dependence are less if people are helped out into the market rather than segregated from it?' (Waldegrave, 1987, p9).

Demunicipalisation partly reflects, therefore, the Government's aim of moving away from a social democratic to a more market oriented model of social policy. However, council tenants seem particularly unwilling to be 'helped out into the market' and to be given the 'choice' of an alternative landlord. And although (as Whitehead and Klienman show in their article) council housing is unlikely to be hived off on a large scale to private landlords, the major recipients of such housing (the housing associations, whether already established or set up for the purpose) are being refashioned so that they more closely mirror the market model of social policy. Indeed, the Government have referred to housing associations and commercial private landlords as belonging together to the 'independent rented sector'. Even so, housing associations (even with the reduced levels of HAG) and many co-operatives, receive extensive state subsidy and Waldegrave has acknowledged that local authorities may be the most economical way of providing homes to rent. Thus the hiving off of council housing will not reduce 'dependency' on the state, only dependence on public, in-kind provision (cf Walker, 1988). Nevertheless, the ideological significance of demunicipalisation lies to some extent in the fact that local authorities not only represent *public* provision, they also have statutory responsibilities, unlike housing associations and other types of landlord. Demunicipalisation, therefore, represents a shift in responsibility from the state to the individual. In this way, citizenship rights are eroded and greater emphasis is placed on the market model of welfare.

Notes

1 In Scotland a separate White Paper was published (SDD, 1987), while the Housing (Scotland) Act is different, in several important respects, from its counterpart south of the border. For reasons of space, this article is confined to the English proposals.

2 For the convenience of readers, the text in this article talks about the 'Housing Act 1988' (as it will be when this volume is published). However, it is important to note that, at the time of writing, the Housing Bill 1987 has not yet returned from the House of Lords and it is possible, therefore, that some details referred to in this article will be amended prior to enactment. The clauses discussed in this article relate to the Bill as it left the Commons on 28 June 1988.

3 The Housing (Scotland) Act makes no provision for HATs, but it does provide for a merger between the Scottish Special Housing Association (which has a stock of 60,000) and the Housing Corporation in Scotland, to provide a large new quango called Scottish Homes. Among its functions, this body is to take over some local authority estates with

the aim of carrying out physical improvements itself or devolving ownership and renewal to housing associations, co-operatives or private landlord such as the recently formed Quality Street.

4 This data is reproduced with the kind permission of Social Surveys (Gallup) Ltd.

References

Audit Commission (1986) *Managing the crisis in council housing.* HMSO.

Cawson, A (1982) *Corporation and welfare.* Heinemann Educational Books.

Clapham, D Kemp, P and Smith SJ (1989) *Social policy and housing.* Macmillan.

CDP (1976) *Whatever happened to council housing?* London, Community Development Project Information and Intelligence Unit.

Department of Employment (1988) *Family expenditure survey 1986.* HMSO.

Department of Environment (1987) *Housing: the Government's proposals.* Cm 214, HMSO.

Department of Environment, (1988a) *Tenants' choice.* Department of the Environment.

Department of Environment (1988b) *Large scale voluntary transfers of local authority housing to private bodies.* Department of the Environment.

Department of Environment (1988c). *New financial regime for local authority housing in England and Wales: a Consultation paper.* Department of the Environment.

Department of Environment (1988d) *Capital expenditure and finance: a consultation paper.* Department of the Environment.

Forrest, R and Murie, A (1986) Marginalisation and subsidised individualism: the sale of council houses in the restructuring of the welfare state. *International Journal of Urban and Regional Research.* 10: 46–66.

Gallup (1988) *Council tenants.* Social Surveys (Gallup) Ltd.

George, V and Wilding, P (1976) *Ideology and social welfare.* Routledge and Kegan Paul.

Hamnett, C (1984) Housing the two nations: socio-tenurial polarisation in England and Wales 1961–81. *Urban Studies.* 21: 389–400.

Hamnett, C (1987) Conservative government housing policy 1979–85. In van Vliet W, (ed) *Housing Markets and Policies under Fiscal Austerity.* Westport, Connecticut, Greenwood Press.

Harloe, M (1987) The declining fortunes of social rented housing in Europe. In Clapham, D and English, J (eds) *Public Housing: Current Trends and Future Developments.* Croom Helm.

Housing Corporation (1988) *Tenants' choice landlords: Criteria for approval and grounds for revoking approval: draft for consultation.* Housing Corporation.

Kemp, P (1987) The reform of housing benefit. *Social Policy and Administration.* 21: 171–86.

Kemp, P (1988) The assured tenancy scheme, 1980 to 1986. In Kemp, P (ed) *The Private Provision of Rented Housing.* Gower.

Malpass, P and Murie, A (1987) *Housing policy and practice.* 2nd ed. Basingstoke.

Merrett, S (1979) *State housing in Britain.* Routledge and Kegan Paul.

Patten, J (1987) Housing – room for a new view. *Guardian* 30 January: 23.

Piven, F (1987) Cities, housing, and the rise of 'hyper capitalist' regimes. *City Renewal Through Partnership.* conference proceedings, Glasgow.

Ridley, N (1987) *Conservative proposals for housing.* Conservative General Office.

Ridley, N (1988) HAs set for leading roles – Ridley. *Housing Associations Weekly.* 24 June: 1 and 6.

Selbourne, D (1987) Why Labour's attacks miss the mark. *Guardian* 18 May: 34.

SDD (1987) *Housing: the Government's proposals for Scotland.* Cm 242, Edinburgh, HMSO.

Waldegrave, W (1987) *Some reflections on housing policy.* Conservative News Service.

Waldegrave, W (1988a) *Extract of speech by Housing Minister, William Waldegrave to CIPFA Services, at Warrington, Cheshire, 8th June 1988.* Department of the Environment.

Waldegrave, W (1988b) A third force enters the market. *Guardian* 29 February: 36.

Walker, A (1988) Dependent relativities. *Times Higher Education Supplement.* 22 April: 36.

Willmott, P and Murie, A (1988) *Polarisation and social housing.* Policy Studies Institute.

5 The private rented sector and the Housing Act 1988

Christine Whitehead and Mark Kleinman

One of the Government's most important aims in the Housing Act 1988 is to provide the basis for a viable independent rented sector. The phrase 'independent rented sector' is intended to cover a range of housing organisations from housing associations and other non-profit-making bodies through to 'true' (i.e. profit-seeking) private landlords. There are two main elements to the Government's approach: easing controls on new lettings to enable private landlords to obtain higher returns and use their stock with greater flexibility; and transferring stock from the local authority sector to independent landlords. Although the overall success of their policy depends on both elements, and the interaction between them, this article concentrates mainly on the first. The second element is discussed in the article by Kemp.

The provisions of the Act

New lettings

This article is being written in August 1988, before the Housing Bill has completed is passage through Parliament, and hence the exact details of the legislation are not yet certain. However, the main thrust is already clear (Department of Environment 1987a and b). All new lettings will be assured tenancies, i.e. the rent will be set freely between landlord and tenant at any level up to that determined by the market. Tenancies may be either periodic or fixed term. Tenants will have indefinite security of tenure in that they may remain as tenants while they are prepared to pay the agreed rent. That rent may be set and reviewed in any way that is acceptable to both landlord and tenant but if no contractual mechanism for review is included either party may apply to the Rent Assessment Committee (RAC) to fix a market rent. Appeal against the RAC's assessment is limited to points of law.

Landlords will have rights of possession under certain specified circumstances. The main mandatory rights include where the landlord provides suitable accommodation; where the landlord wants to use the property for owner-occupation, and notice was given before the start of tenancy; where the property is let on the basis of an out-of-season holiday let; where the landlord wishes to redevelop; and where there are serious arrears of rent or persistent delay in paying rent. Courts may also, at their discretion, give possession either where the tenant is in significant breach of contract or where tenancies are held by virtue of employment. These possession rights are both a simplification and an extension of those specified in the Rent Act 1977. As a result of the changes, the existing balance between the interests of landlord and tenant in terms of possession is tilted towards the landlords.

At the limit landlord and tenant may agree an 'assured shorthold tenancy' where the tenant only has a right to remain in the property for the length of the original contract – a minimum of six months. Such shorthold tenancies may be renewed as often as desired or be replaced by a periodic tenancy with possession on two months notice.

Thus the objective of the Housing Act 1988 is to free up the market for new lettings almost completely. Agreed market rents will reflect a willing landlord's preparedness to provide different levels of security and tenants may in principle choose to pay for the extent of security they desire (*pace* the possibility of possession in specific circumstances). Rents will thus reflect on the one hand tenants' willingness to pay and, on the other, the rate of return required by landlords to supply accommodation.

To some degree, the two types of tenancy – assured tenancy and assured shorthold tenancy – are intended to appeal to different types of landlord. For the large landlord, rates of return are the crucial factor, with security of tenure being less important, while for the smaller landlord, the issue of security of tenure – i.e. the ability to regain possession when desired – looms much larger.

Existing lettings

Through these provisions, creeping decontrol of the sector will be achieved as new property comes on to the market and existing units fall vacant. The position of existing tenants is, in general, left unchanged; they will continue to have security under the Rent Act and the right to a registered fair rent. However, succession rights are reduced. Only the spouse or a member of the tenant's family who has lived in the property for five years before the tenant's death will have succession rights, and any second succession will be on assured tenancy terms.

The private rented sector is thus split into two quite distinct parts, the first working on market principles and the second going out of existence as tenants die or move on. The government recognises that such a split might increase the incentive to landlords to get rid of existing tenants who will be paying lower rents and be more secure than potential tenants. Both for this reason and because it is thought that protection in the past has been inadequate, they intend to strengthen the law against harassment and illegal eviction in two ways. First, there will be an additional offence of harassment knowing that it is likely to cause the occupier to leave home. This is thought to be easier to prove than the current requirement of intent under which there have been very few successful prosecutions. Second, the civil right to compensation will be extended to give tenants who have been illegally evicted or driven out of the home, a right to payment based on the gains made by the landlord. Thus the greater the difference between the tenanted and vacant possession value, the greater the compensation.

In practice these legal changes may not solve the problem of harassment. Taking action against a harassing landlord can be a distressing or even frightening experience for tenants, particularly the elderly. Moreover, many tenants will be unaware of their rights, and the Act contains no provisions for additional resources for local authorities in either publicising tenants' rights or prosecuting instances of harassment. A different approach to curbing 'bad landlordism' might be some form of licensing, but this is not one of the Act's proposals.

There are a number of other more minor changes aimed mainly at simplifying the regulatory framework. For instance, landlords will have to obtain a court order to evict licensees as they now have to for tenants. Special categories of lettings (such as out of season holiday lets) under existing legislation are brought into the simplified basic framework. Other changes reduce tenants' rights notably with respect to resident landlord tenancies where new lettings will be simple market contracts.

Transfer from the local authority stock

Another important aspect of the Act is the emphasis on breaking up local authority holdings and transferring property into the independent rented sector. As this aspect is covered in detail by the article by Peter Kemp we shall not discuss it further here, except to say that it is likely that the vast majority of such transfers will be to housing associations rather than to profit-seeking private landlords. Particular council estates with attractive locational attributes (e.g. river-side or adjacent to city centre) may be of interest to private landlords. However, very few existing council tenants express any preference to transfer to private landlords: the Gallup survey quoted by Kemp found that only one in a hundred council tenants wanted a private company for a landlord.

Housing benefit

Another major area of the Act which affects the private rented sector relates to the provision of housing benefit. The Government has stated as a basic principle that they are prepared to fund the adjustment to market rents on the basis of the current housing benefit system. That implies that any tenant in receipt of housing benefit will have the whole of any rent increase paid by DHSS – because under the system introduced in April 1988 eligibility depends on household circumstances and income but not on rent. This puts severe strain on any system where rent is to be determined by agreement between landlord and tenant because the tenant has no incentive to keep the rent down. Moreover, the existence of unlimited housing benefit must anyway modify demand. At the limit, if a high proportion of tenants are eligible for benefit it is difficult to understand how a market rent could be defined.

To deal with this problem the Government intends to limit subsidy in certain ways. Firstly it is already the case under the April 1988 rules that the rent must not be set taking account of the specific tenant's potential eligibility for benefit. In addition, all rents being met by housing benefit will be subject to scrutiny by the Rent Officer who will be given guidance by the Department of Environment on the principles by which market rent levels may be set. Where the rent is in excess of that adjudicated by the Rent Officer, housing benefit will still be payable, but the local authority will receive central government subsidy only in relation to the adjudicated rent.

Hence there will be financial pressure from central government on local authorities not to pay benefit on rents above that which the Rent Officer considers to be a market rent. The Rent Officer's adjudication will not, of course, impose any ceiling on the rent which the landlord is able to charge, only on what rent will be eligible for housing benefit subsidy. It is for the local authority to determine whether housing benefit will be paid above that level. In one of its more chilling phrases, the Consultation Paper on housing benefit states that where a claimant's rent is above that deemed to be appropriate, the claimant will be free to make up the difference 'should he have the means to do so' (Department of Environment 1987c).

Finally, there will be restrictions as to the quality of accommodation that those on benefit may occupy. It is suggested that these will generally only exclude the highest priced accommodation in any given neighbourhood but there are existing powers to limit space and other standards which could be invoked if necessary.

Thus, in principle, housing benefit will be available on existing terms to cover rents under the new regime. Yet the Government has already recognised that the links between market rents and the benefit system will set up strains and they have already stated that if necessary they will be prepared to deal with these by placing direct limits on the extent of benefit not just upon subsidy. But perhaps the most worrying aspect, made clear during the Committee stage, is that as yet no additional provision has been made in the public expenditure estimates to fund the projected increase in subsidy arising from the shift to market determined rents.

Associated changes

Thus the Housing Act 1988 itself puts in place, at least in principle, two elements perceived to be necessary to revive the private rented sector. On the one hand it allows rents to be determined by the market and to reflect the terms and conditions laid down in each contract – so only willing landlords will be prepared to let. On the other, through the provision of housing benefit and strengthening the law on harassment and illegal eviction, it attempts to ensure that these contracts are carried through and tenants are protected from the relative power of landlords while lower income households are given the capacity to compete in the market through the provision of income related assistance.

However, in practice both the law on harassment and the housing benefit system are unlikely to be able to cope with the strain being placed on them. As far as harassment is concerned, tightening up legal definitions is no substitute for a proper licensing and enforcement system. On housing benefit there are two problems. Firstly, there is no commitment on the part of the government to meeting the revenue implications of higher rents. Moreoever, the housing benefit budget is the responsibility of the DHSS not the DoE, and hence does not come under the control of either the Housing Minister or the Environment Secretary. Secondly, and perhaps more importantly, is the fact that successive cuts to the housing benefit system since its inception in 1981–2 have meant that relatively few of the working poor qualify (Hills, 1987). Hence households in low paid work will in general not be protected against rapid increases in rent levels, as market rents replace regulated rents.

Even in principle, one other element is missing – are landlords going to be prepared to increase supply at the rents determined by the market? The Housing Act is silent on this question – which can anyway only be answered within the context of the overall financial framework.

The Finance Act 1988 does include one element addressing the question – the extension of the Business Expansion Scheme (BES) to the private rented sector. The BES was originally an attempt to give an incentive to the small private investor to provide venture capital for new, high risk, business initiatives. Property development was excluded because of its physical asset base which means that it is not generally regarded as risky. However, the risks in the private rented sector are seen as being those of poor information arising from the lack of past investment opportunities together with lack of confidence in the future. The scheme has therefore been extended to companies of up to £5 million investing in the provision of assured tenancies for at least four years. The properties can either be newly constructed, or vacant existing dwellings purchased for letting. Individual investors benefit from tax relief at their marginal tax rate – so the maximum level of subsidy is 40 %. In addition when the property is sold for the first time, it will be exempt from capital gains tax. The scheme in the first instance will run for five years, in other words it is regarded as a demonstration project.

The effect of the scheme is to give company landlords many of the benefits available to owner-occupiers except to the extent that net income is taxable while the owner-occupier is exempt from imputed income tax. However, there are still significant set up and administrative costs not all of which are financial.

The future viability of the private rented sector

The current position

The private rented sector is currently estimated to contain no more than 8 % of households. The sector is characterised by a heterogeneity of occupants (Whitehead and Kleinman, 1986), including:

- the 'rump' of the traditional private rented sector: households who have remained in the sector (often in the same dwelling) all their lives. These are typically elderly households, living in whole houses (rather than flats or bedsits) which are in poor condition, often lacking amenities. They are usually on low incomes and often pay registered fair rents;
- middle – and higher-income groups seeking short-term accommodation
- students, other newly-forming households and newcomers to an area;
- those obtaining employment-related accommodation.

Of these categories, the 'rump' of the traditional sector remains the largest, although new lettings, particularly in London go increasingly to young, employed households on average or above average household (but not necessarily individual) incomes (Greater London Council, 1986; Whitehead and Kleinman, 1987).

The sector has continued to decline throughout the post-war period. Even in London, where the sector has traditionally played a more important role in the overall housing system, the London Research Centre estimated that in 1986–7, only 10 % of households were private tenants; moreover, the rate of decline in the 1980s was similar to that of the 1970s (London Research Centre, 1988).

The sector's decline relates to factors on both the demand and supply sides. On the demand side, the majority of existing and potential tenants are simply too poor to pay the type of rents that would encourage investment in the sector, while those who could afford to pay such rents would almost always be better off financially, and obtain more choice, in the owner-occupied sector. That is, the current housing finance and subsidy system does not favour private renting as a way of providing housing.

Such demand as there currently is for private rented housing comprises three main groups. Firstly, there are those who actively seek the attributes of private renting (e.g. relatively easy access) and for whom such a choice is logical given their specific circumstances. This group includes students, long-distance migrants, and those seeking employment related accommodation, among others. In many cases, these households will go on to become owner-occupiers, or may even already be owner-occupiers elsewhere. Secondly, there are those who have no specific preference to be private tenants but have remained in the sector largely through inertia and now have no particular desire to move. Thirdly, there are those who wish to be elsewhere but are too elderly or too poor to become owner-occupiers, and do not qualify (or are waiting to qualify) for public housing.

On the supply side, one can identify four main sectors which have undermined investor confidence in the sector:

1 security of tenure;
2 rent control/regulation and the corresponding low rate of return;
3 the public's perception of the image of private landlordism (particularly since the Rachman era);
4 political uncertainty about the future of the sector.

The Housing Act is aimed mainly at the second of these factors, while also attempting somewhat to alter the first and third. Significantly, the fourth handicap to investor confidence still remains. Indeed, by opting for deregulation of *all* future lettings, the Government threw away the existing fragile consensus with the Opposition parties on the more limited experiment restricting assured tenancies to newly-built or newly-renovated properties. On the demand side, the Housing Act does little to alter the existing position, except insofar as the housing benefit system improves the capacity to pay of lower income households. Even so, this begs the question of why any improved capacity to pay among such households should be targeted at the private rented sector, when households' own preferences are likely to be for other tenures.

Transferred property

Perhaps the starkest way of putting the question of the future viability of the sector is twofold: first, can the proposals increase the size of the private rented sector; second, can net investment in private renting be increased?

The answer to be first question must be yes, simply because the name can be changed for a large proportion of housing currently owned by local authorities, especially given the fact that the price paid by landlords for taking over existing council estates may in fact be negative in some cases (see the article by Kemp for more details). However, the government has committed itself to ensuring reasonable conditions for tenants of transferred estates and restrictions on resale into owner-occupation. To the extent that these commitments have teeth, the incentive for private landlords to buy up local authority housing is reduced. To the extent that they do not, private landlords may wish to purchase, especially in estates where they see a good chance of future capital gains. However, both tenants and local authorities can be expected to view the pure private sector with, at best, uncertainty, and, more likely, hostility. Given the choice they are likely to opt for housing associations rather than commercial landlords. The most likely outcome here is therefore that private involvement will mainly be limited to financing housing associations or to the supply of a small number of altruistic private owners of accommodation on conditions very similar to those in the social sector. Thus the type of tenants that are likely to remain will probably be very similar to those already in this accommodation. It appears, however, that local authorities will not be permitted to have nomination rights to the transferred stock. In addition, as Kemp makes clear, under the new financial regime, housing associations are likely to become more risk-averse, as they will bear more of the costs. As a result, future lettings policies may discriminate against poorer and/or more disadvantaged groups, leading to some change in the social mix. In general, though, the main effect will be a change in name together with a wider range of landlords.

What are the benefits and costs of such transfers? On the benefit side, the process can provide capital receipts for local authorities (although according to the DoE's Consultation Paper on Capital Finance [Department of Environment, 1988] future legislation will compel councils to use at least some of these capital receipts to pay off existing debt rather than to undertake additional expenditure). Also, if sale prices reflect the quality of the existing stock, and are consequently low or even negative, for estates in poor repair, transfers will unlock the possibility of funding improvement investment through future rents, which will more than cover the existing capital costs.

Another benefit is seen as being the greater incentive to manage the property in a cost effective fashion and to be more responsive to tenant's demands. Certainly the profit motive provides an incentive for least cost provision but the extent to which landlords must respond to demand depends on the availability of alternative opportunities for tenants – which in many areas are likely to be very restricted.

The major cost is likely to be a leakage of rented accommodation into the owner-occupied sector as this is the most effective way that landlords can realise capital gains. Only if rental conditions are exactly similar to perceived opportunities in the owner-occupied sector will the price of tenanted property be equal to that of property with vacant possession. These conditions are unlikely to be realised in the short or medium term so the incentive to transfer property into owner-occupation will remain, at least in many areas.

New investment

The second and far more relevant question is, can investing in the rented sector as a whole be increased or, at the very least, can disinvestment in what is currently the private rented sector be reversed? The answer to this question seems very uncertain and depends on two linked factors:

1 how far is the existing system out of equilibrium – because the change in the regulatory framework will enable suppressed demand to be met and landlords to adjust supply to the new conditions? and
2 to what extent may there be increases in demand for rented housing as a result of all the changes taking place in provision and subsidy, or increases in supply from reductions in the cost of provision?

In other words, it may be that the current regime is keeping dwellings in private renting which landlords would like to remove. If so, the size of the sector will continue to decline until landlords are satisfied with the rate of return they are achieving. On the other hand there may be demands for different types of dwelling that have been suppressed in the past or demand transferred from other sectors which can be realised as a result of the new regime. In addition, the costs of provision may be modified by the changed regime – for instance because finance can be obtained more cheaply.

From the point of view of commercial landlords the arithmetic here is fairly clear. Such landlords will only be prepared to enter and remain in the sector if they can earn a return equivalent to that available elsewhere. Market rent does not in itself guarantee that this is possible. What determines this is whether the rent covers the long run marginal cost including the interest rate which reflects the relevant risk category (Whitehead and Kleinman, 1988).

Evidence from the housing association sector is relevant here. Housing associations require subsidy on almost all assured tenancy projects and indeed found that they could not work the experimental 'challenge funding' schemes in 1987–8, where there was at least 30 % central government subsidy, unless they were prepared to provide additional cross subsidisation. This shows that, for that quality of accommodation, market rents will not generally cover the cost of provision. In non-stress areas this appears to reflect a lack of demand for additional units. This in turn reflects the fact that most tenants who can afford such a rent will also be able to afford owner-occupation. Those who cannot get into owner-occupation will generally have to be content with lower standards.

The same scenario can be seen in the private rented sector where in many areas landlords are prepared to register fair rents because these are at least equal to market rents – however, at the same time disinvestment is taking place. The only possible implication of both these facts is that, with current levels of effective demand, the equilibrium size of the private rented sector, i.e. the size it would be in a free market, is less than it is at present.

Rather different arguments apply in areas of heavy demand. The evidence for London is that even in those parts of the market where rents are freely set and quite high gross margins are being achieved, the size of the sector is declining. It is unlikely that the fear of finding oneself with a secure tenant is the only problem for landlords. Net rents on vacant possession values that would compare moderately well with returns on other investments would anyway imply gross rents in many cases over 10 %, which with current property values means people simply cannot afford to pay. Or if they can, they are better off in the owner-occupied sector where at least they are not paying management charges and where tax benefits are still concentrated. In these areas demand is generally high enough to induce additional housing investment but it is likely that this will be concentrated in the owner-occupied sector and investment will anyway be a very slow process heavily dependent on the availability of land and planning permission.

Under current conditions therefore the evidence suggests that the long run equilibrium size of the sector would be significantly less than its current level. Unless therefore there are increases in effective demand or reductions in cost it is unlikely that the continuing erosion of the traditional private rented sector will even be fully offset by new investment generated as a result of the changing regime.

Potential demand

Where could such additional demand come from? The most important factor is that the Act does nothing to change the relative incentives to choose different tenures on the part of consumers. If owner-occupation was the preferred tenure in the past both because of its particular attributes and because of the financial regime, higher rents will simply make it relatively more desirable for a larger number of households. And there is no suggestion that rents under the new regime can generally be lower than at the present time. Indeed, excactly the opposite is likely to occur and as a result of these higher rents, demand is likely to be reduced.

Increased demand must therefore arise either from a greater capacity to pay among those unable to enter owner-occupation or from demand which in current conditions has been suppressed. With respect to the first the most important factor is the availability and level of housing benefit. If the benefit system is prepared to pay a rent which will cover the costs of supply of reasonable quality accommodation then demand from those on low incomes could certainly be increased. However, the taper introduced under the new April 1988 rules is so steep that assistance will generally only be available to those outside the labour force. Employed people will have to pay the higher rents themselves which will increase their incentive to become owner-occupiers if at all possible.

Renting among those with the capacity to pay is likely to remain limited to those groups already identified as having positive prefernces for private renting. These include newly forming and mobile households for whom the transaction costs of owner-occupation make it a poor choice; those who do not wish to spend much on housing and want low quality at a low price; those who put considerable emphasis on others doing the management and maintenance and providing the capital; and finally those who are already owner-occupiers elsewhere but for one reason or another require an additional home in which they want no ownership role (Whitbread and Kleinman, 1986).

There are two likely sources of additional demand from these groups. The first is from mobile households looking for relatively short term accommodation of a higher standard than that which has generally been supplied in the past. This could include significant numbers of people looking for second homes especially related to employment. The second is from those who would rather live separately if at all possible but who have low incomes and therefore little capacity to pay for such accommodation themselves. This demand will depend mainly on the eligibility criteria for housing benefit and will be for lower quality older accommodation.

The other major source of demand for private renting could come from those who would traditionally have been housed by local authorities but who can no longer gain access to that sector. As rents will be higher than they would have paid in the past they will demand smaller and lower quality accommodation than before, except to the extent that housing benefit is prepared to underwrite traditional (i.e. relatively high) standards.

Generally therefore, in a market regime one can predict some growth of demand for higher quality, easy access accommodation especially in employment centres, together with a continuing demand for lower quality, higher density, perhaps shared, accommodation at the lower end of the market. The extent of this demand will depend upon ease of access to other tenures, household incomes, the level of rents at which landlords can supply this type of accommodation and, most notably, the availability and level of housing benefit. Thus, on the demand side the viability of the majority of the sector will depend upon central government policy.

The cost of provision

The other side of the coin is whether there is any reason to believe that either the costs of supplying private rented accommodation or the rate of return required could decrease as a result of the new regime. If so the rents that commercial landlords would need to charge to make it worthwhile to stay in business could be less than in the past making it worthwhile for more households to demand rented accommodation.

The costs of supply are basically determined by management and maintenance and the cost of finance. Management and maintenance costs mainly relate to the quality of the basic stock, to expected standards, to turnover, and to the type of tenant. On the whole one can expect such costs to be relatively high for a given standard of accommodation because demand comes mainly from mobile and other marginal households, and because of the age and low quality of the basic stock in the private rented sector. For instance, dwellings in multiple occupation have notably higher running costs than single family homes. So, if current costs are to be held down, the standard of provision is likely to be reduced. Only in the small up-market part of the sector do these arguments not hold.

The two main factors with respect to the cost of finance are perceived risk and expectations of capital gains. If the new regimes can give the private finance market confidence in the long term viability of the sector, large scale funds could be provided at rates which reflect the underlying security of the physical assets involved. So far there is little evidence that the private financial institutions regard the sector in this light – indeed even housing associations are having to pay well over the odds for their long term financing. This situation may change in the medium term as the institutions become more experienced but changing attitudes will take time.

The second question is expectation of capital gains. If landlords expect property values to continue to increase, the return they will require in rent alone will be less, because they receive part of their overall returns from these gains. At the limit, landlords would only need to cover the cost of letting to be prepared to provide accommodation. The difficulties here are obvious; first, if rents are low and letting problematic, they may simply keep the property vacant. Second, to realise the gains they normally have to sell with vacant possession thus generally transferring the property to owner-occupation. Any increase in net investment therefore must depend on a continuing flow of such landlords. Third, if landlords expect such gains, on which they have to pay tax, so do owner-occupiers who receive their gains tax free. The larger the expected gains the larger the incentive on the demand side to transfer to owner-occupation. So landlords are again left with lower income tenants or those whose running costs are likely to be high. So again the incentive to invest is reduced.

It is here that the BES could become important because this provides assistance to landlords which is more comparable to that of owner-occupiers, especially when net income from rent alone is low. It is likely therefore that the scheme will generate considerable interest. On the other hand the level of investment will be reduced by the complexities and costs specific to the scheme, which initially appear quite high. And the underlying question remains – is there adequate suitable demand for BES projects to provide additional supply rather than simply to substitute for other private sector investment? Current estimates suggest that total supply from BES projects is likely to be in the thousands of units rather than even the tens of thousands, and that they will be concentrated in particular areas in the South of England. Moreover, it is not clear what proportion of this supply will be *net* investment; much of it may be substitution for investment by other landlords or even by owner-occupiers.

Overall, then, BES provides an interesting demonstration project. It may help to build confidence and show the private sector what is possible in the medium term but the net effect on provision is likely to be small.

Resident landlords

One sub-sector where the pressures might go the other way is provision by resident landlords. They are to face an even less regulated regime than in the past, notably with respect to rent determination and eviction. This could marginally increase their preparedness to supply. But the most important factor here is that such landlords turn over rapidly and they provide accommodation mainly to help pay the costs of owner-occupation (Todd, 1986). If interest rates rise significantly many owner-occupiers may feel the need to let, but past experience suggests that such effects are fairly short term. The main trend is towards greater privacy, so if the economy is buoyant and incomes are generally rising, the supply of accommodation from resident landlords can be expected to continue to decline.

Conclusion

Overall we can expect to find that market rents will often be far higher than present regulated rents in areas of pressure, but not significantly different to current levels in non-stress areas. The mix of demand is likely to change away from traditional tenants towards those wanting easy access, mainly short term, accommodation while the emphasis in supply will be on provision by commercial landlords who expect to obtain an acceptable return on their investment.

In some ways therefore, the effect of the Act will be to move over time to a more desirable position; one in which willing suppliers provide accommodation to those who are prepared to pay for it. But this scenario does not take into account two basic factors of housing provision; first, supply adjustment is very slow so in areas of pressure, market rents may, to begin with, be far above those necessary to induce additional provision in the longer term. Second, housing is an expensive commodity and those on lower incomes are unable to pay for acceptable standards of housing unless they receive considerable government assistance. Ultimately, the success of the sector depends upon the generosity of government subsidy schemes either to landlords or more generally in the form of income related benefits to tenants. Crucially, though, for the private rented sector to move towards the desirable position outlined above would require an expansion in investment in the social housing sectors (local authorities and housing associations) so that tenants have real choice across the system as a whole.

Nor does the scenario define the size of the sector. Clearly, the traditional part can be expected to continue to decline. Most of the new supply will simply come from parts of that traditional sub-sector transferring into the non-regulated sector. The incentives for net new investment are likely to be very limited unless the contracts and related sale prices of transferred property from the council housing sector allow significant investment and improvement or unless government provides much larger scale supply subsidies than have yet been envisaged. Ultimately the size of the sector depends upon the relative desirability of renting privately compared to living in other tenures. At the present time it is difficult to envisage any large scale shift away from the preference for owner-occupation or, if this is not available, for social landlords. Demand for private renting will always be mainly from those looking for short term accommodation or from those unable to obtain access to other tenures.

Overall, the evidence suggests that under current conditions the equilibrium size of the true private rented sector is less than its current size. Moreover, even property transferred out of the local authority sector could well transfer again into owner-occupation. This does not mean that some sub-sectors will not expand, notably those for newly forming and mobile households and for those who are prepared to put up with low standard, perhaps crowded accommodation. But it is difficult to see where significant extra investment can come from within the existing financial framework. While BES may lead to small additions in net investment, this slight gain is difficult to justify on equity grounds when it is achieved at the cost of yet another tax break for higher income investors.

One relevant area given the government's current concerns is whether this changing mix within a probably smaller sector will help improve the operation of the labour market. Clearly there is no reason under the new regime why supply should not be forthcoming wherever potential tenants can pay the price. Moreover owner-occupiers who move, especially to the North, for job purposes, may wish to keep their investments in the South, increasing the supply of suitable accommodation. Once again the question remains; why should there be tenants who want to rent rather than buy? Again the answer must depend either on their already being owner-occupiers and wanting additional accommodation or on their being too poor or too mobile to want to buy. The basic problem is that in areas of high house prices rents must also be high unless there are expectations of continuing capital gains – in which case those who can afford it will try to obtain these gains themselves.

Thus the Housing Act 1988 changes the regulatory framework but it does little or nothing to change the economic and financial environment or to change preferences. Without such changes the true private rented sector must remain at most of marginal importance. What remains in the future will be economically viable but most of it is likely to be of poor quality and provide relatively low value for money with only a small subsector for the mobile employed (Kemp, 1988a). Ultimately, the position of the majority of both current and future tenants will depend on the government's preparedness to pay for adequate housing standards for the poor.

The Housing Act will not lead to any large scale revival of the private rented sector. However, this is not perhaps the major aim of the Act - which is rather to reduce the role of local authorities as providers of rented housing. In this process, the 'pure' private rented sector will play a role that is marginal in terms of numbers but is of some symbolic significance.

Notes

1 This article is based partly on work funded by the Joseph Rowntree Memorial Trust. The authors would like to thank the Trust for their assistance.

2 Despite the article being written before the Bill has been enacted it is nevertheless referred to hereafter as the 'Housing Act 1988'.

References

Department of Environment (1987a) *Housing: the Government's proposals*. Cmd 214, HMSO.

Department of Environment (1987b) *Private rented sector*. Consultation Paper. Department of Environment.

Department of Environment (1987c) *Deregulation of the private rented sector*. Consultation Paper on the Implications for Housing Benefit. Department of Environment.

Department of Environment (1988), *Local Government in England and Wales: capital expenditure and finance*. Consultation Paper. Department of Environment, Welsh office.

Greater London Council (1986) *Private tenants in London: the GLC survey 1983/84*, GLC.

Hills, J (1987) *Finance for housing associations: a response to the Government's proposals*. Welfare State Programme Research Note No. 8, London School of Economics.

Kemp, P (1988a) *The future of private renting*. University of Salford.

London Research Centre (1988) *Access to housing in London*. London Research Centre.

Todd, J E (1986) *Recent private lettings 1982/84*. HMSO.

Whitehead, C M E and Kleinman, M P (1986) *Private rented housing in the 1980s and 1990s*. Granta Editions.

Whitehead, C M E and Kleinman, M P (1987) Private renting in London: is it so different? *Journal of Social Policy* **16**, (3): 319–48.

Whitehead, C M E and Kleinman, M P (1988) Capital value rents: can the Inquiry into British Housing's proposals work? In Kemp, P (ed) (1988b) *The private provision of rented housing: current trends and future prospects*. Gower.

6 Thatcherism, citizenship and the poll tax

Stewart Miller

The Thatcherite policy project can be thought of as a twin-pronged fork. Both prongs point firmly in the same direction, and they are equally sharp. One represents the substantive changes which are sought directly through legislation and policy decisions, and the other the structuring of future decisions to ensure the continued prosecution of the project. Both prongs are aimed aggressively at the social-democratic norm of guaranteed welfare which had a significant degree of influence on policy for much of the post-war era. The Bill which on 29 July 1988 became the Local Government Finance Act illustrates both prongs in use, particularly in its creation of a community charge, or poll tax. It is designed to make a direct impact on the redistributive element of local public services, and to influence future decisions by local authorities and their electors. Both of these strategies derive from a rejection of the social democratic view of citizenship rights and relations in favour of a new model of citizenship which emphasises the costs of constructing social rights and the obligations which are thought to accompany those rights.

From the perspective of Thatcherite reformism, the experience of forty years of social democratic welfarism has, among others, two important facets. The first is substantial redistribution of resources through the public service system. This is not always highly egalitarian by any means, but undoubtedly cuts across the market distribution of incomes and resources dominated by labour rewards. The second is the operation of public decision-making systems, electoral and organisational, in such a way as to enhance and develop such redistribution. The 'New Right' thinkers from whom Mrs Thatcher draws much of her inspiration have long abhorred, on the one hand, the promiscuity of redistribution by universalist social services, and, on the other, the 'ratchet' mechanism by which the welfare state redefines both normal and acceptable levels of government activity, public expenditure and taxation. The introduction of the community charge is, as we shall see, an assault on both of these in the arena of local government. It is scarcely surprising, then, that the opposition to it has been so fierce, or so broadly based. This article proposes that the arguments for and against the community charge evoke, and stem from, conflicting models of citizenship.

Models of citizenship

In the early post-war years it was plausible to argue that the 'welfare state' legislation of the forties had almost completed the construction of a set of national rights of citizenship for the British people. Whatever the gaps and deficiencies that subsequently appeared in these rights, the thinking behind that legislation was strongly influenced by a perceived need to guarantee tolerable levels of income and access to services, on tolerable conditions, as a badge of full membership of a society which had undergone great collective hardship and was experiencing a new feeling of social solidarity.

It was in a series of public lectures in 1949, just as the post-war welfare system was coming to completion, that the sociologist T H Marshall expounded what we may call a 'social democratic' concept of citizenship, and he saw the moment as one of enormous importance in the realisation of that concept in social organisation. He defined citizenship in terms of 'full membership of a community' (Marshall, 1963, p72) and went on to divide it into three elements: civil, political, and social rights.

> *The civil element* is composed of the rights necessary for individual freedom – liberty of the person, freedom of speech, thought and faith, the right to own property and to include valid contracts, and the right to justice . . . By *the political element* I mean the right to participate in the exercise of political power, as a member of a body invested with political authority or as an elector of the members of such a body. The corresponding institutions are parliament and the councils of local government. By *the social element* I mean the whole range from the right to a modicum of economic welfare and security to the right to share to the full in the social heritage and to live the life of a civilised being according to the standards prevailing in the society. The institutions most closely connected with it are the educational system and the social services (Ibid, p74).

For Marshall, the post-war welfare reforms brought to culmination a radical recovery from the nadir of the mid-nineteenth century, when 'the minimal social rights that remained were detached from the status of citizenship'. Recipients of the cold charity of the Victorian Poor Law lost their personal liberty and, if they had it, their vote too. Thus their social rights could only be obtained at the expense of their political rights. The policy and practice of the Poor Law were an expression of the belief in the forces of the market as a set of guiding principles in social life which characterised the industrial revolution and its liberal ideology.

> The stigma which clung to poor relief expressed the deep feelings of a people who understood that those who accepted relief must cross the road that separated the community of citizens from the outcast company of the destitute (Ibid, p83).

Redistribution was kept to a minimum, and conceded on terms which did as little damage as possible to the natural dynamics of the labour market. Moreover, receipt of aid brought with it disenfranchisement, not only as part of the disincentive to apply, but also for fear that recipients, as interested parties, would exercise improper influence on the level of provision which local ratepayers would have to finance. These latter were treated as citizens largely on account of their preserved self-reliance and their contribution through taxation to the common weal. Their citizenship was earned, and was the less likely to be abused through rash or extravagant decisions by virtue of the fact that it was they who would have to pick up the bill.

The citizen as member of the social democratic 'welfare state', in contrast, experiences two phenomena unknown by his or her Victorian predecessor. One is the legitimacy of redistribution through state intervention in the markets in incomes and in welfare goods; and the other is the exercise of political rights, more or less universally and without conditions and limitations related to the use of public services. Both of these are essential to the social democratic model of citizenship – they have often been evoked as norms by critics of the inadequacy with which real institutions have reflected the model. And in the maturity of Thatcherism, these two elements of social and political citizenship are being renegotiated and adjusted.

Following the economic crisis of 1975–6, policy for citizenship on the social democratic model lost much of its limited momentum. And since the general election of May 1979, perceived financial necessity has been reinforced by ideological enthusiasm for public expenditure cuts and market forces. This reaction against the interventionist, social-democratic 'rights' model echoes some ideological assumptions of the Victorians. (Taylor-Gooby and Bochel in *The Year Book of Social Policy 1987–8* described the reconstruction under way and some of the contesting opinions around it. It is not surprising that the solidarity of the 1940s should have diminished as the years have passed, and the memory and reality of much hardship with them. But the intention of the present government has been to accelerate this process and deliberately to construct a model of citizenship much less solidaristic than competitive and individualistic. It lays stress on the responsibilities of citizenship, and the conditions placed on recognition more than the benefits which were once thought both to stem from the promise of citizenship and to consolidate its reality.

This model is referred to as 'new model citizenship', although it has features which hark back to the years before social democracy. If in the nineteenth century the dominant concern was to reinforce the market and self-help by the conditionality of citizenship rights, in the new Thatcherite model the same end is to be served by reminding voters – including welfare state clients, who can no longer be separated out so categorically – of the responsibilities and costs of citizenship, expressed in terms of spending impact. It is thus intended to mobilise popular pressure to limit redistribution through public services. Current policies in social security and taxation, and the reform of local government in particular, reflect this approach.

Something of the moral imperatives behind the new model of citizenship can be discerned in the speech which Mrs Thatcher gave to the General Assembly of the Church of Scotland in May 1988, while the Local Government Finance Bill and a clutch of others in the Government's reform programme were before Parliament. After a personal declaration of Christian faith, Mrs Thatcher turned to 'the relevance of Christianity to public policy – to the things that are Caesar's'. She laid stress on her belief in the legitimacy of private wealth accumulation; '. . . it is not the creation of wealth that is wrong, but love of money for its own sake', she said. Equally, there was an emphasis on individual responsibility and the limitation of government:

> What is certain . . . is that any set of social and economic arrangements which is not founded on the acceptance of individual responsibility will do nothing but harm. We are all responsible for our own actions . . . We simply cannot delegate the exercise of mercy and generosity to others . . .
>
> In our generation, the only way we can ensure that no-one is left without sustenance, help or opportunity, is to have laws to provide for health and education, pensions for the elderly, succour for the sick and disabled. But intervention by the State must never become so great that it effectively removes personal responsibility. The same applies to taxation, for while you or I would work extremely hard whatever the circumstances, there are undoubtedly some who would not unless

the incentive was there. And we need their efforts too (*Observer*, 22 May 1988.

In comparison with post-war orthodoxy, all of this implies a much less collective view of social relations and of the potentialities of social achievement; and a much less collective conception of citizenship. In particular, the anxiety to limit state activity to what is unavoidable, and to leave as much responsibility as possible with the individual, militates for selectivity and against universalism in social provision. Universalism has been seen since the time of the Beveridge Report as a means of avoiding obstacles to the realisation of social rights such as the stigmatisation of those dependent on public provision, and thus as a way of preserving claimants' citizenship. It has been regarded widely as a failure of the British social security system that it has come to depend heavily on selective, means-tested benefits in respect of needs which Beveridge intended to be met universally. But the social security reviews of 1984–5 mark the official abandonment of any attempt to perfect universal benefits so as to render means-testing redundant. The social security reform is rather an attempt to make means-testing work well enough to reduce the need for universal benefits (such as child benefit and the state earnings related pension scheme). There is a strong presumption that, beyond a basic set of guarantees, 'social' provision is best provided privately through the market, and that as many services as possible ought to be paid for by their users, not by the community at large.

An elaboration of Conservative citizenship had been spelt out a few weeks before the Prime Minister's speech by the Home Secretary, Douglas Hurd, in a *New Statesman* article. This began by asserting the desirability of voluntarism in social organisation and activity. The Conservative Party was expanding the scope for 'voluntary acts of citizenship', in contrast to the Left's 'bureaucratic definition of citizenship as something to which we are compelled by the state' (Hurd, 1988).

The diffusion of power is a bulwark against despotism and corruption, and the key to active and responsible citizenship . . . So the thrust of government policy is to shift power outwards, away from the corporatist battalions to the small platoons. (Hurd, 1988).

One might infer from this a devolutionary speech to central–local relations in government. But local authorities figure among the 'big battalions', not the 'small platoons', so 'some aspects of our policy, like the national curriculum or the business rate, involve taking power from local councils to the centre in order to prevent its abuse or atrophy'. And in a passage which suggests a reinterpretation of Marshall's sociological account of the development of citizenship, and which also finds echoes in the government's approach to local taxation, Hurd argues that with the spread of political rights and prosperity, 'we need to encourage the notion that civic responsibilities, too, are the property of all. They have been democratised'. (Hurd, 1988).

Nevertheless, the spectacle of a Conservative government engaged, as this one is, in a strenuous effort to shift radically the balance of power from local to central government is a surprising one – not just in terms of Conservative tradition but especially in the context of the decentralisation which has been a part of the Reaganite conservative strategy in the United States. An American commentator struck by this paradox explains it thus:

> Viewed from a broader perspective, both governments see themselves in populist terms, decentralising power to the grass roots. In both cases, there is an effort to provide individuals with more 'power', in effect bypassing local government institutions, which are seen as distorting true citizen preferences. In this view, the local political elites are unrepresentative and are able, because of the inability of local general elections to enforce conformity between public opinion and public policy, to impose tax/spending packages at a higher level than the citizenry actually prefer (Wolman, 1988, p433).

This illustrates a crucial shift in perceptions of power relations and progress. As many commentators have pointed out, the social democratic consensus was forged in the peculiar circumstances of wartime and after. Moreover it assumed a large proportion of the population in conditions of poverty or near-poverty, likely to see themselves as benefiting from collective provision. Poverty was the oppressor, and progress meant giving citizens the right to a better life. In the majority affluence of the 1980s, it is not difficult for the notoriously monolithic, bureaucratic and expensive welfare machine to be presented as the oppressor against which citizens' rights ought to be realised and exercised. With low turnouts in local government elections, the legitimacy of the councils is more tenuous than that of central government and they (the councils) present a target for a centrally-directed citizenship campaign. So 'new model' citizenship emphasises not only social obligations rather than social rights, but also a 'progressive' set of political rights which are largely perceived as enabling individuals to protect themselves from the cost implications of expensive communal provision. This inevitably brings this conception of citizenship into conflict with the expansion of social rights on the social democratic model.

Of course, it would be nonsensical to argue that there is no room in the Government's thinking for redistribution, or for popular or authoritative decisions which run counter to that thinking. But the direction of policy inspired by the thoughts expressed above is clearly anti-redistributive, and that policy is accompanied by a high degree of sensitivity to what is perceived as the 'abuse or atrophy' of power. Local government, largely controlled by the Labour Party, spending large amounts of money raised through a combination of the unpopular local 'rates' and subvention from central government's own coffers, was an obvious case for treatment on both counts.

Accountability and reform

The Local Government Finance Bill acquired the soubriquet of 'flagship' of the Government's third-term project, a *flota armada* if ever there was one. In the wake of the flagship sailed galleons of education, housing and further local government reform, and more. The Bill reflected, perhaps even more clearly than any of its fellows, the new model citizenship of 1980s Conservatism, and some of its practical implications.

The Conservative version of citizenship involves the heightening of popular consciousness of the costs of services, as a guard against public extravagance. This has led the Government into conflict with the supporters of the social democratic model on the grounds both of redistributive policy and of the terms of political participation. An important element of this strategy involves the wide distribution of tax-paying, so that as many people as possible have a vested interest in low tax rates. This is a central theme of the reform of local government finance, and it revives in a new form a connection which had seemed to be severed, between representation and taxation. We have seen that Marshall pointed out how the granting of one set of rights might be conditional on the loss or modification of another. On the whole, such conditions have tended to be removed or overridden in the twentieth-century development of citizens' rights. However the present local government finance reform can be seen as an attempt to reverse this tendency, or at least to exact a price for it. The Government has drawn a particular connection between the provision of local authority services and liability for local taxation which adheres to its concept of accountability.

The Government's argument on accountability is spelt out most fully in its Green Paper, *Paying for local government* (Cmnd 9714), which contains the proposal to replace domestic rates with the community charge. A summary of and commentary on both the argument and the proposals are in Bramley's article, 'Paying for local government' in the *Year Book of Social Policy 1986–7* (Bramley 1987). In essence the strategy is to construct a flat-rate tax on all adults, modified by rebates for the poor, which will be so simple and visible to its payers that they will be highly sensitive to variations and movements in local expenditure affecting it. This will promote accountability by enhancing the direct interest of local voters in the performance of their authorities. It is also designed to reduce the redistributive element of local taxation in favour of an overall charge as a contribution to the costs of local services. If the social democratic citizen is a member of a community, the new model citizen is essentially a paying customer.

The community charge proposal is a critical move on what has become the battlefield of central–local government relationships. As an undergraduate student of politics in the 1960s the author was told that, although central government provided about half of local councils' finance, it was loath to use the 'power of the purse' over these authorities to excess, and there was a general consensus on the value of local democracy. Needless to say, the economic stringency of recent times has placed a massive strain on relationships in this area, but the post-1979 Government has added an ideological commitment to the Whitehall side of the struggle.

It was argued by ministers in the early 1980s that local councils were not democratically entitled to levy whatever rates they felt appropriate. Their commercial ratepayers were not enfranchised, and therefore not part of the constituency to which councils could be forced into accountability through the ballot-box, whereas the personal recipients of welfare assistance did have the vote, even though their housing benefit might release them from their entire ratepaying liability. It was therefore necessary for central government to intervene and restore the balance by preventing local councils from spending excessively on services, placing unacceptable burdens on ratepayers. This intervention would have to be of a very thorough-going kind. It began with limits to central government aid to local authorities, it proceeded by way of controls on their revenue raising and it has now moved into the use of the tax and benefit structure to influence the political dynamics of local government. The vehicle chosen for that influence is the community charge and it has been justified chiefly in terms of accountability. It is important, particularly in the context of citizenship, to examine critically the Government's use of the concept of accountability.

Accountability is about responsible representation. The relationship between taxation (and spending decisions) on the one hand, and representation (in its electoral aspect) on the other, has two facets. Firstly, representation influences taxation directly:

any elected body is bound to be influenced in its decisions to spend and tax by the way the electorate votes. Secondly, taxation influences representation: the subjection to tax is part of the voters' experience of the consequences of their electoral decisions. So there is a real sense in which the electorate is accountable for its exercise of representation. To use the tax (and benefit) system to create incentives towards voting for particular patterns of local spending is to emphasise the second of these facets at the expense of the first, and that is exactly what is proposed. Through the community charge, voters are to pay such an obvious and penal price for high spending on the part of their local authorities that they will check it electorally and, presumably, by the exercise of acute vigilance between elections.

The penal nature of this price is to be enhanced by the device of 'gearing'. Under the new legislation, central government will determine some 75 % of local councils' revenue (a far higher proportion than at present because of the nationalisation of non-domestic rates). But *all* of any local variation from centrally-set norms will be reflected in the community charge. So a council wishing to spend 5 % more than the norm will have to increase its community charge by 20 %. Chargepayers will thus experience, in proportion, hugely magnified variations in the level of their liability, according to the amounts their councils raise to cover their expenditure once central grant has been set. This is calculated to produce in the electorate a heightened sensitivity to council spending – as well it may.

There has been concern among commentators and local political actors, both about the principle and about the differential gearing effects likely to occur up and down the country. This concern is heightened by doubt as to whether the 75 % of 'normal' revenue that central government controls will be determined in a politically neutral way, and the White Paper, *A new public expenditure planning total,* published in July 1988, is not entirely reassuring on this matter. Superficially this paper proposes a liberal regime, in which locally determined expenditure – community charge and some other receipts – will be excluded from the national expenditure planning total. The rationale for this is highly characteristic:

> The changes in local government finance will greatly increase its transparency and so enhance accountability. This process can be further enhanced by redefining the planning total, so that it distinguishes expenditure which is the responsibility of central government from that which is the responsibility of local government (Cmd 441, p5).

So central government will be able to distance itself publicly from the bits of local expenditure over which councils have formal control. This has been taken to imply that the powers of 'charge-capping', by which the government has enabled itself to continue to punish high-taxing councils as it did under the rating system, will be redundant. As a writer on local government affairs put it, 'If the previous local financing system was a swamp surrounded by mists . . . then capping is a dinosaur from these same swamps' (Davis-Coleman, 1988, p1594). Crucially, however, the Government makes it clear in the White Paper that it remains highly interested in the totality of public expenditure, even beyond the new formal planning total. 'Spending by local authorities of their own resources' will continue to attract the active concern of central government:

> . . . if the Government felt that this expenditure was growing too rapidly . . . the Government would need to consider whether to take action to moderate the growth of spending within the planning total, whether its own spending or *grants to local authorities* (Cmd 441, p6, emphasis added).

It is evident, then, that the Government has less than total faith in the automatic operation of the particular political market it is striving to create. In the Scottish legislation which was enacted just before the general election it was felt necessary to include two 'fall-back' provisions. First, section 22 of the Abolition of Domestic Rates etc (Scotland) Act empowers the Secretary of State for Scotland to reduce community charges where he is satisfied that local authority expenditures are 'excessive and unreasonable'; and second, under section 31, 'Such provisions as appear to the Secretary of State to be necessary or expedient for the purpose of rendering this Act of full effect may be prescribed'. In England and Wales, part VII of the Local Government Finance Act provides for financial penalties to be visited on those councils who, in the opinion of the Secretary of State, attempt to spend to excess. The effect on these provisions of the new planning proposals is not clear, but it seems likely to be greater in appearance than in substance.

The centralisation of local taxation on business premises, as well as the creation of the 'geared-up' community charge, is largely prompted by the Government's concern to protect 'disenfranchised' business from the depredations of unchecked local authorities – or of their voters. However, as Thomas Wilson (who has advised the Government on local government finance, and is sympathetic to this part of the plan) points out, there is no more a formal business vote at central government level than there is at local, so the tax will still be levied without electoral representation.

> Presumably it is argued that the central government will behave more responsibly than some, at least, of the local authorities because there may be less likelihood of an extreme ideological position being adopted and also because there will be no higher authority to rescue the central government from the consequences of its actions – apart from that severe disciplinarian, the IMF! (Wilson, 1987, p48).

All in all, it will become more difficult for local councils to behave in certain ways that may be seen as 'accountable': particularly to follow the desires of their electorates when these desires do not conform to those of a central government committed to expenditure cutting. What is being promoted, critics have suggested, is effectively the electorate's accountability to central government for its (the electorate's) behaviour in local elections, and, through this, the incentive to vote for low spending. The effect of spreading tax-paying throughout the electorate is to put the exercise of the political rights which citizens already enjoy into a carefully constructed economic framework. This is as serious a hindrance to the social-democratic model of citizenship as the register of liable charges which it is proposed to maintain and update frequently, or the use of the electoral register as its base.

The debate

As the reform process developed, it was possible to discern a number of major sources of opposition. Obviously, among the most ardent opponents were the official parliamentary opposition, and in particular the Labour Party, which was trying to defend its position in the local authorities up and down the country from the effects of the loaded political incentives with which the Bill is designed to present the local electorate, and the control over local affairs which it gives to central government. The Labour Party's alternative proposals – to include rates based on property values and a complementary local income tax – emerged at a fairly late stage of the process. The Democrats were committed to a local income tax from the beginning.

There was also a fairly sustained opposition within the Conservative Party, particularly in the parliamentary party of both Houses, in which the attempt of a number of 'wets' led by George Young and Michael Mates to convert the flat-rate poll tax into a modified local income tax was of particular interest. The authority of the whips, undermined by an earlier confrontation over the reform of the Official Secrets Act, was severely tested.

The local authority associations saw the future of local government as bleak and restricted, particularly as the implications of councils' reduced administrative role began to dawn on commentators and policy-makers. They foresaw the possibility of a gradual transition to American-style, small-scale local boards with restricted functions. The lobby of welfare and civil rights pressure groups were allies, nervous of the welfare implications of a basically flat-rate tax whose means-tested adjustments are designed to maintain the political incentives of the whole tax, as well as the civil rights implications of a general tax on electors, with concomitant register. Alongside them were also the trade unions likely to be affected by the trimming of local government staffs which is one of the objectives both of the Local Government Bill and of a number of others which were in the process at the same time.

Obviously, there is a strong element of self-interest in elements of the opposition to the community charge, and to its support. But in the battle for parliamentary and public opinion the arguments have had to be put in terms of values which are more broadly shared. These have centred largely on explicit and implicit models of citizenship. Two documents produced by the local authority associations may serve to illustrate the criticisms aimed at the proposals from an early stage. The Association of Metropolitan Authorities (AMA) rejected the Government's version of accountability in plain terms: 'To link voting with paying – as this Green Paper does in its underlying arguments and in the detailed administration of poll tax – is narrow and dangerously anti-democratic' (Association of Metropolitan Authorities, 1986, pi). The document contrasted the 'benefit principle' on which the government sought to base local taxation with the principle of 'ability to pay', and argued that the former was inappropriate and incompatible with fairness in taxation, citing no less than Adam Smith and John Stuart Mill in support (ibid, pp1–5). Similarly the Association of County Councils (ACC) opposed the reform package, arguing that true accountability required local authorities to be freer of central control and more capable of responding to local influence than the Green Paper's proposals would allow. Again, the unfairness of the community charge was asserted, along with the 'serious problems of determination and enforcement' to which it would give rise (Association of County Councils 1986, pp 1–3). Civil as well as political and social rights are involved in such arguments.

When the Local Government Finance Bill was introduced into Parliament, it was not long before the strength of opposition to it, particularly in the government's own ranks in both Houses, became apparent. After a December division in which the

Government's majority had been reduced to 72 by a Tory rebellion, the *Guardian,* an implacable opponent, remarked that the flag ship was 'holed but still afloat'. The paper's parliamentary sketch writer developed the metaphor. Mrs Thatcher, who was not present during the debate, 'has a nose for a sinking ship'; when the Secretary of State Nicholas Ridley gesticulated at the Opposition, 'it looked less like waving than drowning' *Guardian,* 18 December 1987).

However, the Bill survived this and other assaults and insults, and if the crunch came it was in May, when the amendment proposed by the Conservative backbencher Michael Mates was put to the Commons. This proposed a banding of the community charge by income level, linked to income tax liability. This challenged the government's anti-redistributive stance on the charge, and raised the fundamental principles of the reform.

The day before the vote on the Mates amendment, the debate between Mr Ridley and his critics was carried into the columns of the *Sunday Times.* The Secretary of State defended his Bill and Mr Mates his assault on it. Mates, predictably, was critical of the flat-rate charge in the context of an earlier Conservative promise to replace the rates with 'taxes more broadly based and related to people's ability to pay'. He emphasised that rebates for the poor, on their own, did not meet this criterion, even after the improvements announced by the government some days before the debate.

> The Government said that it had now dealt with the problem, but it has only taken care of the *inability* to pay. This misses the greatest point: for the overwhelming majority – for anyone above the poverty line – we are still left with a flat-rate charge. (Mates, 1988; emphasis added).

Mr Ridley felt obliged to defend his Bill on ground not far removed from this. Although he did not suggest that the charge would be more related to ability to pay than the rates, he did argue that the new system of local government finance would be fair. This was, of course, partly because of the rebate system; but also because 50 % of local spending will come from central government funds and 25 % from the business rate, so that 'the top 10 % of households will pay far more towards local spending through national taxation than the 10 % of households with the lowest incomes' (Ridley, 1988).

It was interesting to see this attempt to defend the charge in the traditional terms of redistributive citizenship, not least because it took Mr Ridley on to very weak ground. The characteristics he emphasised figure rather more strongly in the pre-reform system than in the new; and his argument, repeated in Parliament and by other defenders of the Bill, pointed if anything to the low priority given to redistribution in the new scheme. This is characteristic of the 'new model' citizenship. It also highlights an ironic aspect of the Government's position. The original pledge to reform the rates was made in the election manifesto of October 1974, when Mrs Thatcher was the Party's spokesperson on local government. It was expressed in the terms, still current at that time, of social-democratic distributive justice.

> The rating system itself has come under criticism . . . we shall abolish the domestic rating system and replace it by taxes more broadly based and related to people's ability to pay (Craig, 1975, p436).

Since that time the centre of gravity of practical Conservative policy has shifted substantially, and the particular emphasis of local government finance reform has come to be on new model accountability. So the redemption of the pledge is taking place in a context of a quite new set of values, and indeed is a very different kind of reform from what might have been expected as an enhancement of 'ability to pay' in local taxation. But Mrs Thatcher's early commitment is psychologically important to the Government; and even if it wished to forget it, it would not be allowed to by its critics. It is scarcely surprising, then, that the new model reform and some old-fashioned elements of its defence seem occasionally to part company.

In the House of Commons, Mr Mates attacked the unfairness of the tax, and reiterated his point that 'ability to pay' must go beyond a residual rebate scheme *(House of Commons Debates* 131, col.580). On the other hand Mr Norman Tebbit, who claimed to have invented the poll tax, remarked that Mr Mates 'has still not accepted that it will only account for one quarter of local government finance, with the other three quarters being paid according to ability to pay' (Ibid, col.600). This actually suggested the abandonment of 'ability to pay' as a guiding principle in this part of the taxation scheme. More explicit was a remark of Mr Ridley's to his constituency association, reported in the local newspaper and quoted by John Cunningham from the Labour benches:

> He added that there was no reason why local services should be paid by people according to their incomes. 'Why should a duke pay more than a dustman?' he asked. 'It is only because we have been subjected to socialist ideas for the last 50 years' (*Wiltshire and Gloucester Standard,* 1 April, cited at ibid, col. 590).

In the debate, Mr Ridley coined a phrase which, if less than totally clear, seemed to epitomise the link between democratic participation and taxation embodied in the reform: '...it makes everyone contribute, at least a little, to local resources, so that *all can contribute in democracy at local level*' (Ibid, col.581; emphasis added).

The Government has been fairly consistent in defining the limits of this demand for contribution on grounds of accountability. The Housing Benefit provisions in the Social Security Act 1986 constituted the first stage in the local taxation reform, anticipating crucial aspects of the community charge. The recipients of housing benefit, which provides aid with housing-related rates as well as direct housing costs, now receive the benefit in respect of only 80 % of these rates. This flies in the face of the recommendation of the Housing Benefit Review Report of 1985, but, according to the subsequent Social Security Green Paper, 'will strengthen local accountability by ensuring that everyone pays something towards their rates' (Cmnd,9517, p46). In *The Year Book of Social Policy 1986–7,* Bramley argued, regarding the 80 % proposal, that:

> if it were simply about accountability the Government would restore the average income of claimants by an increase in basic scale rate equal to the national average rate bill/community charge (Bramley, 1987, p191).

Sure enough, the Government subsequently announced a substantial amendment to its social security reform plans in this respect. Recipients of selective income maintenance benefits under the reformed system of social security now receive compensation for the 20 % contribution to the rates and will eventually receive similar treatment in respect of their contribution to the community charge. Since the principle of accountability requires that their marginal liability for local tax be real and that it vary with the full amount of the tax, the compensation is at a flat rate, this being, according to a Government spokesperson, 'the average amount that we expect householders who are income support claimants to have to meet' as their residual contribution (*Guardian* 16 May 1987). During the passage of the Local Government Finance Bill itself, exemption was extended to the mentally impaired but not to the physically handicapped, again consistently with the principles of the reform. There is a clear assumption of electors as rational and self-interested 'economic persons'.

The new model, then, is one in which citizenship is a status to be attained largely by the payment of tax, placing the benefits of welfare services firmly in a context of costs and incentives. We are well used to social benefits which are designed to maintain *economic* incentives; and this remains a major element in the current thinking. But now the controllers of the welfare state, in a closely related and interdependent strategy, are also seeking to construct something like the *political* dynamics of an earlier stage. It would be unthinkable to return to a situation where, through either specific disqualification or a narrow franchise, those who had an interest in extensive public services were to be disenfranchised. But if the 'paupers' of the late twentieth century cannot be excluded from citizenship, they are to be pressed into it on the Government's 'new model' terms. The incentives with which *all* voters are faced are to be more like those which confronted Victorian electors and citizens. We are all – even the recipients of the most selective social benefits – to experience some of the pangs felt by the propertied electorate of the nineteenth century when faced with swelling demands for publicly-financed sewerage and Poor Law provision. This is what will make new model citizens of us. (Ironically, property is being abandoned as a basis for personal local taxation. But this, says the Government, is because local services are now predominantly personal services, not services to property. So the shift to people-taxation is merely an act of modernisation).

Of course, all this is actually quite a long way from the form that conditional citizenship took in the nineteenth century, when the receipt of aid automatically disenfranchised those few men – women being utterly excluded from the electorate – who would have had the vote but for the ministrations of the Poor Law. But when T H Marshall, in 1949, looked back on that practice as an example of the linking of social rights to political conditions and of the vulnerability of social rights in earlier times, he thought he was documenting a whole concept of conditional citizenship which had been finally abandoned. It seems he may have overestimated the resilience of its redistributive and less conditional social democratic successor. Of course, he could know nothing then of the weapon to be used against that model in the 1980s: the sharp fork of Thatcherism.

References

Abolition of Domestic Rates Etc. (Scotland) Act 1987. HMSO.

Association of Metropolitan Authorities (1986) *The AMA's response to the Government's Green Paper 'Paying for local government'*. AMA.

Association of County Councils (1986) *Paying for local Government: response to the Green Paper*. ACC.

Bramley, G (1987) Paying for local government. In Brenton, M, and Ungerson, C (eds) (1987) *The Year Book of Social Policy 1986–7*. Longman.

Craig, F W S (ed) (1975) *British general election manifestos 1900–1974*. Macmillan.

Davis-Coleman, C (1988) How the treasury mandarins conjured up a curate's egg. *Municipal Journal* 29 July.
Department of the Environment, Scottish Office and Welsh Office (1986) *Paying for local Government* (Cmnd, 9714). HMSO.
H M Treasury (1988) *A new public expenditure planning total* (Cmd 441). HMSO.
Hurd, D (1988) Citizenship in the Tory democracy. *New Statesman,* 29 April
Local Government Finance Act 1988. HMSO.
Marshall, T H (1963) *Sociology at the crossroads, and other essays.* Heinemann.
Mates, M (1988) Fighting for fair play. *Sunday Times,* 17 April.
Ridley, N (1988) A community tax is the best way forward. *Sunday Times,* 17 April.
Taylor-Gooby, P and Bochel, H (1988) Parliament and the politics of welfare. In Brenton, M and Ungerson, C (eds) (1988) *The Year Book of Social Policy 1987–8.* Longman.
Wilson, T (1987) Paying for local government. *Policy Studies* 7 (2): 45–65.
Wolman, H (1988) Understanding recent trends in central–local relations: centralisation in Great Britain and decentralisation in the United States. *European Journal of Political Research.* 16 (4): 425–35.

7 Yet another NHS crisis?

Alan Maynard

Introduction

Every five or six years the continuing conflict between the holders of mutually incompatible ideologies generates a 'crisis' concerning the funding and provision arrangements of the National Health Service. The collectivistic ideology which influenced the creation of the NHS in 1948 requires that access to health care should be determined by the need of patients. The market or liberal ideology requires that access to health care should be determined by the consumers' willingness and ability to pay. The former group defends the NHS by demonstrating its *theoretical* strengths and the *actual* weaknesses of market provision. The marketeers advocate the *theoretical* virtues of the market and highlight the *actual* weaknesses of the NHS (Maynard and Williams, 1984).

The most recent manifestation of the conflicts in ideology concerning the NHS is evident in the Thatcher Government review of the NHS. In late 1987 the parsimonious funding of the NHS and the increasing demands for care and cure led to hospital ward closures and the explicit rationing of health care resources in a way which led provider and user groups to unite in protest. After initial repudiation of demands for increased funding the Prime Minister decided to divert political pressure on her administration by setting up a review.

The alleged under-funding of the service and the establishment of the review led to a flood of advocacy from adherents of the liberal (market) ideology in particular. Green (1988) advocated the replacement of the NHS by private (insurance) funding and competitive (private) market provision of care. The advocacy took all too little account of the problems of such solutions as evidenced by US experience, cost inflation and inequalities in access in particular.

Brittain (1988) advocated the replacement of tax finance with (earmarked) social insurance contributions but again, as Ludbrook and Maynard (1988) showed, the distributional impact of this was to make the poor pay more and the rich pay less, and the effects on the efficiency of the supply of care were ambiguous.

Various contributions to the debate were made by the Tory 'think-tank', the Centre for Policy Studies. Goldsmith and Willetts (1988) advocated the maintenance of tax-funding but the creation of competitive mechanisms in the supply of health care. A similar approach was advocated by Pirie and Butler (1988) of the Adam Smith Institute. A critical appraisal of three proposals is set out in Brazier, Hutton and Jeavons (1988). These proposals had much in common with those of the American economist Enthoven (1985) and the mechanisms put forward by Maynard (Maynard 1985, Maynard et al 1986). The objective of all those ideas is to improve the efficiency of the supply of health care in the NHS.

Whilst the Thatcher review of the NHS was confidential, the House of Commons Select Committee on Social Services held their deliberations in public and cross-examined the protagonists. Their report (House of Commons, 1988) provides cross party support for the maintenance of tax funding but with experimentation with market mechanisms in the supply of health care. In particular they advocate more spending on health care, the more careful evaluation of the effects of the NHS on citizens' health and the integration of clinicians into the management process of the NHS.

The outcomes of the Government review are likely to be modest as this debate has educated the politicians into recognition of the fact that no easy solutions to the problem of health care system exist. However its conclusions are unlikely to vitiate the long run conflicts over ideology.

The regular conflict of the mutually incompatible ideologies, together with the confusion of the theoretical and actual strengths and weaknesses of the competing models by the contestants, often with all too little recourse to empirical evidence, ensures that the problems of how to finance and provide health care will not be resolved easily. Only if there is a consensus about ideological goals can the problems associated with achieving them be tackled effectively. But such a consensus will be continually fluctuating and be challenged by those seeking different social objectives. The difficulty which must be resolved in any debate about health is the identification of social goals and the illumination of the actual problems of the health care market in Britain.

What are the objectives of British health care policy?

Policy goals are usually set in an ambiguous and general fashion. In part, this may be due to the reluctance of policy-makers to be held accountable for clearly defined goals. In part, the ambiguity may be due to the difficulty of framing difficult concepts in the tumult and rhetoric of the political debate.

It was, no doubt, difficult to formulate objectives when the Coalition Government of the day with a Conservative Prime Minister adopted an ideology inconsistent with the liberal market tradition of the Conservative Party. Thus, Churchill's Coalition Government stated in the 1944 White Paper:

> the Government...want to ensure than in the future every man and woman and child can rely on getting...the best medical and other facilities available; that their getting them shall not depend on whether they can pay for them or on any other factor irrelevant to real need (Ministry of Health, 1944, p5).

This statement that need, not ability to pay, would determine access to the NHS was iterated by another adherent of the Conservative ideology, Prime Minister Margaret Thatcher, at the Party Conference in 1983:

> The principle that adequate health care should be provided for all, regardless of ability to pay, must be a foundation of any arrangements for financing health care (M.Thatcher, Conservative Party Conference, 2 October 1982).

However, it is not only Conservative Prime Ministers who can adopt apparently alien ideologies. The architect of the NHS, Aneurin Bevan, adopted a clearly liberal position in an argument in the 1946 Parliamentary debate about the NHS in relation to charging for social services:

> I really must resist this amendment. Does the Hon. Member suggest that everything shall be free?...It is a perfectly reasonable proposition that, where domestic help of this sort is needed and the persons concerned are able to provide it for themselves, they should do so, and, where they are able to make a contribution, they should make it...it seems to me to be wholly unjustified that we should provide a service of this sort without any payment whatever.
>
> Our objection to the means test was that it was devised for the purpose of withholding money from people. This means' test is for the purpose of giving services to people who are in need of these services...and where people can make a contribution towards the cost, they should make it (House of Commons Debate, 1946).

Despite ideology swaps between the contending political parties and continual debate about the objectives of health care policy, there seems to be some degree of adherence in the UK to the goal of allocating care on the basis of need. But what is need? This can either be a demand (patient) or supply (a professional judgment by a doctor) concept. For the purpose of analysing the NHS the definition of need used here is a supply side, technical judgment of the capacity of competing patients to benefit from health care inputs. If benefit is measured in terms of enhancements in the length and quality of life, then patients will get access to care in the NHS in relation to its cost and the benefit they get from it.

Instead of determining access on the basis of whether patients are willing and able to pay for care, only those patients with the greatest expected benefit from care per unit of budget will be treated. Patients with positive but low expected benefits from care or with substantial expected benefits at great cost are unlikely to get care. The NHS budget will be allocated on the basis of maximising expected improvements in the health status of patients regardless of whether they are rich or poor.

This definition of the objective of the NHS: maximisation of expected health benefits for patients from the given budget, may not be accepted at all. It discriminates against groups or patients with inferior capacities to benefit from care. Such people may be poor and this may bias resource allocation away from them towards the rich who can benefit more. But to remedy this inequality, health benefits for the poor have to be bought by forgoing more health benefits to the rich than are given too the poor, i.e. the resource allocation would be inefficient.

It is assumed here that inefficiency is unethical: it deprives potential patients of care from which they could benefit. Furthermore, it is assumed that efficiency is equitable: the best distribution of care is that which maximises the production of expected health benefits from the NHS budget. Thus, the objective of the NHS, to allocate care on the basis of the patients' expected benefits from care from a given budget, is ethical, equitable and efficient. Such a conclusion is clearly based on the utilitarian perspective: the pursuit of the greatest happiness of the greatest number.

Is the NHS under-financed?

The current funding situation

There is continual argument about the funding levels of the NHS and this is fuelled by the absence of good data for all aspects of the Service and by the difficulties of deflating budgets to take account of NHS pay and price changes. The data in Table 7.1 were supplied by the Department of Health for the House of Commons Select Committee on Social Services and pertain to England.

Table 7.1 Real growth in NHS expenditure[1]

	HCHS[2] (hospitals)	FPS[3] (primary care)	Total[4] NHS	LASS[5] (PSS)
1982–3	0.1	7.8	1.7	2.0
1983–4	0.4	2.6	1.2	3.4
1984–5	1.2	5.3	2.8	1.7
1985–6	-0.6	-0.6	-0.1	-0.1
1986–7	4.0	4.1	4.2	8.1
1987–8	4.9	5.7	4.8	4.4
1988–9[6]	na	5.7	4.6	na

1 After adjusting for pay and prices increases
2 Current HCHS spend.
3 Current FPS spend.
4 Total NHS spend (current and capital, all activities).
5 Total PSS spend (current and capital).
6 Planned expenditure where available.

Source: *The Future of the National Health Service*, Select Committee on Social Services Fifth Report HC 613, July, House of Commons, 1988

The first column is for the Hospital and Community Health Services (HCHS) budget. This is cash limited and from this limited run of data there is evidence of a political cycle: note how expenditure increased around the time of the 1987 general election. Prior to April 1986 the rate of growth of the HCHS budget was meagre, with negative (a fall) growth in 1985/6.

The Family Practitioner Services (primary care) budget is not cash limited by HM Treasury. It is open-ended with its size determined in large part by the number of general practitioners and their prescribing habits. Again, the Government succeeded in holding down the rate of growth of this budget in 1985/6, but by and large, and not unexpectedly, given its open-ended nature, the rate of growth of this budget exceeded that of the hospital sector (HCHS).

The Local Authority Social Service (LASS) budget, like the HCHS budget, is cash limited. It grew rapidly around the period of the 1987 general election and was held down prior to that period, especially in 1985/6.

Sources of increased demand

From Table 7.1 it can be seen that, apart from 1985/6, NHS funding has increased in real terms in total every year and for each component part of the service (HCHS, FPS, and LASS). Furthermore, Government ministers insist that resources have been freed up within the hospital services by 'efficiency gains' totalling cumulatively, according to DHSS evidence to the Select Committee in 1988, over £800 million.

Despite some increase in funding and these efficiency gains, it is possible that the gap between the demand for care and its supply is widening. A variety of factors are causing this, all of them are ill-understood and poorly researched:

1 Demographic change: the officials of the Department of Health guestimate that in each of the last five years a real growth rate of approximately 1 % was required to meet the consequences of the 'greying of the population'.
The increased burdens of physical and intellectual deterioration in the elderly people affect the over 75s particularly. However, the precise nature of the onset of dementia, the decline for a variety of caring activities is ill-understood and poorly chronicled. Thus, whilst the numbers of elderly people can be forecast with reasonable degrees of certainty, their dependency and care needs over the last two decades of their lives are largely unknown. It could be that a 1 % increase in real resources in recent years and lower levels of increase in future years as the stock of elderly people stabilises, will be inadequate to meet the needs of those who are highly dependent and their burdened carers, often spouses.

2 Technological change: the officials of the Department of Health, when bargaining with the Treasury, argue that they need a real growth increase of about 1 % to take account of the increased needs of elderly people and another 0.5 % increase in real funding to meet the pressures of technological change.
This factor is rarely defined and its effects are very difficult to quantify. Technology may refer to Zimmer frames to assist elderly people, new pharmaceutical products or large magnetic resonance imaging scanners which, including bunkers to house them, may cost £2 million each. The impact of changing technology on the funding of the Service is difficult to identify. New materials to repair hernias or new techniques for the treatment of breast cancer or heart disease may increase the costs of these procedures insidiously and unequally across the country as surgeons

alter their practices. Whether a 0.5 % increase in real funding is adequate to meet these pressures is unknown, but these influences, whilst difficult to quantify, are very evident.

3 Community care: since the 1970s the official policy of successive governments has been to de-institutionalise people who are mentally handicapped and mentally ill. The majority of NHS expenditure on these client groups is still spent on institutions, but gradually community care is developing. Some of this is publicly financed (from the board and lodging payments of social security) and provided in private residential and nursing homes. Some is publicly financed and provided.

What is becoming clear is that good quality community care is not cheap. For instance, an average cost of £12,000 a year to care for a mentally handicapped person in the institution may be transformed into a bill in excess of £16,000 per year for community care for the same patient. Such community care is provided typically in small units, with the consequent loss of any economies of scale that exist in large institutions. Furthermore, the hospital savings, unless wards or institutions are closed, may be small in the early years of the de-institutionalisation policy. This means that Health Authorities may face increasing costs from community care as they begin to discharge patients, but little savings from reduced hospital costs to finance their community care policies. Whether such increased expenditure purchases improved quality of care and less dependency in the patients, has been little researched.

4 AIDS: The HIV infection is spreading steadily and by the late summer of 1988 over 900 people had died from it. There is no cure and treatment of the symptomatic disease is very expensive. The HIV infected person presents with treatable skin cancers and pneumonia during the last 400–500 days of life. These problems, together with the use of Retrovir, a drug which appears to delay the infection's spread, mean that the cost of care per patient is between £25,000 and £30,000.

Thus, the total cost of treating patients with this disease in 1989 may approach £100 million. Furthermore, the distribution of this infection and its costs is very unequal geographically with high prevalence in Lothian and areas of London. The cost of this infection will increase steadily in the 1990s.

5 Nurse training: the nursing market is being affected radically by two factors. Firstly, the size of the cohort of

16–18 year olds from which nurses are recruited is shrinking rapidly. To persuade people to become nurses in sufficient numbers it will be necessary to increase relative wages. This pressure for increased finance will be supplemented by the desire of the profession and the Government to reorganise the training of nurses. Instead of 'learning by doing' on the ward, and as a consequence, providing care for patients, nurses will be translated into students trained in colleges and not available to provide much patient care. Thus the resource consequences of these proposals are twofold: pupil nurses will have to be replaced on the ward and student nurses will have to be paid as they train. At present, there is argument about the precise costs of these changes but they are unlikely to be insignificant.

These five factors, demography, technology, AIDS, community care and nurse training, will make very heavy demands for additional resources in the 1990s. Most of these demands are ill-defined due to the failure to evaluate practice and inform policy choice with better information about the costs and benefits of policy options.

Is the NHS under-financed?

The financing of the NHS has generally been parsimonious during the last ten years. There are treatments and care packages available which, if financed, would provide patients with improvements in the length and quality of their lives. In this sense the NHS is under-financed, although this argument merely says we could do more to improve health but we choose not to do so. Is this rational?

Scarcity, choice and efficiency

Distinguishing between inputs, processes and outcomes

It is essential to distinguish between inputs, processes and outcomes in any discussion of the under-financing of the NHS:

1 inputs are expenditures on doctors, nurses, hospital beds, equipment and pharmaceuticals;

2 processes of care are combinations of inputs used to produce health care activities such as GP consultations, inpatient stays and outpatient visits;
3 outcomes: inputs combined to produce processes of care may (or may not) affect patient outcomes, i.e. enhance the length and quality of life of the beneficiaries of the health care process.

Much of the political debate about the NHS (and other health care systems) concentrates on input and process measures because they are easy to measure. The Department of Health provides health authority managers with performance indicators which show where particular authorities are located in the distribution of various processes.

Thus, Scarborough Health Authority appears to perform well on these performance indicators: its expenditure per capita is low, its doctor population ratio is low, its pharmaceutical expenditure per capita is low and its administrative expenditure per capita is low relative to other health authorities. But such measures of input and process tell us nothing about outcomes: is Scarborough cheap with good outcomes or cheap with poor outcomes?

Obviously, outcomes are very difficult to measure. One indicator of success is hospital mortality. Florence Nightingale advocated evaluation of the hospitals' activities in three categories: dead, relieved and unrelieved. She went on to argue, in phrases reminiscent of the NHS in 1988, that:

> I am fain to sum up with an urgent appeal for adopting this or some uniform system of publishing the statistical records of hospitals. There is growing conviction that in all hospitals, even in those which are best conducted, there is a great and unnecessary waste of life. In attempting to arrive at the truth, I have applied everywhere for information, but in scarcely an instance have I been able to obtain hospital records fit for any purpose of comparison. If they could be obtained, they would enable us to decide many other questions besides the ones alluded to. They would show subscribers how their money was being spent, what amount of good was really being done with it, or whether the money was doing mischief rather than good. (Florence Nightingale, 1863).

More recently, Kind (1988b) has used routine NHS mortality data to compute the crude (actual) and adjusted (by age and case mix) mortality rates for English NHS Health Authorities in 1985. A selection of his data are shown in Table 7.2 and from them it can be seen that there are great variations in crude and adjusted mortality rates. Also, it can be seen that Scarborough, which performs 'well' on performance indicators, has an adjusted mortality rate over 20 % above the national average. If Grimsby, 41 % above the adjusted national average rate of mortality, was at the national average, 360 fewer deaths would have been expected in 1985.

Table 7.2 Variations in mortality rates across health authorities 1985

District	Crude mortality rate	Standardised mortality rate
North Tees	6.4	1.317
Grimsby	6.4	1.414
Scarborough	6.9	1.214
Sheffield	4.7	0.829
Harrow	3.4	0.577
North West Hertfordshire	5.9	1.510
Brighton	5.6	0.891
North West Surrey	9.3	1.500
Macclesfield	8.8	1.330
Central Manchester	2.8	0.695

All data are percentages.

Source: Kind (1988b, table 4).

The variations in this crude and incomplete measure of outcome may be caused by a variety of factors. Firstly, hospital consultants may not make mortality returns accurately or completely, ward clerks may collate returns inaccurately and data may get mistranscribed into computer tapes. All too little effort is made by NHS managers to control the quality of the data of the type used by Kind, although its publication in this form (Table 7.2) may provide a sharp incentive to achieve greater quality in data collection.

Another explanation of the variations may be differences in the socio-economic background of patients. There are no suitable national data to use to control statistically these effects in these data.

Another explanation of mortality variations may be differences in the performance of doctors: some doctors may be less proficient than others.

Thus linking inputs, processes and hospital mortality outcomes raises new policy questions and provides crude insights into input-outcome (efficiency) relationships. But is hospital mortality an adequate measure of the outcomes of the NHS.

Measuring outcomes

Are mortality data alone sufficient?

Whilst mortality rates for hospital stays are, suitably adjusted for risk factors, useful indicators of one aspect of hospital outcome, they are incomplete unless they are augmented with both survival (mortality) data (after episodes of hospital care) and quality of life data.

Without linking hospital survival data into the community it is impossible to determine whether the patient lived one day, one year or twenty-five years after leaving the hospital. Such data-linking is difficult and expensive. Typically hospital administrators have little knowledge of survival variations once the patient leaves hospital. The general practitioner may have better information because, for instance, she may have to sign the death certificate. However, routinely there is little in the way of mortality data-linking, although efforts are being made to remedy these defects in places like Oxford.

However, even if mortality data were linked and it was possible to identify variations in post treatment survival, would such data alone be an adequate measure of outcome? If data about the duration of survival was used to prioritise options, and thus 'need' was interpreted as those who get the greatest enhancement in the duration of life, investments would be made in mortality-avoiding therapies such as organ transplants and no resources would be allocated to procedures such as hip replacements which have little effect on the duration of survival but much effect on its quality.

Adding in quality of life (QoL) measures

So duration of survival (mortality) data alone are inadequate as measures of outcome or as a means of prioritising competing care options. However, defining and measuring the quality of life (QoL) is complex.

The first step is the acquisition of agreement amongst researchers, as derived from social investigation of peoples' attitudes, about the nature of quality of life. What descriptors should be used? Factors such as physical functioning, pain, psychological function and social integration all seem relevant but can be measured in very different ways. The objective is to select a set of descriptors which reflect appropriately peoples' attitudes so that a global measure can be derived which is generally accepted and can be used across a wide variety of health care activities (e.g. cancer, transplants, screening and health promotion) to identify which therapies or interventions have the most significant effect on these measures.

There is no agreement about the 'best' set of descriptors or the 'best' QoL indicator (Kind, 1988a) and, equally, different investigators use different methods to value different combinations of descriptors.

This process is illustrated in Table 7.3 which sets out a set of descriptors, ranking different levels of disability and distress. Rosser and Kind used psychometric techniques to get 70 respondents to rank different combinations of distress states (A to D) and disability states (I to VIII). This ranking was then translated into a one (healthy with no disability and distress) to zero (dead) scale. The values for the alternative combinations on the zero to one scale are set out in Table 7.4

Table 7.3 Rosser's classification of illness states

	Disability	Distress
I	No disability	A No distress
II	Slight social disability	B Mild
III	Severe social disability and/or slight impairment of performance at work. Able to do all housework except very heavy tasks.	C Moderate D Severe
IV	Choice of work or performance at work very severely limited. Housewives and old people able to do light housework only but able to go out shopping.	
V	Unable to undertake any paid employment. Unable to continue any education. Old people confined to home except for escorted outings and short walks and unable to do shopping. Housewives able only to perform a few simple tasks.	
VI	Confined to chair or to wheelchair or able to move around in the house only with support from an assistant.	
VII	Confined to bed	
VIII	Unconscious	

Source: Kind, Rosser and Williams, 1982.

From duration and QoL measures to QALYs

Williams (1985; 1986) took the data in Table 7.4 and acquired expert judgments and information from the clinical evaluation literature to estimate how patients progressed from pre to post treatment across the Table 7.4 states, e.g. a patient might start at VD and go VID (one week after treatment), IIIC (ten days after treatment) and eventually to IIB (or IA if fortunate).

Table 7.4 Rosser's valuation matrix: all seventy respondents

Disability rating	Distress Rating			
	A	B	C	D
I	1.000	0.995	0.990	0.967
II	0.990	0.986	0.973	0.932
III	0.980	0.972	0.956	0.912
IV	0.964	0.956	0.942	0.870
V	0.946	0.935	0.900	0.700
VI	0.875	0.845	0.680	0.000
VII	0.677	0.564	0.000	-1.486
VIII	-1.028		not applicable	

Source: Kind, Rosser and Williams, 1982.

Figure 7.1 The effects of alternative procedures on the quality and quantity of life

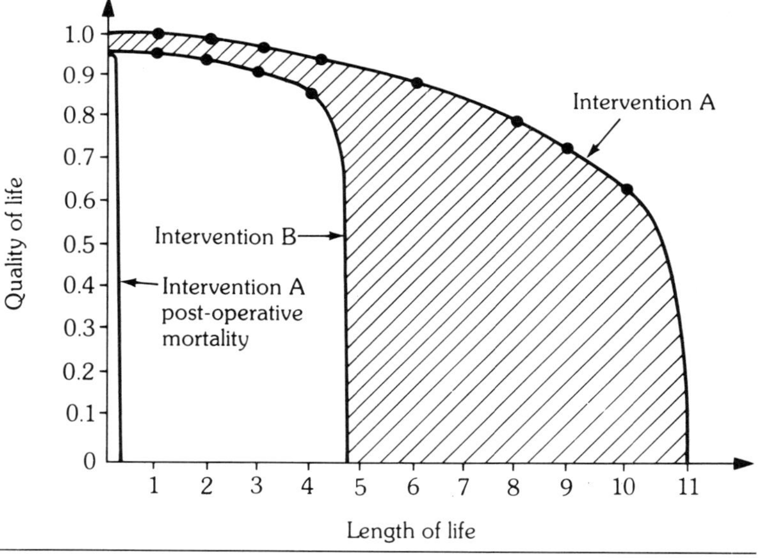

Using this technique, Figure 7.1 can be constructed. The quality of life (0 to 1) is measured on the vertical axis and duration of survival is measured on the horizontal axis. For a patient with end stage renal (kidney) failure, there are two treatments, dialysis (i.e. maintenance on a machine) and organ transplant. Illustratively the quality and duration of the transplant (intervention A) are shown in Table 7.1, as are those for dialysis (intervention B). The difference between the two treatments, the shaded area in Figure 7.1 can be translated into a composite unit of outcome which measures the duration and quality of life of treatment A relative to treatment B. This measure is the quality adjusted life year or QALY.

Table 7.5 UK data on costs and QALYs (Williams)

	£ per QALY
GP advice to stop smoking	167
Pacemaker implantation for atrioventricular heart block	700
Hip replacement	750
Valve replacement for aortic stenosis	900
CABG for severe angina with LMD	1,040
CABG for severe angina with 3VD	1,270
CABG for moderate angina with LMD	1,330
GP control of hypertension	1,700
GP control of total serum cholesterol	1,700
CABG for severe angina with 2VD	2,280
CABG for moderate angina with 3VD	2,400
CABG for mild angina with LMD	2,520
Kidney transplant	3,200
Breast cancer screening	3,300
Heart transplant	5,000
Hospital haemodialysis	14,000

Source: Williams 1985; 1986; Department of Health and Social Security 1987.

Table 7.6 The QALY output of competing therapies from a given budget*

Therapy	QALY output
GP advice to stop smoking	5,988
Hip replacement	1,333
Breast cancer screening	302
Heart transplant	200
Hospital dialysis	71

*From a budget of £1 million

Source: Table 7.5

Some estimates of the cost of producing one quality adjusted life year (or QALY) from different procedures are set out in Table 7.5. This technique permits prioritisation to be made. Let us imagine that a health authority can choose only between those procedures in Table 7.6 and that it has a budget of £1 million to spend. Which option gives the greatest QALY benefit from the £1 million budget? Using the data in Table 7.5

and assuming constant returns to scale, the answers are set out in Table 7.6.

Scarcity, choice and efficiency

There are two certainties in life: death and the scarcity of resources. In health care these two certainties come together and difficult choices have to be made about how to allocate scarce resources so that death can be delayed and the quality of survival enhanced. It is impossible to meet all health care demands and resources have to be rationed: choices have to be made about who will not be treated and left to die or live in pain and discomfort. Not everyone agrees with this perspective:

> **Cost Should not be a Factor in Medical Care**
> ...Of late an increasing number of papers in this and other journals have been concerned with 'cost effectiveness' of diagnostic and therapeutic procedures. Inherent in these articles is the view that choices will be predicted not only on the basis of strictly clinical considerations but also on the basis of economic considerations as they may effect the patient, the hospital and society. It is my contention that such considerations are not germane to ethical medical practice, that they occupy space in journals that would be better occupied by substantive matter, and that they serve to orient physicians towards consideration of economics, which is not their legitimate problem. It is dangerous to introduce extraneous factors into medical decisions, since considerations of such factors may eventually lead to consideration of age, social usefulness and other matters irrelevant to ethical practice. The example of medicine in Nazi Germany is too close to need further elucidation (Loewy 1982).

Loewy's individualistic perspective, trying always to do whatever is possible for his patient, clashes with the social opportunity cost perspective which emphasises that if the budget is finite, it should be spent on those patients who will benefit most. A decision to use the available budget and to produce only 7.5 QALYs from treating Mrs T is inefficient if treatment of Mr K with the same budget produces ten QALYs.

Such rationing decisions have to be made every day by practising doctors. An example of the criteria established and used by clinicians when making choices about which patients with end stage renal failure they will treat are set out in Table 7.7. Exclusion from treatment means death for an untreated patient within six months.

Table 7.7 Reasons for patient rejection for treatment

Taylor et al	Parsons and Lock
Age	Age
Heart disease	Psychiatric illness
Blindness	Social situation
Types of renal disease	Blindness in a diabetic
Other complicating disease	
Annual income	
Sex	

Source: Taylor et al 1975, Parsons and Lock 1980.

Whilst it is clear that doctors ration resources, it is unclear how alternative treatments are to be ranked unless economic evaluation (e.g. cost-QALY estimates) is undertaken. At present, decisions about the level of funding the NHS and individual areas of care are determined in an implicit and ad hoc fashion, often with much 'shroud waving' by providers seeking to defend or augment their budgets.

The cost-benefit (QALY) framework is logical and explicit; it challenges practitioners to prove their therapies are cost effective. Unfortunately, the bidding process by which clinicians compete for resources is not informed by evidence about costs and benefits. Cochrane (1971) argued that the majority of health care therapies had never been evaluated scientifically. Fuchs (1984) asserted that 10 % of health care reduced health, 10 % had no effect and 80 % of health care improved health. The problem, argued Fuchs, was that no-one knows which therapies lie in the 10 and 80 % categories!

The 'crisis' in the NHS

The crisis in the NHS consists of advocacy of more spending, often articulated most vigorously by provider groups (doctors, nurses and the pharmaceutical industry) whose incomes and employment prospects are enhanced by higher levels of health care spending. The demand for health care is escalating rapidly and the capacity to improve the health of the population with known and perhaps efficacious therapies exists.

So the NHS is under-funded in the sense that more health (QALY) benefits could be produced from targeted increases in spending. However, this argument is incomplete. The impacts of many therapies in use in the NHS today are unknown yet their provision is expensive.

Increased funding of the NHS can be vindicated only if evaluative evidence (cost-QALY) is available to substantiate the claim for scarce resources. Until it can be demonstrated that the £22 billion spent on the NHS is used efficiently, the case for additional funding is flawed.

Such a conclusion may be unpopular but it is logical and supported by available evidence. No reform, either of the NHS or by privatisation, will resolve this issue. What is needed is evaluative evidence to demonstrate that clinicians' claims for additional funding are valid.

Conclusion

From a collective (ideological) perspective, a plausible goal for the NHS is maximisation of improvements in health (QALYs) from the available budget. Care should, with this objective in mind, be allocated on the basis of the best cost-QALY solution which can be achieved.

Unfortunately, care in the NHS is not allocated in this way. One reason for this is that the cost-QALY characteristics of most therapies are unknown. Another reason is that the adoption of this approach would require a radical departure from existing therapies and potentially disadvantage powerful interest groups, both patients and providers.

There is a reluctance amongst politicians of both major parties to confront these issues because alienated producer and user groups might withdraw vital voting support. The medical market place is inevitably influenced by the political market place where politicians seek to maintain or acquire power. These processes make it inevitable that NHS 'crises' will be regular occurrences as competing groups seek to gain advantages. Perhaps in time, the waste of time and resources induced in this rhetoric will decline into a more constructive investigation of the costs and benefits of alternative therapies and policies and the use of the results of such evaluation to prioritise health care options. However, maybe such hopes are naïve as an administrator of the Roman Emperor Nero, Caius Petronius is alleged to have written in AD 66 (English translation from the *Satyricon:)*

> We trained very hard, but it seemed that every time we were beginning to form up into teams, we would be reorganised. I was to learn in life that we tend to meet any new situation by reorganising and a wonderful method it can be for creating the illusion of progress, while

producing confusion, inefficiency and demoralisation (Caius Petronius, AD 66, quoted in Westminster Hospital, 1986).

Over 1,900 years later we prefer 'crisis' and 'redisorganisation' in the NHS rather than the application of logic and evidence.

References

Brazier, J, Hutton, J and Jeavons, R (eds) *Reforming the UK health care system: an analytical framework and a review of some recent proposals.* Discussion paper 47, Centre for Health Economics, University of York.

Brittain, L (1988) *Financing the NHS.* Conservative Party Central Office.

Cochrane, A L (1971) *Effectiveness and efficiency: random reflection on health care.* Nuffield Provincial Hospitals Trust.

Department of Health and Social Security (1987) *Breast cancer screening.* The report of the Forrest Committee. HMSO.

Donabedian, A (1971) Social responsibility for personal health services: an examination of basic values. *Inquiry.* 8(2): 3–19.

Enthoven, A C (1985) *Reflections on the management of the National Health Service: an American look at incentives to efficiency in health services management in the UK.* Nuffield Provincial Hospitals Trust.

Fuchs, V (1984) The rationing of medical care. *New England Journal of Medicine.* 311 (24): 1562–73.

Goldsmith, M and Willetts, D (1988) *Managed health care: a new system for a better health service.* Health Review No. 1, Policy Challenge, Centre for Policy Studies.

Green, D (1988) *The potential for a competitive market in health in Britain.* Paper given to the Health Economist Study Group, January.

House of Commons Debate, Committee Stage of the National Health Service Bill, 18 June 1946, cols 1561–2.

House of Commons (1988) *The future of the National Health Service,* Select Committee on Social Services, Fifth Report, HC613, July.

Kind, P (1988a) *The design and construction of quality of life measures.* Discussion paper 43, Centre for Health Economics, University of York.

Kind, P (1988b) *Hospital deaths – the missing link: measuring outcomes in hospital activity analysis.* Discussion Paper 44, Centre for Health Economics, University of York.

Kind, P Rosser, R and Williams A (1982) Valuation of quality f life: some psychometric evidence. In Jones-Lee M W (ed) *The value of life and safety.* North-Holland, Geneva.

Loewy, W (1982) Cost should not be a factor in medical care. *New England Journal of Medicine.* 302,(12): 697.

Ludbrook, A and Maynard, A (1988) *The funding of the National Health Service: what is the problem and is social insurance the answer?* Discussion Paper 39, Centre for Health Economics, University of York.

Maynard, A (1985) Performance incentives. In Teeling Smith (ed) *Health, Education and General Practice,* Office of Health Economics.

Maynard, A Marinker, M and Gray, D P (1986) The Doctor, the Patient and their contract III: alternative contracts: are they viable. *British Medical Journal.* 292: 1438–40.

Maynard, A and Williams, A (1984) Privatisation and the National Health Service. In LeGrand, J and Robinson, R (eds). *Privatisation and the Welfare State.* George Allen and Unwin.

Ministry of Health (1944) *A National Health Service.* Cmd 6502, HMSO

Nightingale, F (1863) *Notes of Hospitals,* 3rd Ed. Longman, Roberts and Green.

Parsons, V and Lock, P (1980) Triage and the patient with renal failure. *Journal of Medical Ethics.* 6: 173–6.

Pirie, M and Butler, E (1988) *The health of nations: solutions to the problems of finance in the health care sector.* Adam Smith Institute.

Taylor, J R, Aitcheson, J, Parker, L S, and Moore, M T (1975) Differences in selecting patients for regular haemodyalisis. *British Medical Journal.* 1:380–1.

Westminster Hospital (1986) *The Westminster Hospital is threatened with closure.*

Williams, A H (1985) Economics of coronary artery bypass grafting. *British Medical Journal* 291: 326–9.

Williams, A H (1986) Screening for risk of CHD: is it a wise use of resources? In Oliver, M Ashley-Miller, M and Wood, D (eds) Screening for risk of coronary heart disease. John Wiley and Sons.

8 Primary health care: the way forward?

Roland Petchey

The publication of the White Paper *Promoting better health* (Secretaries of State for Social Services, Wales, Northern Ireland, and Scotland, 1987) on 25 November 1987 marked the end of a period of gestation which had effectively begun in July 1982 with the establishment of the (suppressed) Binder Hamlyn study into the feasibility of applying cash limits to Family Practitioner Services (FPS). It had continued with the publication of the Green Paper *Primary health care: an agenda for discussion* (DHSS, 1986a) and the report of the Cumberlege Review of Community Nursing in England (DHSS, 1976b) in April 1986 and culminated in ten public ministerial roadshows around the country in the latter part of 1986.

The White Paper, the Health and Medicines Act (1988), and circulars (HC [87] 29) and (HC (FP) [87] 10) on community nursing detail the programme by which the Government intends to achieve its aim of a more responsive, efficient, prevention-oriented primary health care system. Some of the more radical and controversial proposals aired in the Green Paper have been dropped (the idea of for-profit health-care 'shops' offering the full range of primary health care services, for example, or the proposed 'good practice allowance') but the White Paper is otherwise little modified. In particular, it remains wholly faithful to the principles which underlay the Green Paper, continuing to assert the necessity and desirability of: increasing consumer (sic) choice; promoting competition among FPS providers; and linking the remuneration of practitioners more directly to the level of their performance. Thus, it requires Family Practitioner Committees (FPCs) to provide more detailed information about practices in their areas, to simplify the arrangements for changing doctors and to simplify complaints procedures. It explicitly states its view that the freedom of patients to choose their doctor might be an effective influence on the quality of services. It also proposes a variety of measures aimed at making practitioners' incomes more dependent on the range and quality of services they provide. The proportion of income derived from capitation fees will be increased from 47 % to 50 % in the first instance, thus making practice income more sensitive to changes in the size of the panel, and providing a greater financial incentive to practices to attract more patients or to compete to retain those they already have. In addition, a range of new item of service fees is to be negotiated with the medical profession including health checks and any necessary follow-up for patients registering for the first time and the provision of regular comprehensive care for the elderly. The Government also intends to negotiate a system of incentives to achieve locally set target levels of vaccination, immunisation and screening and to encourage doctors to undertake minor surgery.

Finally, although the good practice allowance has been abandoned in the face of opposition from the medical profession, the Government proposes instead to tighten the qualifications for the award of the full basic practice allowance by increasing the minimum list size (currently 1,000 patients) and the average number of hours spent in surgery sessions (currently twenty hours per week). The award of the allowance will also be made dependent on doctors performing health promotion and prevention work. In effect, these changes in the remuneration system will mean that the good practice allowance has been retained in its essentials but not in name.

Other central proposals relate to manpower and staffing. The Government has introduced compulsory retirement at 70 and abolished the '24 hour retirement' arrangements under which doctors who have reached retirement age could retire, draw their pension and return to practice the next day without loss of pay or pension. Since the White Paper estimates that there are currently around 500 general practitioners around 70 years or over out of a total of over 30,000 (Fry and Stephen, 1986, p488) the effects of these changes are likely to be quite minor by comparison with other proposals affecting manpower. Although, as has already been stated, the Green Paper suggestion of one-stop 'health shops' has been abandoned, the Government continues to be intent on breaking down traditional lines of demarcation between the various health professions and encouraging the development of multidisciplinary primary health care teams. To this end it proposes to remove restrictions on the types and number of staff who may be employed, although the funds allocated for this purpose will be cash limited – the first time that cash limits will be imposed in FPS. The role of pharmacists in health promotion is to be increased, and the Government is to embark on negotiations with a view to pharmacists playing a role in advising patients with minor symptoms. To create the time for this, it is proposed that some of pharmacists' present responsibilities for dispensing be delegated to appropriately trained assistants. On community nursing the Government announced its intention of examining further the legal status, functions and qualifications of nurse practitioners, and of increasing their freedom to prescribe a limited range of items.

Discussion

These, then, are the essentials of the Government's proposals relating to primary health care. Many of the objectives which the Government has set itself are entirely laudable – health promotion and preventive medicine, for example, the improvement of provision in inner cities and other deprived areas, increased information for patients, the development of primary health care teams – but reservations must be expressed about the appropriateness of the strategy by which those objectives are being pursued. Although, as has already been stated, some of the more radical proposals contained in the Green Paper have been abandoned, the White Paper remains entirely faithful to the principles which underlay it, and which inform Conservative social policy across the board – in particular the belief in the inherent superiority of the market as a mechanism for allocating resources and imposing financial discipline and a corresponding mistrust of any institution (be it a state monopoly of provision or a professional one) which is seen to operate as a restraint upon competition. There are, therefore, a number of implications, some immediate, others which are more long-term and conjectural, which require examination.

The role of Family Practitioner Committees

Many of the changes proposed imply a significant extension of the responsibilities exercised by FPCs in their oversight of the primary health care sector. Inter alia, they are being required to 'exercise a leadership role in developing more effective and economic prescribing' (Secretaries of State, 1987, p55) and to encourage good practice in the referral of patients to hospitals: 'Doctors with abnormally high or low rates of referral will be invited to take part (sic) in an assessment of their approach to help them (sic) in making effective use of hospital resources' (ibid, p23). In other respects as well, their role in setting targets and monitoring performance is being expanded: it is they who (in collaboration with district health authorities) will be responsible for setting targets for disease prevention. They will also be responsible for awarding (or withholding) the basic practice allowance and encouraging doctors to improve sub-standard premises: 'The sanction of withholding rent or rates...in cases where there is reluctance to raise premises standards will be applied more vigorously by FPCs' (ibid, p53). On them will fall the burden of providing their local population with more information about practices and the services they offer and of receiving annual reports from practices. Conversely, they will also be expected to consult consumers directly on the quality of service by means of periodical local public opinion surveys. Interestingly, the House of Commons Social Services Committee had recommended that the community health councils be given these responsibilities. The Government's longstanding antipathy towards CHCs ensured that this recommendation was not adopted.

These changes not only involve a substantial addition to the workload of FPCs, they also amount to a transformation of primary health care from an administered to a managed service. Instead of being responsible for providing mainly administrative services to the practitioners who are contracted to them, FPCs are now being expected to play a central role in the planning of services and the evaluation of service delivery. The White Paper explicitly recognises this, and promises FPCs additional funds to enable them to carry out these functions, but even so it must still be questioned whether, as presently constituted and organised, they are capable of sustaining the new burdens being imposed on them. It must be remembered that it was only in April 1985 that FPCs were granted independence as health authorities, amidst considerable ambiguity and confusion from the DHSS downwards about their powers and duties. They thus have relatively little experience of exercising responsibility and authority for FPS. Moreover, a recent study (Huntingdon and McClenahan, 1987) has identified a number of organisational weaknesses, particularly a lack of corporateness arising from unresolved tensions between their traditional bureaucratic functions and personnel, and the more recently grafted-on entrepreneurial functions associated with service planning. In many cases, this lack of corporateness is felt to amount effectively to the emergence of quite distinct subcultures within FPC organisation. A further threat to their ability to manage effectively arises from the fact that practitioners have far greater representation (50 %) on FPCs than do clinicians on management committees in the hospital sector. In many cases, a practitioner occupies the chair of the FPC. The present management arrangements in FPS, in other words, are highly reminiscent of the system of consensus management which existed in the hospital sector before Griffiths. Although the White Paper expresses the Government's belief that it is too early for major organisational change (in response to a Social Services Committee recommendation that FPCs and district health authorities be amalgamated), one may still speculate on how much time will elapse before a managerial revolution comparable with the Griffiths reorganisation of hospital management will be found to be necessary in FPS.

Practice size, organisation and staffing

Hitherto, policy on practice size has been guided by the assumption that quality of service is best assured by reducing the number of patients on a family doctor's list. The result of an annual increase (about 1.7 %) in the numbers of newly-qualified doctors choosing general practice as a career has been a reduction in the average number of patients per family doctor from 2,291 in 1976 to 1,988 (estimate) in 1986. Certainly, the position adopted by the medical profession has been that fewer patients per doctor will result in more time and attention per patient, and the Social Services Committee found the case for continued reduction in GP list size 'unanswerable'.

The White Paper proposals, however, imply a significant shift in policy on list size in a number of respects, both directly and indirectly. First, directly, there is the proposal to raise the level at which a practice qualifies for the full basic practice allowance from the present 1,000 by an unspecified amount. If it is assumed (as seems likely) that these smaller practices are also the single-handed ones, the effect of this proposal will be to add fresh impetus to the existing trend towards larger group practices which is revealed in Table 8.1.

Table 8.1 General practitioner units in England 1965 and 1985

Numbers of GPs per unit	Percentage of GPs 1965	1985
1	24	12
2	32	16
3	24	21
4	12	18
5	5	15
6 or more	3	18
	100	100
Total GP principals	1,8784	2,4035

Source: Calculated from DHSS 1987, Table 3.23.

Second, indirectly, the proposals to enlarge patient freedom of choice on the one hand, and on the other to increase the proportion of practice income which is sensitive to patient choice are quite explicitly designed to stimulate competition for patients among practices in the belief that this will serve to raise standards of care. In other words, 'successful' practices will now have an incentive to expand their list while the less successful will be sanctioned by the threat of the patients they currently have moving elsewhere. Effectively, the Government is proposing to reverse the inverse relationship which has traditionally been presumed to obtain between list size and quality of care.

Although it is as yet regrettably fragmentary, research evidence on list size and service quality does not appear to substantiate this presumed relationship between the two. Butler, in a pilot study (1986) reports that list size was not systematically associated with standards of care. However, it should be noted that 'standard of care' in this study was self-rated by the practitioners themselves, and that no attempt was made to measure it objectively. Another study, this time part of the DHSS submission on GP workload to the Doctors' and Dentists' Review Body in 1987, again reports no systematic relationship between workload and list size, although once more data on the outcomes of care were not collected (cited in Bosanquet, 1987). Bosanquet claims that number of consultations and their length bear little relationship to list size and concludes that

> There seem to be few distinctive changes in service patterns as list size falls: the main effect is in terms of falling hours of work and a rising consultation rate. Reducing list size is simply shrinking the current model of general practice (ibid, p753).

Perhaps the only conclusion which may be safely drawn is that, in spite of recent manifestations of interest (Royal College of General Practitioners, 1981, 1985; Pendleton et al., 1986), the primary health sector lags woefully behind the hospital sector in terms of the development of performance indicators and output measures.

That the Government is serious in its intention to break down the traditional division of labour between the medical and nursing professions is indicated by its announcement that doctors, in common with other professions, will lose their current legal exemption from legislation against restrictive trade practices, with a view to increasing competition. Obviously, the main reason that the Government favours the development of nurse practitioners is that they are cheaper than doctors, but there is also accumulating evidence that, in some respects, they might also prove more effective. A survey carried out as part of the Cumberlege review of community nursing found that 60 % of patients would prefer to see a nurse rather than a doctor as their initial contact. This greater willingness to consult a nurse could mean that certain groups (notably the elderly and Asian women) might receive earlier diagnosis and treatment. The Royal College of Nursing in its evidence to the select committee on social services cited research showing that nurses were more skilled than doctors in tasks such as health assessment, preventive health care and counselling, with a higher success rate than doctors in anti-smoking counselling (Warden, 1988a).

The concept of nurse practitioners has already been welcomed in general terms by the medical profession, subject to such safeguards as an agreed definition of their role and suitable training. However, against this general welcome of the concept needs to be set the fact (unkindly pointed out by Edwina Currie during a House of Commons debate) that hitherto GPs have been reluctant to translate the concept into practice, preferring to employ receptionists (15,000 currently employed) rather than practice nurses (only 3,000) (reported in Warden, 1988). One can also reasonably anticipate extremely tough bargaining by the medical profession on this issue, since, mindful of their traditional monopoly over prescribing and treatment, they will be anxious to limit the scope of any change in legislation for fear that nurse practitioners might prove to be the thin end of a very large wedge. The final factor which will obviously help to determine whether doctors will embrace the concept of the nurse practitioner in practice will be the size of the cash limits being introduced in respect of GP premises and staff.

This is not the only proposal about which this fear might be expressed. Precisely the same reservation could be voiced about the special allowance for practices in deprived areas in the context of the de-regulation of healthcare. The American experience of de-regulation (which is discussed more fully below, p137 suggests that it has tended to accentuate rather than to redress existing inequalities in the distribution of resources, particularly the imbalance between deprived inner city areas and the more affluent suburbs. The fear must be that this might occur here also, with more able, articulate and mobile patients switching from inner city practices, depriving them of funds and leaving behind those elements of the community which, for whatever reason, are unable to exercise their freedom of choice. The White Paper recognises the additional demands imposed on practices in deprived areas, hence its proposal for the special allowance. Whether it will prove sufficient to counteract market forces pushing in the opposite direction will depend on the size of the allowance (not specified in the White Paper, but to be determined in negotiation with the profession) and the extent of market freedom.

A further cause for concern in this connection is the proposal to privatise the General Practice Finance Corporation which, since 1966, has provided loans for the purchase and improvement of practice premises, and to invite the private sector to provide the necessary capital. The White Paper presents only two arguments in defence of this change: the desirability of reducing the public sector borrowing requirement, and the belief that the regeneration of inner cities should be led by private investment. Be that as it may, if normal commercial criteria are to govern the availability of this finance, this could well proved an additional obstacle to raising the standards of practices in areas of deprivation.

These anxieties about the future of such practices are in large part confirmed by research carried out by Bosanquet and Leese (1988) into practice organisation and orientation as a means of investigating the likely responses to the professional and economic incentives contained in the White Paper. Practices were classified as innovative, traditional or intermediate according to whether they employed a nurse, participated in the cost rent scheme and the vocational training scheme. All of these criteria were regarded as indicators of a practice's willingness to incur costs and to expand services by investing in salaries or premises. Innovative practices satisfied two of the criteria, traditional practices none; the remainder were classified as intermediate.

The survey revealed large and significant differences in the distribution of the different types of practice among the areas studied – differences which were clearly related to the social characteristics of the areas. Innovative practices were more likely to be found in rural or affluent suburban areas; traditional practices were more common in urban and working class areas. Traditional practices were more likely to be in rented premises; *and* the value of the premises they owned was two to three times higher than the value of the premises occupied by the traditional practices. Doctors in innovative practices were more likely to have further qualifications, to have access to microcomputers, and to employ a practice manager. In general, their net earnings were higher. And their practices were more likely to be located in an area which had experienced an increase in population.

These results suggest quite clear differences in strategy between practices in terms of their response to the incentives to innovate already available, and also that it is the area in which a practice is located which is the main influence on its choice of strategy.

> There were distinct differences in strategy, with a third or more practices taking decisions that allowed them to be described as innovative; but innovative practices were found disproportionately in affluent areas. The response to incentives was much greater in areas of an expanding population or a middle class population. Innovation was found typically in large practices in places that were environmentally attractive (op cit, p1580).

Bosanquet and Leese concluded that innovative practices in affluent areas are, accordingly, in a much stronger position to respond to the financial incentives contained in the White Paper.

> They face a heavier demand for the services; are under less pressure from a high rate of consultations; and are better able to organise the recall and information system that are (sic) required to increase income from such fees, especially as our results showed that they are more likely to have computers. A swing towards charging fees for services is likely to mean a further widening of the differences in net income between practices in the affluent areas and elsewhere (ibid).

Conversely, practices in areas of developmental difficulty had been much less able to respond to existing incentives, and had a smaller margin available for development in response to the White Paper.

> ...our study has shown how the margin for development available to practices differs between areas in a systematic way. The strategy of a practice is affected by economic forces and constraints operating locally as well as by national policies. It may be more sensible to concentrate resources in local primary care budgets, which could be targeted on areas of developmental difficulty rather than to extend the system of charging fees for service (ibid).

Bosanquet and Leese concede that the results of their study may not be generalisable, since it was carried out on a small area basis and covered only 260 practices. Nevertheless, the areas which were selected for study covered a wide range of types of area, and considerable differences in strategy were uncovered. This study, in spite of its limitations, at least offers some empirical basis for the formulation of primary health care policy. Its findings offer little encouragement to the belief that the Government is adopting the most appropriate means to the achievement of its stated objectives. Quite the contrary, they confirm the suspicion that the changes in financial incentives, combined with increased patient mobility between practices, will have the effect of aggravating the problems confronting areas of deprivation, rather than ameliorating them.

Paying for change

The proposals we have been considering so far may all be regarded as being directed principally at modifying the behaviour of suppliers, by altering the system of financial incentives, professional monopolies, organisational factors and the like which are seen as currently distorting the supply of health services. Even the increased rights being granted to consumers must, I believe, be viewed in the light of the attempt to subject suppliers to the disciplines of the market place. As has already been observed, the White Paper is in this respect entirely consistent with the supply-side emphasis of Government policy elsewhere.

There is, however, one further strand to the proposals contained in the White Paper which has not yet been identified. I refer to the belief that goods and services which are supplied free at the point of use, by exposing the consumer to what Americans have termed 'moral jeopardy' show a tendency to be overconsumed. Economic orthodoxy requires that where the cost of a service is zero, demand for it will be infinite.

If this analysis is correct, how do we reconcile it with the fact that the White Paper, far from seeking to reduce moral jeopardy is seemingly proposing to increase it by expanding the range of services and making available 'large sums of extra money' for FPS? The answer to this paradox lies in an investigation of the Government's plans for financing the changes. Over the three years 1988–91 the Government was already planning for expenditure on FPS to rise in real terms by some 11 %, or £570 million at 1987–8 prices (HM Treasury, 1987). The White Paper announces the Government's intention 'to invest substantial extra resources...to develop positive health promotion activities, raise standards and make the service more sensitive to the needs of the consumer' (Secretaries of State for Social Services, 1987, p8).

However, two caveats needs to be entered against this commitment. First, the objectives just referred to (health promotion, higher standards, more responsive services) effectively exhaust the proposals contained in the White Paper. Second, nowhere in the White Paper are the proposals costed on the grounds that 'the exact amount to be spent will depend on the outcome of negotiations with the profession(s)' (ibid, p8). What is stated quite explicitly in following paragraphs is that the changes which are being proposed are to be financed at least in part by increasing user charges elsewhere in the primary care sector. Accordingly it proposes to abolish free sight testing and free dental examinations and to relate all dental charges more closely to the cost of treatment (except for categories who are already exempt). In his statement to the House of Commons the Minister of Health,

Mr Tony Newton, estimated that these extra payments towards ophthalmic and dental care would contribute some £170 million by 1990–1. Since the White Paper proposals are uncosted, it is not possible to calculate what proportion of the additional finance will be raised by these new charges, but other passages of his statement seem to imply that the Government is contemplating perhaps no more than an extra £50 million on top of the £570 million already budgeted. If this is the case, it suggests that dental and optical fees will, in effect, be funding the vast majority of the changes proposed in the White Paper.

As Birch argues (1986) these new charges have to be seen as a continuation of the Government's policy of requiring patients to pay an increasing proportion of the costs of their own treatment. Between 1979 and 1985 the prescription charge was increased by 590 % in real terms, while the maximum charge per course of routine dental treatment doubled in real terms. This policy of raising user charges faster than the rate of general inflation represents a significant departure from the policy of previous administrations – Conservative as well as Labour. Nor is there any sign that the Government intends to relent on this policy. The latest public expenditure plans reveal that revenue from health charges will continue to rise at almost double the anticipated rate of inflation during the period 1988–91 (HM Treasury, 1987).

Table 8.2 Total Government expenditure and proportion of expenditure financed by patient charges for NHS dental and pharmaceutical services, 1978/9–1983/4

	General dental service		*Pharmaceutical service*	
Year	*Expenditure £million*	*% Charges*	*Expenditure £million*	*% Charges*
1978/9	330	19.7	880	3.2
1979/80	400	19.5	986	5.0
1980/1	494	21.5	1,213	7.3
1981/2	562	23.5	1,394	7.7
1982/3	629	25.9	1,599	7.8
1983/4	692	27.7	1,769	7.7

Source: Central Statistical Office (1985).

Table 8.2 demonstrates the steady increase in the proportion of the total cost of services met by patient charges. However, as Birch points out, these figures are distorted by averaging charges across the entire population. In fact, almost three-quarters of prescriptions and half of courses of dental treatment are not subject to charges, since the recipients belong to one of the categories exempted either on grounds of medical priority or poverty. As a result, those patients who are subject to charges actually pay a significantly higher proportion of the cost of their own treatment. In 1985, the DHSS estimated that the average contribution towards prescription costs was around 45 %. Continuation of this policy would result in the services concerned (pharmaceutical, dental and ophthalmic) being effectively privatised to patients not exempted from charges, with provision coming to be 'characterised by two tiers of both finance and type of provision' (Birch, 1986, p169).

The argument advanced in the White Paper in support of these new charges is that they will enable patients who can afford it to contribute towards their own treatment. However, it should be observed that it is only in the low-income category that exemption is related to (in)ability to pay. The other exempt categories (children, expectant mothers, the elderly) are exempted irrespective of their means. Further, it has been estimated that the rate of take-up of exemption on the grounds of low income is 'probably less than 10 %' (Deacon and Bradshaw, 1983, p130). It is likely, therefore, that in practice payment of charges is only loosely related to means.

However, although it is rarely mentioned by ministers, there is another rationale offered for user charges in the NHS, namely that they act as a disincentive to over-utilisation or frivolous use of services and thus contribute to the more efficient use of resources. The effectiveness of charges in reducing utilisation is adequately demonstrated by Birch (1986) and Birch and Ryan (1988). Birch calculated that, in the period 1979–83:

> In terms of the number of prescriptions per capita, the non-exempt population has experienced a 7.5 % reduction in consumption compared with a 1 % increase for the exempt population (Birch, 1986, p174).

Birch and Ryan conclude that:

> ...in the case of NHS prescribed drugs the main source of the revenue effect is not the increased per item charge, which is estimated to have produced an extra £90 million revenue in 1985, but the resources released as a result of reduced utilisation, estimated to have saved around £290 million 1985 (Birch and Ryan, 1986, p24)

However, while it is apparent that user charges deter utilisation, Birch and Ryan point out (ibid, p23) that with available data it is not possible to estimate the opportunity costs of this policy in terms of health improvements forgone. In other words, it is impossible to determine whether or not the utilisation deterred by the charges is, indeed (whether partly or wholly) frivolous. Nevertheless, even though empirical validation of the policy may not be possible, Birch identifies two theoretical arguments in favour of subsidising health care provision – what he terms 'consumer ignorance' and 'external benefits' (1986, p170). He argues that:

> anything that delays the point at which the uninformed individual seeks the advice of the better-informed doctor should be avoided since it may lead to an inefficient allocation of health care resources (ibid)

by reducing the benefits of treatment or increasing its costs when it is eventually obtained. Secondly, he points out that it is not just the individual who benefits from improved health status but society more generally (as a consequence of the individual's increased productivity, perhaps, or a reduction in the risk of disease through immunisation).

> Since society is to benefit from the improvements in health status on offer, it is in society's interest to remove any barriers (such as the cost of treatment incurred by the patient) to the production of those improvements (ibid).

He concludes that this 'backdoor privatisation' of services is not compatible with the objectives of the NHS, and that the motivation for the policy is controlling or reducing public expenditure on the NHS, rather than raising revenue for it.

Health maintenance organisations (HMOs)

As has already been stated, the Green Paper proposal for one-stop, for-profit 'health shops' which aroused speculation about the possible introduction of HMOs here has been dropped from the White Paper. Nevertheless, in spite of this, it might be premature to conclude that they have been dropped entirely from the agenda. There are three reasons for this conclusion. First, pressure for the introduction of HMOs (or some variant of them) continues unabated from various right-wing pressure groups and individuals (e.g. Butler and Pirie, 1988a, 1988b; Goldsmith and Willetts, 1988; Whitney, 1988). Second, while minimal movement is currently being made in the direction of HMOs, none of the White Paper proposals is inconsistent with their eventual introduction. Finally many of the problems to which they have been advanced as the solution in the USA – uncontrolled health spending, provider monopoly, erosion of the discipline of market forces – remain firmly on the political agenda in Britain. For these reasons, even though the White Paper does not make explicit reference to HMOs, brief consideration of the American experience remains appropriate.

As has been argued elsewhere (Petchey, 1987), although HMOs in the US date back to 1929, their recent advances in the health care delivery system have to be seen in the context of American attempts to reduce health spending since the 1970s.

Proponents of the HMOs have generally claimed three advantages for them. Firstly, they would reverse the 'perverse incentive' to overmedicalise which was built into the traditional fee for service payment system. Because HMO revenues are generated by a prospective payment system, providers would have a direct financial incentive to minimise treatment, since all the costs would have to be met out of pre-paid membership subscriptions. Not only would this reduce expenditure, it would also contribute to more rational and efficient resource allocation in that, for the first time, doctors would have a financial incentive to practise preventive medicine in order to avoid the expense of treating an acute episode at a later stage. Secondly, because HMOs were responsible for comprehensive health care delivery, for prophylaxis and, from screening through to convalescence, they would contribute to the vertical integration of the health care delivery system. No longer would patients be left free to wander through the system finding hospitals and doctors where they might: once they were enrolled with an HMO, it would determine where and by whom they were treated by providing treatment directly or buying it in from elsewhere as appropriate. Thirdly, HMOs would facilitate the extension into the primary care sector of the sophisticated financial information and control systems being developed in the acute sector (Salmon, 1984). Although these were in the expectations surrounding the promotion of HMOs it must be recognised that they have not all been fulfilled in practice. Earlier estimates were that by 1993 membership would be almost fifty million (Iglehart, 1984), but more recently these estimates have been revised downwards.

> The current assumption that at least two of every five insured persons will be enrolled in a prepaid plan by 1990 is probably too optimistic in the face of the steeply growing costs of marketing, the absence of large savings to employers, the difficulties of structuring and managing large prepaid plans, and the growing insistence of employers and consumers on quality controls (Ginzberg, 1987, p1152).

Actual membership in 1987 was 27.7 million (Levinson, 1987).

Just as earlier expectations of growth have been modified, so have the initial estimates of HMO performance. Cost savings of 25 % over the traditional FFS system have been claimed, but such claims have been queried by recent research. First, there is evidence (e.g. Jackson-Beeck and Kleinman 1983; Siminoff, 1986) that HMO enrolment is biased in favour of the younger and healthier, whose health costs would be lower under any system. Second, the validity of HMO utilisation data has been called into question by Mott's

(1986) study of 'out of plan' utilisation by HMO subscribers (i.e. treatment whose cost is either not claimed by the subscriber, or else not reimbursed by the HMO). He identifies fifteen ways in which subscribers may be hospitalised without the fact finding its way into the HMO's records, and concludes that 'true HMO rates are unknown' (ibid, p406).

However, other authors have estimated them to be 7 % (Roemer and Shornick, 1973) or as much as 39 % (Donabedian, 1969) higher than the reported figure. Similarly, Luft (1980) warns that the lower operating costs claimed for HMOs may be offset by a heavier burden of out-of-pocket expenses borne by subscribers, either directly or indirectly. McLaughlin (1987) casts further doubt on the efficiency of HMOs. He concludes from his national study of HMO growth and the pattern of hospital use that, although they would appear to be associated with reduced admission rates and length of stay, they are associated with higher expenses per day per admission. Thus they have not led to decreased hospital expenses per capita, and would not appear to be the 'systemwide hospital cost-reducing policy tool' that their supporters have claimed them to be.

A similar picture – of early optimism giving way to greater caution – emerges when one considers the medical performance of HMOs, which has been investigated by the Rand Corporation Health Insurance Study. Earlier Rand HIS papers reported that cost sharing was effective in reducing utilisation of health services (Newhouse et al, 1981; O'Grady et al, 1985; Valdez et al, 1985). Moreover, the HMO which they studied (the Group Health Co-operative of Puget Sound) was reported as being 25 % cheaper than the FFS plans included in the study, largely because of a 40 % lower hospital referral rate (Manning et al, 1984). Just as importantly, lower utilisation and lower hospitalisation were apparently being achieved without any adverse effect on the health status of the patients concerned.

This earlier optimism has, however, been called into question by two more recent Rand studies. The first study (Siu et al, 1986) investigates the impact of cost sharing on hospital use and reveals that although it reduced costs it did not improve efficiency, since it was *all* utilisation that was reduced and not inappropriate utilisation selectively. It concludes that 'Cost sharing reduced inappropriate hospital use, but at the price of reducing appropriate use' (ibid, p1265). In other words, it is not just unnecessary treatment which is being denied to patients but necessary treatment as well. The second study (Ware et al, 1986) concentrates on HMOs and raises serious doubts about the equality of treatment they offer. It reports that although high-income, high-risk subjects enjoyed an improvement in health, low-income, high-risk subjects were actually disadvantaged by HMO membership. They reported significantly more bed days per year due to ill health, and presented with more serious symptoms that the control group. Their risk of death was much higher than low-income members even of cost-sharing FFS schemes. Another recent study (not part of the Rand HIS) of mortality rates among hospital inpatients has reported a significant positive correlation between mortality rate and market penetration by HMOs (Shortell and Hughes, 1988).

Although there is thus accumulating evidence that HMOs disadvantage the lower-income sick, so far little is known about precisely how and why they should do so.

Luft (1982, p282) speculates that the centralised location and large, bureaucratic structure of some forms of HMO may create barriers for the less mobile or the less educated, while the need to make an appointment might deter those (e.g. the hourly paid) who have little control over their daily timetable. He concludes that 'it appears that to some degree the style of service provided by the HMOs does not match that desired by the poor enrolees' (ibid, p285). Dutton (1986) reports that the average distance from poor patients to HMOs was significantly greater than to other sources of care. Since HMOs concentrate on enrolling the younger employed population, it is likely that they will be less accessible (both socially and geographically) to patients from deprived inner city areas.

Conclusion

Even though the prospects of the early introduction of HMOs into Britain receded significantly with the publication of the White Paper, their performance in the US continues to hold important lessons for anyone interested in anticipating the effects of the White Paper proposals for the organisation and financing of primary health care. Admittedly, there are obvious differences which must be borne in mind in the course of any such comparison. The White Paper proposals are, for a start, markedly more modest in the short term at least, while the longer term strategy remains unclear. In addition, the British and American administrations might appear to be converging on a similar solution from entirely opposite directions. For, whereas in Britain change is being pursued in the name of expanding patient choice and disintegrating the NHS monopoly, in the US it has been pursued essentially as a means of limiting patient choice, and vertically integrating a hitherto uncontrolled and unregulated primary health care market.

Nevertheless, despite these differences there remain important similarities, not the least of which is the common belief that the 'financial crisis' of health care provision in both countries can ultimately be traced back to the fact that both consumers and providers have far too long been sheltered from the economic consequences of their choices. 'Third party provision' – by the state in Britain, by insurance in the US and latterly by the state there, too, via its financing of Medicare and Medicaid – has resulted in the removal of the discipline of the marketplace, and created the conditions in which provider monopoly could flourish unchecked. The remedy, in both countries, has been to attempt to restore the market in order to bring the supply and demand for health back within the control of market forces.

What, then, are the lessons that can be derived from recent American experience? There are, I believe, several difficulties which have tended either to be ignored by advocates of a grater role for market forces in the provision of health care, or else to be dismissed as problems of implementation only. On the contrary, it is, in my view, more realistic to see them as symptoms of fundamental dissimiliarities between health care and other goods and services (for further discussion, see e.g. Siminoff, 1986; Vladeck, 1976; Macklin, 1985).

In America, there is now growing recognition that in practice the deregulation of health care has led to consequences which are becoming socially and politically unacceptable. Among those which have been identified are: a 'medical arms race' between hospitals which has contributed to the unnecessary duplication of sophisticated technology (Robinson et al., 1988; Hampton 1987); the 'dumping' of patients with inadequate insurance cover (Schiff et al., 1986); the pauperisation of inner-city hospitals (Broyles and Rosko, 1985; Rosko, 1984; Dunham and Morone, 1983); the increase in under-insurance among the poor (Berk and Wilensky, 1987); the growing reliance of insurers on terms and conditions (often covert) which restrict the coverage they contract to offer their subscribers (Ginzberg, 1987; Kinzer, 1988).

It might be objected that such problems may be discounted (given the reduced likelihood of the adoption of full deregulation of health care here) and that the strategy of limited competition being pursued in the White Paper will enable us to enjoy the benefits while avoiding the costs which have been incurred in the US.

This objection, however, overlooks the evidence of the studies cited earlier (Bosanquet and Leese, 1988; Birch, 1986; Birch and Ryan, 1988) which document the adverse impact of even the relatively modest modifications which have already been made to the system of financial incentives and disincentives to which suppliers and consumers of primary health care services are liable.

Further practical difficulties have been identified by Marinker, Wilkin and Metcalfe (1988) in the course of a discussion of a variety of possible strategies for achieving the White Paper objective of more rational and cost effective referral by GPs of patients to hospital. One of the possibilities they consider is that the referring behaviour of GPs might be altered by means of restructuring their contracts so as to provide them with appropriate incentives to maximise the quality of the hospital services they were purchasing on behalf of their patients and to minimise unnecessary or costly referrals. (Such a system has been envisaged by Maynard (1986) who proposes that the GP should become the budget holder for both primary and secondary care). A number of difficulties with this system are identified. As has been shown earlier, even FPCs are experiencing problems in coping with the more managerial role which has been created for them. Not surprisingly, therefore, Marinker, Wilkin and Metcalf conclude that the greatly enlarged role which Maynard envisages for GPs is far beyond the current managerial capacity. They conjecture that practices might be able to buy in such skills, but even this possibility must currently be reckoned remote given the rudimentary development of the information systems which would be required for the management of such an internal market.

Admittedly, some initiatives are being undertaken in this area with the publication of data on, for example, hospital mortality rates or GP prescribing patterns. However, there is still a considerable way to go before reliable and valid data are available which will serve as the basis for rational decision making. As Roland points out, at the moment most hospital information systems do not relate referral to the referring general practitioners. Substantial changes in hospital computing practices will be required before valid data on referrals can be provided (Roland, 1988, p437). Similarly, Marinker, Wilkin and Metcalfe express scepticism about the likelihood of genuine competition between practices, given that in many parts of the country patients have virtually no choice of practice. No doubt they have rural practices mainly in mind, but one could add that even in urban areas problems of transportation and access may mean that for a significant proportion of the population the local practice may well exercise an effective monopoly. They also point out that, even if patients were to begin to exercise their right to change practices, the financial impact of an individual or even a family so doing is likely to be small by comparison with the US where the vast majority of HMO subscribers are enrolled not as individuals but by employers or insurance companies. Finally, they observe that contractual arrangements of this kind, under which doctors have a direct financial incentive to minimise or restrict treatment, posit important ethical considerations. Changes of the sort proposed by Maynard would entail radical shifts in the organisation and culture of general practice.

While many of the detailed proposals contained in the White Paper are entirely laudable in their own right, it is difficult to extend an unreserved welcome to the document as a whole. Its potential for good is reduced and its potential for harm simultaneously increased, in my view, by a central conceptual error that health is a commodity like any other and that the transaction between patient and doctor is essentially the same as that between any supplier and any consumer and thus is (or should be) subject to the same economic forces. This economic reductionism not only overlooks the crucial features which distinguish health care from the market, it also jeopardises the achievement of the central objective of the White Paper. The changes it proposes are, I fear, likely to lead not to the raising of standard for all, but to increasing inequalities in the provision of primary health care.

References

Berk, M L and Wilensky, G R (1987) Health insurance coverage of the working poor. *Social Science and Medicine* **25**(11): 1183–7.

Birch, S (1986) Increasing patient charges in the National Health Service; a method of privatising primary care. *Journal of Social Policy.* **15**(2): 163–84.

Birch, S and Ryan, M (1988) *Estimating the effects of health service charges; evidence of the utilisation of prescriptions.* Centre for Health Economics, University of York.

Bosanquet, N (1987) Fresh light shed on GP's workload, *Health Service Journal* 2 July: 753

Bosanquet, N and Leese, B (1988) Family doctors and innovation in general practice. *British Medical Journal.* **296**: 1576–80.

Broyles, R W and Rosko, M D (1985) A qualitative assessment of the Medicare prospective payment system. *Social Science and Medicine.* **20**(11): 1185–90.

Butler, E and Pirie, M (1988a) *The health of nations.* Adam Smith Institute. (1988b) *The health alternatives.* Adam Smith Institute.

Butler, J R (1986) List-size, standards and performance in general practice; a pilot study. In Pendleton, D Schofield, T and Marinker, M (eds) *In pursuit of quality.* Royal College of General Practitioners. Central Statistical Office (1985). *Annual Abstract of Statistics 1985.*

Deacon, A and Bradshaw, J (1983) *Reserved for the poor.* Basil Blackwell and Martin Robinson.

Department of Health and Social Security (1986a) *Primary health care; an agenda for discussion.* Cmnd 9771, HMSO.

Department of Health and Social Security (1986b) *Neighbourhood Nursing – A focus for care.* Cumberlege Report. HMSO.

Department of Health and Social Security (1987) *Health and Personal Social Services Statistics for England.* HMSO.

Donabedian, A (1969) An evaluation of prepaid group practices. *Inquiry.* **6**:3

Dunham, A and Morone, J (1983) *DRG evaluation: political evaluation.* Health Research and Education Trust of New Jersey, Princeton.

Dutton, D (1986) Financial, organisation and professional factors affecting health care utilisation. *Social Science and Medicine.* **23**(7): 721–35.

Fry, J and Stephen, W J (1986) Primary health care in the United Kingdom. *International Journal of Health Services.* **16**(4) 485–95.

Ginzberg, E (1987) A hard look at cost containment. *New England Journal of Medicine.* **316**:(18) 1151–8.

Goldsmith, M and Willetts, D (1988) *Managed health care: a new system for a better health service.* Centre for Policy Studies.

Hampton, J R (1987) MRI and hospital politics. *Hospital Update.* November 1987: 889–90.

HM Treasury (1987) *Public expenditure estimates, 1988–91.* HMSO.

Huntingdon, J and McClenahan, J (1987) *Report of a project to investigate the training and development needs of Family Practitioner Committees with particular reference to their management development needs.* King's Fund College, London.

Iglehard, J K (1984) HMOs (for profit and not-for-profit) on the move. *New England Journal of Medicine.* **310**(18): 1203–8.

Jackson-Beeck, M and Kleinman, J H (1983) Evidence for self-selection among health maintenance organisation enrolees. *Journal of American Medical Association.* **250**(20): 2826–9.

Kinzer, D (1988) The decline and fall of deregulation. *New England Journal of Medicine.* **318**(2): 112–6.

Levinson, D F (1987) Towards full disclosure of referral restrictions and financial incentives by prepaid health plans. *New England Journal of Medicine.* **317**(27): 1729–31.

Luft, H (1980) Trends in medical care costs; do HMOs lower the rate of growth? *Medical care.* **18**(1): 1–16.

Luft, H (1982) Health maintenance organisations and the rationing of health care. *Milbank Memorial Fund Quarterly.* **60**(2): 268–306.

Macklin, R (1985) Are we in the lifeboat yet? Allocation and rationing of medical resources. *Social Research.* **52**(3): 607–23.

McLaughlin, C G (1987) HMO growth and hospital expenses and use: a simultaneous equation approach. *Health Services Research.* **22**(2): 183–205.

Manning, W G, Leibowitz, A, Goldberg, G A et al. (1984) A controlled trial of the effect of a prepaid group practice on use of services. *New England Journal of Medicine.* **310**(23): 1505–10.

Marinker, M, Wilkin, D, and Metcalfe, D H (1988) Referral to hospital: can we do better? *British Medical Journal.* **297**: 461–4.

Maynard, A (1986) Performance incentives. In Teeling-Smith, G (ed) *Health Education and General Practice.* Office of Health Economics.

Mott, P D (1986) Hospital utilisation by health maintenance organisations. *Medical Care* 24(5): 398–406.

Newhouse, J P, Manning, W G, Duan, N et al. (1987) The findings of the Rand Health Insurance Experiment – a response to Welch et al. *Medical Care.* **25**(2): 157–99.

Newhouse, J P, Manning, W G, Morris, C N et al. (1981) Some interim results from a controlled trial of cost sharing in health insurance. *New England Journal for Medicine.* **305**(25): 1501–7.

O'Grady, K F, Manning, W G, Newhouse, J P and Brook, R H (1985) The impact of cost sharing on emergency department use. *New England Journal of Medicine.* **313**(8): 484–90.

Pendleton, D, Schofield, T and Marinker, M (eds) (1986) *In pursuit of quality approaches to performance review in general practice.* RCGP.

Petchey, R (1987) Health maintenance organisations: just what the doctor ordered? *Journal of Social Policy.* **16**(4): 489–507.

Robinson, J C, Luft, H S, McPhee, S J and Hunt, S S (1988) Hospital competition and surgical length of stay. *Journal of the American Medical Association.* **259**(5): 696–700.

Roemer, M I and Shornick, W (1973) HMO performance, the recent evidence. *Milbank Memorial Fund Quarterly.* **51**(2): 27.

Roland, M (188) General practitioner referral rates. *British Medical Journal.* **297**: 437–8.

Rosko, M D (1984) *Cost-shifting under prospective payment.* Paper presented to the International Health Economics Conference, San Juan, 1984 cited in Broyles, R W and Rosko, M D (1985).

Royal College of General Practitioners (1981) *A survey of primary care in London.* Report prepared for the RCGP (coordinator B Jarman). RCGP.

Royal College of General Practitioners (1985) *What sort of doctor? Assessing quality of care in general practice.* RCGP.

Salmon, J W (1984) Organising medical care for profit. In McKinley, J B (ed) *Issues in the political economy of health care.* Tavistock.

Schiff, R L, Ansell, D A, Schlosser, J E et al. (1986) Transfers to a public hospital. *New England Journal of Medicine.* **314**(9): 552–7.

Secretaries of State for Social Services, Wales, Northern Ireland and Scotland (1987) *Promoting better health.* Cmnd 249, HMSO.

Shortell, S M and Hughes, E F X (1988) The effects of regulation, competition and ownership on mortality rates among hospital inpatients. *New England Journal of Medicine.* **318**(7): 1100–7.

Siminoff, L (1986) Competition and primary care in the United States: separating fact from fantasy. *International Journal of Health Services.* **16**(1): 57–69.

Siu, A L, Sonnenburg, F A, Manning, W G et al. (1986) Inappropriate use of hospitals in a randomised trial of health insurance plans. *New England Journal of Medicine.* **315**: 1259–66.

Valdez, R B, Brook, R H, Rogers, W R et al. (1985) Consequences of cost-sharing for children's health. *Paediatrics.* **75**(5): 952–61.

Vladeck, B C (1976) On cutting the cost of medical assistance. *Policy Analysis.* **24**(2): 497–8.

Warden, J (1988a) Rise of the nurse practitioner. *British Medical Journal* **296**: 1478.

Warden, J (1988b) Changing the script. *British Medical Journal* **296**: 726.

Ware, J E, Brook, R H, Rogers W H et al. (1986) Comparison of health outcomes at a health maintenance organisation with those of fee-for-service care. *Lancet*. 3 May 1986: 1017–22.

Welch, B L, Hay, J W, Miller, D S et al. (1987) The Rand Health Insurance Study: a summary critique. *Medical Care*. **25**(2): 148–56.

Whitney, R (1988) *The National Health crisis – a modern solution.* Shepheard-Walwyn.

9 The Griffiths Report on Community Care

Sally Baldwin and Gillian Parker

Introduction

On 16 March 1988, some three months later than expected, the Griffiths Report *Community care: agenda for action* was published – the day after the Budget and when its author, Sir Roy Griffiths, was in hospital. On a cynical view the publication date (the report was known to have been with ministers for some time) was chosen to ensure that it would have a low profile. If so, the attempt failed. It generated – and continued to generate – a torrent of discussion. In Sir Roy's own words:

> The interest shown in the report since its publication has been such as to convince me that I have done a great deal already for job creation within both the journalistic and the conference field (Speech to the Association of County Councils, 9 May 1988).

Recognition of the value of a life outside institutions for people who are mentally ill or mentally handicapped has a long history (Parker, 1985). Articulation of community care as a policy for such people dates from the 1930s, gathering momentum after the 1957 Royal Commission on Mental Illness and Mental Deficiency and Enoch Powell's 1962 Hospital Plan.

Since then the use of the term has expanded, to include people who are elderly or physically disabled as well as those mentally disabled; the prevention of entry to institutions as well as the exodus from them; and life in small institutions rather than simply in one's own home or with relatives. A consensus has developed that for anyone requiring long term support, but no acute medical care, the ideal is to provide this in settings as close as possible to ordinary homes, and preferably in the individual's own home (Henwood, 1986).

Why this consensus? Arguably the reason is that community care can be presented as both best and cheapest. Its appeal in professional and academic circles derives from work on the dehumanising effects of institutions and on their political significance (Scull, 1984). The emergence of the equal opportunities movement and its application in the field of disability provided further support for community care, while the hospital scandals of the 1960s and 1970s publicised the issues and gave the debate a higher political profile. (See, for example DHSS, 1969; 1971; 1974; 1977).

The ideal of community care also features in policy documents from the 1950s on, and increasingly after 1962. However as economic and demographic pressures begin to bite in the 1970s and 1980s the idealism of earlier statements is increasingly tempered with notions of financial expediency. (Parker, 1985). Best is subordinated to cheapest, care in the community becomes care by the community, boundaries between statutory and non-statutory support begin to shift, welfare pluralism becomes the dominant paradigm. Hence, while consensus about community care as 'best' remains, community care policy has become, as Henwood notes (Henwood, 1986) the site of deep ideological conflict: between central and local government, between right and left, between informal carers and policy makers both centrally and locally.

Anxiety about the implications of community care policy has existed for almost 30 years (see, for example, Titmuss 1963). In the early 1980s, however, it emerged as a major concern, prompting a series of investigations and reports which continues even after Griffiths (Audit Commission, 1986; National Audit Office, 1987; House of Commons Committee of Public Accounts, 1988). Why, after simmering for more than 30 years has it finally come to the top of the policy agenda?

For the newly established House of Commons Social Services Committee the decision in 1984 to choose community care as their second topic for investigation reflected anxieties about the accelerating process of 'decanting' people from long stay hospitals and the circumstances of people discharged from or unable to enter them (House of Commons Social Services Committee, 1985). The Committee's concern, strongly influenced by what they had seen at first hand of American and Italian experiences of 'decarceration' was primarily with the quality of life of former patients and their families. They found that long-stay hospitals in Britain were being run down and patients discharged before reasonable, or in some cases any, community services had been established. Mechanisms for the joint planning and financing of community service were inadequate or non-existent while the social security budget was emerging as a major, it not wholly reliable, source of support. The Committee warned:

> We are now...at a crucial stage in the development of community care policies...The stage has now been reached where the rhetoric of community care has to be matched by action (ibid, para. 223).

For the Audit Commission (1986), picking up the issue in 1985 the primary concern was value for public money. Community care was by now an accepted policy goal; was 'generally considered better' and also more economical in many cases. However progress towards the goal was in fact both slow and uneven, hampered by fundamental underlying problems of financing and responsibility:

- mechanisms for transferring funds from the NHS to social services were inadequate:
- responsibilities for community based services were fragmented between agencies with different priorities, structures and budgets, able to request but not require co-operation from each other;
- essential bridging finance was limited;
- penalties on over-spending incurred under the block grant system created disincentives for local authorities to develop new services;
- crucially, social security payments introduced 'perverse incentives' for people to choose more expensive and often less suitable forms of care, frustrating both community care objectives and attempts to equalise the allocation of public resources across the country. (Expenditure on supplementary benefits payments to people in private and voluntary homes had risen from £6 million in 1978 to £499 million in 1986. It rose further to £727 million by the end of 1987).

The Commission concluded:

> Joint planning and community care policy are in some disarray. The result is poor value for money (Audit Commission, 1986, p3).

While bringing forward proposals of its own (including the allocation of responsibility for mentally ill people to the NHS, physically and mentally handicapped people to local authorities and the creation of a new 'lead' authority for services for older people) the Audit Commission called for the setting up of an independent, high level, review:

> What is not tenable is to do nothing about the present financial, organisational and staffing arrangements (Audit Commission, 1986, para. 177).

The Government's response was swift, prompted no doubt by the escalating social security budget. In December 1986 Roy

Griffiths was appointed by the then Secretary of State, Norman Fowler 'to review the way in which public funds are used to support community care policy and to advise me on the options for action that would improve the use of these funds as a contribution to more effective community care' (Griffiths Report, piii, para.2).

The choice of Griffiths was predictable. As Managing Director of Sainsburys he fitted with the Prime Minister's view that the public sector had much to learn from successful private enterprise. Already an adviser on health policy he had been responsible for the 1983 NHS Management Review (House of Commons Social Services Committee, 1984). This resulted in a move away from the consensus management style adopted after the 1974 NHS reorganisation towards a stronger management structure – with the creation, centrally, of the NHS Management Board (of which Griffiths was deputy chairman) and the creation of general manager posts at Regional, District and Unit levels.

The choice of Griffiths also had an ironic appropriateness in that the incentive system within which general managers have worked since 1983, with its use of closures, bed reductions and patient throughput as performance indicators had undoubtedly strained joint planning and finance systems and fuelled the expansion in social security expenditure which finally brought community care to prominence. In the remainder of this article we look at the approach he adopted and at his recommendations.

The approach

As with his review of NHS management, Griffiths operated in a highly individualistic mode – supported by a small team of civil servants and professional advisers but essentially reaching his own conclusions on the basis of previous enquiries, informal soundings of his own and a large volume of unsolicited submissions. His remit had been to be brief and geared towards advice on action. The 28 page report was both.

In a memorable line from his review of NHS management structures Griffiths observes:

> If Florence Nightingale were carrying her lamp through the corridor of the NHS today she would almost certainly be looking for the people in charge (House of Commons Social Services Committee, 1984, para.41).

A similar spirit pervades the review of community care which is dominated by the prime objective of filling the current vacuum of responsibility Griffiths identifies at both central and local levels of Government.

> At the centre, community care has been talked of for thirty years and in few areas can the gap between political rhetoric and policy on the one hand, or between policy and reality in the field have been so great...The problem is compounded by the responsibility for inputs to community care at the centre being divided between the two arms of the DHSS...and the Department of the Environment (Griffiths Report, piv, para.9).

> (At the local level) crucially at present there is no-one who is responsible for identifying the needs of individuals and for arranging and delivering services to them (Speech to the Association of County Councils, 9 May 1988).

Griffiths' approach to the problem is rational, simple, and strongly underpinned by a commitment to consumer sovereignty and by a managerial ethos whose key elements are: clearly defined objectives and financial resources in line with these; clear lines of responsibility and accountability; agreed timescales for action; and continuous monitoring of performance to ensure cost-effectiveness and value for money.

Applied to the public sector this approach, Griffiths contends, goes well beyond the radical restructuring of service delivery advocated in the Audit Commission Report and in a number of submissions to his enquiry:

> Nothing could be more radical in the public sector than to spell out responsibilities, insist on performance and accountability, and to evidence (sic) that action is being taken; and, even more radical, to match policy with appropriate resources and agreed timescales (pvi, para.20).

How well this rational, value-neutral, managerialist approach fits with the 'realpolitik' of community care is a question we return to below.

Griffiths' declared starting point is not administrative structures but the vulnerable individual 'in his or her particular situation'. In a speech to the Association of County Councils a month after the publication of his report he identifies the three broad principles on which his report is based:

- The need to establish clear responsibility for identifying the needs of individuals and for the arrangement of services to them.
- The need for a suitable mechanism to ensure that the policies and the resources available to carry them out are compatible.

- The need to guarantee that as far as possible care is provided to the individual by the most suitable agency.

Hence his principal recommendations.

Community care is to be identified and separately financed for the first time as a separate and distinct area of service provision. *Central Government* would assume a more visible, more strategic role, with the appointment of a minister of state at the DHSS 'clearly and publicly identified as responsible for community care' (pvi, para. 22). The minister's responsibilities would include promulgating the Government's objectives and priorities, monitoring local authorities' plans and performance, and overseeing the allocation of finance.

At the local level responsibility for ensuring the delivery of community care is placed firmly with local social services authorities.

> I believe that it is entirely appropriate that local communities, through their elected councillors, should be able to take decisions about community care (Speech to the Association of County Councils, 9 May 1988).

Crucially, however, the role of the local authority is to arrange the delivery of services, not to provide them. In line with the philosophy of consumer choice, Griffiths makes a strong plea for a more mixed economy of care:

> The primary function of the public services is to design and arrange the provision of care and support in line with people's needs...The proposals are therefore aimed at stimulating the further development of the 'mixed economy' of care. It is vital that social services authorities should see themselves as the arrangers and purchasers of care services – not as monopolistic providers (para 2.4).

The local authority's responsibility will, then, be for assessing the community care needs of their locality, setting local priorities and developing local plans. They will assess and prioritise the needs of individuals and ensure that services are provided 'within the appropriate budgets by the public or private sector according to where they can be provided most economically and efficiently' (p vii, para.24).

Following his commitment to matching policy with appropriate resources the financing of community care would be restructured:

> I recommend that community care needs, including the implications for revenue and capital, should be considered separately in the public expenditure planning process (para. 6.22).

In a radical departure from the existing block grant system managed by the Department of the Environment, Griffiths proposes the introduction of specific grants for community care. These would be managed by the now Department of Health and, subject to the approval of local community care plans, would meet between 40 and 50 % of the cost of agreed plans. The remainder of the cost would be met from the block exchequer grant together with locally raised finance – rates or community charge and charges levied for services. Additional targeted grants would be available in specific circumstances – to enable them, for example, to prepare for hospital closures. (Social service authorities would also receive finance currently allocated to jointly funded projects and money currently allocated to the community care grant element of the Social Fund.)

For Griffiths this formula has the merit of protecting financing for locally defined community care priorities and introducing a measure of stability to the planning of services while ensuring that local policy fits with national objectives.

The exponential growth of social security expenditure on private and voluntary sector residential care was, as noted above, what finally forced Government to take the 'disarray' of community care policy seriously. Here Griffiths concurs with the views of the Audit Commission and the Firth Committee (Audit Commission, 1986; DHSS, 1977) that the present situation has to change:

> The separate funding of residential and nursing home care through social security, with no assessment of need, is a particularly pernicious split in responsibilities and a fundamental obstacle to the creation of a comprehensive local approach to community care (para. 4.21).

The need is for a system which supports community care objectives and gives value for public money. Essentially this means assessing the need for care and neutralising the financial implications for local authorities of different forms of care. Griffiths recommends that everyone applying for public finance towards the cost of residential care be dealt with in the same way – regardless of whether the home they want to enter is public or private, offers residential or nursing care. The social services authority would be responsible for assessing the client's need for residential care. If this is judged appropriate a social security residential care benefit would be paid, subject to a test of financial need. This would, however, have a maximum considerably lower than at present (Griffiths suggests 'the average total of income support and housing benefit to which someone living other than in residential care would be entitled'). It would be topped up by the social services authority to meet the remaining costs of residential care, balancing the client's needs and preferences against available resources. Where residential care was not judged to be in the client's best interests an appropriate package of domiciliary services would have to be provided. In both cases those who could afford to do so would contribute to their care costs. Savings from the social security budget would be transferred to the local authority.

An important by-product of this proposal is the recommendation that the current fragmentation of responsibility for regulating different types of residential home would disappear. All, including nursing homes and the small homes currently exempt from regulations, would be regulated by the social services authority, homes being registered and regulated in relation to their stated objectives and the care they sought to provide. To safeguard the interests of the independent sector, finance for community care plans would be conditional on evidence that the private sector is being 'stimulated and encouraged' and involved in the planning process.

An important subset of recommendations concerns the relationship between social service authorities and the other statutory agencies involved in community care. Here again the guiding principle is the identification of responsibility. Acute and community health care will be the responsibility of health authorities; general practitioners will be responsible for notifying the social services authorities of patients' community care needs; public housing authorities will be responsible for the 'bricks and mortar' of housing needed for community care while social services authorities will provide the necessary support service. None of this precludes responsibilities being devolved on an agency basis where appropriate. For example health authorities who have developed expertise in the social care of people with a mental illness might be sub-contracted by the social services authority to continue doing so. Final responsibility would, however, lie with the social services authority.

The number of agencies involved in the actual delivery of community care would, then, be no fewer than at present – and probably greater given Griffiths' enthusiasm for experimentation. Clearly, then, the need for joint planning would be greater than ever – though for health authorities in particular the incentives for collaboration might, paradoxically, be less. Recognising this, Griffiths stresses that arrangements for joint planning will be 'a central area for scrutiny as part of the conditions of grant'.

Response – and critique

Hailed as 'the most significant statement about community care since the Seebohm Report' (Hunter and Judge, 1988) the Griffiths'

Report has been the subject of prolific commentary (see for example Etherington, 1988; Hardingham and Morris, 1988; Henwood and Wistow, 1988; Mitchell, 1988; Oldman, 1988; Westland, 1988). With notable exceptions the verdict so far has been one of 'cautious optimism': optimism about the clarity of the strategy and choice of social services; caution deriving from anxieties about funding mechanisms and the levels of finance allocated and also about the will and the ability of both central and local government to implement the proposals. It is recognised that a great deal remains to be worked out, but at this stage the broad consensus appears to be that the strategy *itself* is right – that, in Griffiths' own words 'these are ideas whose time has come.'

The remainder of this chapter does not deal, to any extent, with problems of implementing and financing Griffiths' recommendations. Others have done that (see, for example, Hunter and Judge, 1988; Henwood and Wistow, 1988). We have chosen instead to look critically at the Report's subtext: at assumptions its author makes without question but which are in fact contestable; at the tensions which underlie (and belie) its skilfull presentation as common sense; at the real possibilities of meeting the expectations it raises for vulnerable people and their carers; and, crucially, at the kind of public service it seems likely to deliver to them – in terms of equity and of adequacy, equality of access and the rights of users.

Issues of consumer choice

Griffiths explicitly states in his 'Dear Secretary of State' letter that his brief was not, 'except in one or two rare instances' to recommend changes in the *content* of policy. Rather, his work was 'geared to ensuring that the machinery and resources exist to implement such policies as are determined' (Griffiths Report, p iii, para.6). Given this objective, coupled with his background in retail management, it is not surprising that he should see issues of 'consumer satisfaction in the field' and of consumer choice as paramount. Nor is it surprising that he should see expanded provision of services through the private sector as an essential prerequisite of improved consumer choice. What *is* surprising is that he should so uncritically transfer the option of consumer choice from market transactions to public services.

Recent work on consumerism in the public service sphere (Pollitt, 1988) identifies a number of ways in which public services differ essentially from market transactions and questions the appropriateness of applying similar notions of consumerism in the two spheres. Indeed for Pollitt the whole character of consumerism in the public services is problematic. The term carries multiple and often incompatible meanings but the conceptions of public service 'consumer' most frequently in use are 'stultifyingly narrow and apolitical'. Attempts to give real power to service users are, moreover, frequently blocked by resistance from professionals or lack of finance. Hence, Pollitt argues, the concept of consumerism needs to be rethought within the concept of the values associated with public services and with ideas of citizenship.

There is no sign that Griffiths regards consumerism as a problematic or even a complex notion. Nor is there any hint that its application to public services is in any way questionable. Moreover, as Twigg has pointed out there is an essential tension between Griffiths' consumerism and his objective of establishing mechanisms for distributing support in relation to need:

> Reviewing the debate the nub of the issue becomes clear: how can we increase choice, and thus by implication quality, within the field of community care, while at the same time...establishing a system that is, first, rational in its distribution of support in relation to need and, second, rationed both in its scope and cost? (Twigg, 1988, p 191).

Consumer choice as a principle conflicts with an approach to service provision based on meeting needs through externally defined criteria, using professionals as gate keepers. When principles of cost-containment dominate, as they have done in recent years and professionals are involved in rationing access to services, the consumer's freedom of choice is highly circumscribed.

Griffiths does not acknowledge these tensions. His somewhat naïve use of the concept of need ignores throughout the fact that needs depend on who is defining them and that the definitions of 'consumer', professional and resource manager frequently conflict. His resolution of the tension is clear, however. Professional authority and cost-containment are to take precedence over consumer choice.

These issues are well illustrated in relation to the private provision of services, firstly in relation to the general diversification of service provision recommended in the report and, secondly in regard to the specific provision of residential care.

The diversification of service provision generally

One of the key tenets of the report is that social services authorities' plans 'should encourage a proportionate increase in private and voluntary services, as distinct from directly provided public services'. This increase is seen as the *sine qua non* of increased consumer choice, derived both from a greater range of services and from increased competition between service providers.

Social services authorities are to ensure that they make readily available information about services provided by the voluntary sector and private businesses, as well as those provided by public bodies. In addition to developing and sustaining the informal sector and voluntary organisations they are, further, to *encourage* development of private services (Griffiths Report, para. 6.9). There should be arrangements for consulting the private and voluntary providers of care in joint planning arrangements – they are mentioned specifically in this respect in the summary (para. 1.3.1) but not in the main body of the report – and the establishment of local plans and the funding of community care is to take into account the amount of private care available in an area (para. 6.29.ii). In sum, the social services authorities are given the responsibility of showing that 'the private sector is being fully stimulated and encouraged and that competitive tenders or other means of testing the market, are being taken' (p viii, para 24).

The outcome of this encouragement is, clearly, to be an increasingly residual role for the local authority as a provider of services and an increased, or in some cases new, role as 'designers, organisers and purchasers of non-health care services...making the maximum possible use of voluntary and private sector bodies to widen consumer choice, stimulate innovation and encourage efficiency' (para. 1.3.3).

This anticipated move towards 'a more mixed economy' of provision raises a number of questions.

Firstly, for whom is consumer choice increased? Incentives to generate new voluntary and private provision, coupled with the social services authorities' obligation to collect and disseminate information about this provision, will undoubtedly enhance consumer choice for those with the financial resources to put together and pay for their own packages. It is not difficult to imagine a competent middle-class son or daughter arranging suitable packages of services to help maintain an elderly patient in his or her own home. Similarly a younger person with physical disabilities and a substantial income from, say, accident compensation payments, with the increased diversity of provision and the information provided, could negotiate a package of services, appropriate to his or her own needs with much less difficulty than is now the case. This is all to the good and is likely to lead to substantial improvements in the quality of life of both carer and cared-for person.

For the individual without the resources to pay for services, however, the position is quite different. In such circumstances the social services authority will have an obligation to *assess* the needs of the individual within the context of his or her own situation, to *decide* what packages of care would be best suited to meet these needs (albeit after 'taking account' of the views of the 'to be cared for' person and any informal carers, to *determine the priority* to be given to the case, and to *arrange delivery* of the services decided upon (para. 3.8)). This seems to indicate anything but consumer choice; indeed it is positively 'dirigiste'.

Secondly, who will or, perhaps more importantly, will not belong to 'priority groups'? In determining the priority to be given to any particular case, social services authorities will have to be guided by some pre-determined definition of 'neediness', as stated in para. 3.5:

> A fundamental purpose of the proposals is to ensure that someone is in a position to apply priorities in a way that maximises the chances that those in most need will receive due care, and that eliminates the possibility of low priority need being met while higher priorities are neglected.

In situations where resources are 'finite' it is almost inevitable that the most 'needy' will be defined as frail elderly people without informal carers. Consumer choice and the definition of priority groups make very strange, if not totally incompatible, bedfellows.

Thirdly, how is the creation of a two-tier service to be avoided if Griffiths' proposals are enacted? In affluent areas it is anticipated that 'more people will be able to buy from both the private sector and social services authorities' (para. 6.29.i). In such areas private business will be likely to seek to develop high quality and relatively expensive services. Local authorities could then find themselves in the situation of having to buy into services which were more 'luxurious' than necessary and consequently not the best value for money. Given that this would run counter to the philosophy of Griffiths – and would probably contravene any legislation or regulations established to enact the proposals – authorities would then have either to encourage private providers to set up lower quality but 'adequate' services or to set up services themselves. In either case those reliant on state support would become visibly different from those not and they would not be able to exercise the same degree of choice as their more affluent counterparts.

The provision of residential care

Griffiths' proposals on residential care are set within a context of substantially increased numbers of elderly and other dependent people being cared for within private residential and nursing homes. Between 1979 and 1986 the numbers of residents in such homes rose from 35,000 to 108,000. At the same time the number of places in local authority provision rose by only 5 % and in voluntary homes by 9 % (Bradshaw, 1988). The reasons for this increase in private provision are various – Bradshaw (1988) suggests demography, care in the community policies, financial pressures on local authority social services departments, the emergence of a new entrepreneurial class, and the payment of supplementary benefit to people in residential care – and their relative contributions as yet unmeasured. It is clear, however, that one of Griffiths' major concerns was with the reduction of the social security bill. Supplementary benefit currently provides finance for around half of all people in private care and the proportion receiving help with their fees has increased from 14 % to over 50 % between 1979 and 1986 (DHSS, 1987). To what extent would the proposals in the report change the current position, and what are their implications for consumer choice?

As noted above, Griffiths recommends that public finance for all forms of residential care should be conditional on both financial assessment and the need for care. The financial assessment would presumably be much as now, using a 'means test consistent with that for income support' (para. 6.39).

It is with the assessment of the 'appropriateness' of residential provision as a care option that the proposed system most departs from current provision and it is here that most opportunity for the development of substantial inequity arises. The social services authority is to establish a system whereby it decides whether residential care is appropriate for a given individual. While consultation with others closely concerned, including the individual herself, will be encouraged the final decision will lie with the authority. Whether the decision making system adopted by authorities is that of case management (Davies and Challis, 1986) or some other model it is clear that it must be underwritten by financial commitment from local politicians via the social services budget. Thus the 'appropriateness' of residential care for any given individual might be determined as much by the finance available to the social services department as by 'objectively' defined measures of need or, indeed, the wishes of the client herself. Residential care might be deemed less 'appropriate' particularly in those areas where it was most expensive and where the local authority had to make up a greater proportion of the cost. This would lead not only to straightforward inequity – where people reliant on state support would be disadvantaged relative to those in similar need but with the resources to pay for their own care – but also to a new form of territorial inequity whereby people with similar needs *and* resources might be offered very different choices depending on where they lived.

It also seems likely that the 'appropriateness' of residential care would be determined, in part at least, by the availability of informal care to the client (see below for a fuller discussion on informal carers). In authorities which clearly acknowledged the burden carried by informal carers and underwrote that acknowledgement with money, residential care might be offered more often than in authorities where the burden was unacknowledged or ignored in the interests of saving money.

Griffiths' proposals do not make clear what will happen to people who decide to enter residential care when their assessment has indicated that they do not 'need' it, but who then run out of money to pay the difference between the 'residential allowance', to which they are entitled, and the full cost of residential care (para. 6.44). These people will have given up their homes and any community networks they might have had, so are unlikely to be capable of reintegration into the community. Indeed, as they *chose* to move into residential care they are unlikely to want to return. Yet if the social services authorities then pick up the bill they are reducing the resources they have available for other, more 'needy', clients. They will, further, be giving preferential treatment to previously affluent individuals against similarly 'needy' people who might like to move into residential care but who do not have the resources to make up the difference in cost.

It may seem strange to have concentrated this part of the discussion on people *not* being able to go into residential care when received wisdom supports care in the community at all (or most) costs. Yet although some of the effects of social security support for private residential care have been 'perverse' and some private care of poor quality, it is still the case that the payment of social security does/did enable many elderly people to obtain a level of care that was previously unattainable and that not always, or indeed very often, was that care 'inappropriate' (Bradshaw and Gibbs, 1988).

It may of course be the case that, with the enhanced range of domiciliary support options which Griffiths envisages as the outcome of his proposals, many of those who in the past preferred a residential option will in the future have both the desire and the opportunity to stay at home. The report states unequivocally that the outcome of any assessment of the need for residential care 'should not be a choice between residential care and very little else'. Instead, residential care will be one means of providing care and support, with packages of other possibilities costing the social services authority nearly as much as residential care also being serious options (para. 6.5.1). The critical question remains of the weight given in the assessment process to the views of the dependent person and those involved, on an informal basis, in her care.

It seems clear, however, than in spite of the prominence it gives to issues of consumer choice the Griffiths report is far from being a consumers' charter. Its version of consumerism is weak, and essentially cosmetic. It contains no strong commitment to the involvement of service users in planning services or monitoring their effectiveness, no emphasis on rights to services, no mechanisms for challenging professional decisions. In important respects, moreover, consumer choice would actually be reduced by the proposals. It can be seen as a move in the right direction, but there is clearly still a long way to go.

Informal carers

In policy documents and statements about community care it has always been the fate of informal carers to be everywhere seen but nowhere regarded. Despite the fact that the vast majority of caring for dependent people takes place within the community and is carried out by members of the community, policy rarely manages more than a fleeting glance towards and a pat on the back for informal carers (Parker, 1985). Consequently carers inhabit a strange Alice-in-Wonderland place where they are the main providers of community care but never the subjects of policy that deals with the provision of care.

However, given the recent upsurge of interest in, and information about, informal carers Griffiths could not have been seen to continue this tradition of neglect. Indeed, throughout the report there are references to the need to support informal carers, to provide them with information about the availability of services and about 'how they can be helped with their onerous responsibilities' (para. 4.13), and to consult them as part of the joint planning processes (para. 6.15). Those who plan packages of care are, further, enjoined to take into account the views and wishes of informal carers, as well as those of the person to be cared for (para. 3.8.11).

Despite all this, Griffiths has not really managed to move away from a view of carers similar to that rehearsed in previous policy documents. Indeed the report contains a clear reiteration of the primacy of informal carers and networks assumed in, for example, the White Paper *'Growing Older'* (DHSS, 1981). Griffiths states:

> Publicly provided services constitute only a small part of the total care provided to people in need. Families, friends, neighbours and other local people provide the majority of care in response to needs which

> they are uniquely well placed to identify and respond to. This will continue to be the primary means by which people are enabled to live normal lives in community settings. *The proposals take as their starting point that this is as it should be, and that the first task of publicly provided services is to support and where possible strengthen these networks of carers.* (para. 3.2, our emphasis).

Thus the position of informal carers, and the 'rightness' of dependent people living in close relationships with those who provide them with intense practical and physical care, are taken to be largely unproblematic. So, for example, while a failure to support carers is acknowledged to diminish their quality of life and that of the people they care for it is 'also potentially inefficient as it can lead to less personally appropriate care being offered' (para. 4.3). In other words if the carer is not maintained within the role, social services authorities might have to take over some of the responsibility; if they do, this is an inappropriate use of their resources.

That Griffiths does not have in mind any wholesale relief of the burden carried by informal carers is given its clearest articulation in paragraph 6.5 where he outlines what social services authorities might do after carrying out their assessment of the dependent person's needs:

> The social services authority must decide then what action to take itself. *At the lowest level, support for informal care may be all that is needed.* At the other extreme, multiple services may have to be arranged (our emphasis).

The obvious implication is that informal carers are a substitute for the provision of multiple services.

Of course we should not really be surprised that the Griffiths Report has been unable to break away from the idea of informal carers as a substitute for service provision. In a cost-neutral exercise it is clearly impossible even to start talking about opening the 'Pandora's box' of carers' service requirements. Thus the report risks the occasional acknowledgement of carers but for the most part regards them as an unquestioned part of the 'given world within which community care will take place' (Twigg, 1988). Considerably greater rights to assessment and support for carers is given in the Disabled Persons (Services, Consultation and Representation) Act 1986 currently in the early stages of implementation.

Relationships between central and local government

At the heart of Griffiths' proposals lies a paradox – the proposal that a Government suspicious of, and intent on curbing, the autonomy of local authorities should assign to the same authorities a pivotal role in the delivery of community care, together with freedom to define their own priorities and 'sufficient' resources to meet their objectives.

His resolution of this paradox – the douceur for central government – lies in the price to be exacted for the enhanced role, which local authorities by and large welcome. As we have seen, this has two elements. Firstly, there will be a measure of control over local authority expenditure, via the formula adopted for the allocation of community care grants and the procedure for approving an authority's plans. The power to ratecap 'high spending' authorities will presumably also remain. Secondly, local authorities are to move from the direct provision of services to orchestrating service delivery. These measures, together with a stronger managerial style of operation – more forward planning, the use of option appraisal and cost effectiveness techniques, the use of performance indicators and the development of better management information systems – promise a transformation. Operating thus, it is implied, local authorities would fit more closely with the present Government's idea of how they ought to behave, and hence pose less of a threat.

It is an adroit manoeuvre. We do not yet know at the time of writing, in October 1988, whether central government is persuaded; the local authorities, however, appear willing to enter into negotiation. It is easy to understand why, after a long period of difficulty and denigration, they should welcome a clearer, more authoritative, role and the possibility of a more strategic mode of operation.

Nevertheless doubts remain at two levels: about whether the strategy proposed for reconciling central and local government interests would actually work; and about the consequences of the new role proposed for local authorities.

Would the strategy work? Griffiths strongly believes that community care plans must reflect local, democratically determined, priorities.

> If community care means anything, it is that responsibility is placed as near to the individual and his (sic) carers as possible...where priorities between different groups may differ widely according to local needs, the right and indeed obligation to determine that should be as local as possible and with the locally elected authority. It cannot be managed in detail from Whitehall, but it has to be managed (p viii, para.30).

The tension between this belief and his proposed use of financial control by central government is very strong, as the local authority associations recognise. Griffiths acknowledges the anxiety, but holds that the degree of control proposed need not be a stumbling block:

> The control is actually intended to be a minimum consistent with there being any national policy in this area...(p viii, para.29).
> The move to specific grant is important. It should be seen as liberating to local authorities to have more certainty. It will provide an instrument of central control but it should not be seen as an instrument of constraint (p viii, para.31).

Nevertheless the potential is there, and the creation of specific grant a hostage to fortune. On the credit side it establishes community care as a distinct area of policy, protecting resources for groups who have in the past lost out. Against this it opens the way, for the first time, for direct central government control of expenditure on social services.

It is difficult, given the history of the last ten years, to believe that disputes will not arise, not least given the inevitably political dimension of deciding local priorities and drawing up expenditure plans. What will happen when, for example, the community care plan submitted by a labour-controlled local authority is vetoed because it shows insufficient use of private sector provision? Or, again, how will community care services be affected if a local authority is rate-capped?

The fears are two-fold. Firstly that, pace Griffiths, central government will significantly reduce local authorities' freedom to define their own priorities – and provoke political confrontation. Secondly, that local authorities will find themselves manoeuvred into responsibility for community care but starved of resources to deliver the 'appropriate' service the report promises. Griffiths does not adequately address these fears. Why is this?

The charitable view is that his rationalist-managerialist approach to policy making has simply led him to underestimate the importance of politics in this domain – to forget that community care is only one policy goal among many, and secondary to the present Government's objective of controlling public expenditure. After all, nothing in his dealings with health policy will have prepared him for dealing with party politics and elected authorities. Conspiracy theory, on the other hand, would have him actively colluding in the present Government's assault on local democracy by further promoting what Walker describes as its 'twin-track policy of decentralising administration and operations while centralising control over resources' (Walker, 1988a). On balance excessive rationality seems the more likely explanation. It remains possible, nevertheless, that the managerialist approach and structures he proposes for social services authorities would, if adopted, reduce the role of elected members in the formulation of policy, and ultimately weaken the influence of local people on community care in their area.

Local authorities' new 'enabling' role also warrants more scrutiny than it has so far received. In general the concerns authorities themselves have expressed relate to the practicalities of the new role, rather than the role itself: the administrative structures they will need to develop for assessing needs and organising services; how these relate to obligations like child care; the role of case-manager and the levels to which budgets would be devolved; training needs, especially for new management roles; mechanisms for constructing community care plans and involving health and housing authorities; relations with the private and voluntary sector; and, perpetually, the question of finance.

Questions less often tackled are what is to happen to publicly provided services – what, in the jargon of the moment, will be their market share? What principles will guide the decision and what will be its consequences? The concept of welfare pluralism is not itself new: social services have always been provided by a multiplicity of agencies, most of them outside the formal system. What is relatively new is the proposal to reduce dramatically the volume of services provided by social services authorities, replacing them with services provided by the private and voluntary sectors. This proposal predates Griffiths by several years. Reducing the volume of publicly provided services has been high on the present Government's agenda for some time, while support for mixed economies of care can be found at all points on the political spectrum.

The arguments for and against welfare pluralism and the residualisation of public services have been rehearsed at length elsewhere (see, for example LeGrand and Robinson, 1984; Klein and Day, 1987; Walker, 1988a, b). This debate is confounded by large, and usually unacknowledged, elements of personal and political bias on both sides. It does, nevertheless, generate questions about mixed economies of welfare which need to be addressed seriously in the context of the radical changes proposed by Griffiths: the difficulty, for example, of matching service provision with need, where the quest for profit may direct private agencies away from poorer areas or difficult client groups leaving these to be picked up by public services; the possible creation, thereby, of residual and stigmatising services for people or areas with less money or more intractable problems; the demoralising effect of working in such services; the absence of public accountability and democratic control in the private sector; the difficulty of facilitating access by members of the public to private facilities, or of fostering a sense of public responsibility for the services they provide with public money.

These are questions about equity and reliability, access and coverage, quality and quality control, about the values that attach to public services, whether provided or merely financed by society at large. They reflect anxieties that increasing the role of the private sector will widen, rather than reduce, social and geographical divisions. Neither the anxieties, nor indeed the existence of a debate, is acknowledged by Griffiths where the case for a more mixed economy of social care goes by default.

There is, of course, no logical reason why adequate regulation should not solve many of these anxieties. The problem is, however, that the regulation of both public and private services in Britain is widely acknowledged to be in a rudimentary state of development at present (see, for example Klein and Day, 1987; Hunter and Judge, 1988; Walker, 1988a). Moreover the present Government's hostility to the regulation and control of private enterprise may actively impede the development of more effective regulation. Hence deciding the public sector's market share of community care services may be more difficult and more politically contentious than Griffiths acknowledges.

Conclusion

Viewed as a strategy for improving the organisation and delivery of community care services – of creating, in Griffiths' own words 'a better chance than exists now of providing the proper help for those in need of community care' – Griffiths' proposals have much to recommend them. Most of the principles on which the report is based are unexceptionable. There is obvious sense in avoiding the chaos of administrative restructuring and placing overall responsibility with social services authorities. Identifying these as the single gateway to all forms of publicly financed residential care again seems sensible.

Anxieties inevitably remain about implementation and, crucially, about the willingness of Government to accept the proposals as a whole rather than piecemeal. At the time of writing no decision had been made. The signs were, however, that the move to specific grant was proving a major stumbling block. On balance, as we note in the introduction to this article, the prevailing judgment on Griffiths remains positive.

We have argued in this article that a critical reading of the report and the assumptions on which it is based nevertheless prompt substantial reservations. What should we make of the fact that consumer choice might be reduced rather than increased if the report were implemented as proposed? Do we mind that informal carers would at best be little better off than at present? Is rationalising the delivery of community care services a reasonable price to pay for a possible reduction in local democratic control of services, whether arising from central government control or the creation of managerialism in social services authorities. (This last is no chimera. Democratic control over local health services is virtually non-existent; the performance indicators used by NHS general managers take little account of local or consumer views; the current review of the NHS is completely uninformed by local preferences). Finally, are we prepared to live with the increased social and territorial inequity that might result from pressures to direct the poorest clients to the cheapest acceptable services?

The important point to make here is that these are possibilities, not inevitabilities. It is possible to envisage a much more optimistic scenario with, for example, the minimum of control by central government, full participation by local councillors and increased consideration of the preferences of clients and carers. If accepted in principle Griffiths' proposals would need to be worked out in detail. At this stage local authorities could exercise considerable influence on central government. At the local level pressure could be brought to bear on how social services authorities interpreted their own brief.

The purpose of this article's, at times negative, analysis has not been to dismiss Griffiths' proposals out of hand. On balance (one of the authors being more optimistic than the other) we believe they have the potential dramatically to improve the delivery of community care. Achieving that potential will, however, depend on confronting the kinds of issue discussed here, as well as the more immediate problems of implementation.

References

Audit Commission (1986) *Making a reality of community care.* HMSO.

Bradshaw, J (1988) Financing private care for the elderly. In *Social security and community care.* Baldwin, S, Parker, G and Walker, R (eds) Avebury.

Bradshaw, J and Gibbs, I (1988) *Public support for private residential care.* Avebury.

Davies, B and Challis, D (1986) *Matching resources to needs in community care*. Gower.
DHSS (1969) *Report of the committee of enquiry into allegations of ill-treatment and other irregularities at Ely Hospital Cardiff*. Cmnd 3785, HMSO.
DHSS (1971) *Report of the Farleigh Hospital committee of enquiry*. Cmnd 4556, HMSO.
DHSS, (1974) *Report of the committee of enquiry into South Ockendon Hospital*. HMSO.
DHSS (1977) *Report of the committee of enquiry into Normansfield Hospital*. Cmnd 7357, HMSO.
DHSS (1981) *Growing Older*. Cmnd 8173, HMSO.
DHSS (1987) *Public support for residential care, Report of a Joint Central and Local Government Working Party*. (Chairman Mrs Firth) HMSO.
Etherington, S (1988) Taking the Griffiths lead on training. *Social Services Insight* **3**(14): 6.
Griffiths, R (1988a) *Community care: agenda for action. A report to the Secretary of State for Social Services. HMSO.*
Griffiths, R (1988b) Community care: agenda for action. Speech to the Association of County Councils, 9 May 1988.
Hardingham, S and Morris, B (1988) Reactions to Griffiths. *Social Services Insight*. **3**(11): 4–5.
Henwood, M (1986) Community care: policy, practice and prognosis. In Brenton, M and Ungerson, C (eds) *The Year Book of Social Policy in Britain 1985–6*. Routledge and Kegan Paul.
Henwood, M and Wistow, G (1988) Making a reality of care in the community – really! *Social Services Insight* **3**(13): 6–7.
Hospital plan for England and Wales. (1962) Cmnd 1604, HMSO.
House of Commons Committee on public accounts (1988) *Twenty-sixth report, Community care developments*. HMSO.
House of Commons Social Services Committee (1984) *First report: Griffiths NHS management enquiry report*. HMSO.
House of Commons Social Services Committee (1985) *Second report: Community care with special reference to adult mentally ill and mentally handicapped people*. HMSO.
Hunter, D J and Judge, K (1988) *Griffiths and community care: meeting the challenge*. King's Fund Institute.
Klein, R and Day, P (1987) The business of welfare. *New Society*. **80**(1277): 11–13.
Legrand, J and Robinson, R (1984) *Privatisation and the welfare state*. George Allen and Unwin.
Mitchell, A (1988) Griffiths: will this be the gateway to privatisation? *Community Care*. 7 April 1988:6.
National Audit Office (1987) *Community care developments*. HMSO.
Oldman, C (1988) More than bricks and mortar. *Housing*. **24**(5): 13–15.
Parker, G (1985) *With due care and attention*. Family Policy Studies Centre.
Pollitt, C (1988) Bringing consumers into performance measurement: concepts, consequences and constraints. *Policy and Politics*. **16**(2): 77–87.

Report of the Royal Commission on mental illness and mental deficiency. (1957) Cmnd 169, HMSO.

Scull, A (1984) *Decarceration: community treatment and the deviant – a radical view* (2nd ed). Polity Press, in association with Basil Blackwell.

Titmuss, R (1963) Community care: fact or fiction. In Freeman, H and Farndale, J (eds) *Trends in the mental health services*. Pergamon Press.

Twigg, J (1988) Social security, community care and the Griffiths Report: reflections on a debate. In Baldwin, S, Parker, G and Walker, R (eds) *Social Security and Community Care*. Avebury.

Walker, A (1988a) Tendering care. *New Society* **83**(i308): 18–19.

Walker, A (1988b) A state of confusion. *Community Care*. 3 March: 26–7.

Westland, P (1988) A double-edged weapon. *Community Care*. 31 March: 8.

10 Not her own income: the reform of the taxation of marriage

Andrew Dilnot

Introduction

Reform of the taxation of marriage has been on the agenda for well over a decade, but successive governments have found it much more difficult to introduce change than to talk about it. The Thatcher Government first produced a Green Paper on the subject in 1980 when Sir Geoffrey Howe was Chancellor. This was followed by a fairly vigorous debate, but no action. Nigel Lawson returned to the subject in his 1985 Budget speech, promising a Green Paper, and declaring himself to be in favour of a particular reform, transferable tax allowances. A Green Paper was published on Budget Day 1986, which set out the Government's arguments in favour of trasferable allowances. Unfortunately for the Government, the Green Paper was greeted by a good deal of criticism, and relatively little support. No action was taken in the 1987 Budget.

The question of the appropriate tax treatment of married couples continued to be an important subject for political debate. Both major opposition parties in the 1987 election campaign opposed the suggestion of a move to transferable allowances, preferring a shift to fully independent taxation. The Conservative Government said rather little about the taxation of marriage during its campaign. Action finally came in the 1988 Budget, in a reform which few had expected. Individuals were to be taxed independently, but a new married couple's allowance was to be introduced, which would leave married couples with the same total allowances as at present. The proposals were not fully understood by those commenting immediately after the Budget, and the debate since then has been rather thin. This perhaps has much to do with the fact that the reform will not be introduced until 1990. This lag is inevitable given the requirement for new legislation. However, if the experience of the social security reforms is any guide , we may see a revival of interest when the reform is implemented. By then, any adjustment to the scheme may be difficult to achieve for purely practical reasons.

This article aims to set out the problem with the current system, analyse some of the proposals made in the 1980s for reform, and then look in more detail at the changes announced in the 1988 Budget, which take effect in 1990. The next section describes the current system and some of its perceived problems. The following section examines the 1980 Green Paper, responses to it, and then the 1986 Green Paper and its reception. In the following section the 1988 Budget proposals are set out, and in the final section these proposals assessed. The conclusion reached is that while the 1988 reforms broadly achieve their stated aims, they fail even to tackle the worst problem identified in the preceding decade, that of the distribution of tax allowances amongst different types of tax unit.

The current system

The structure of personal tax allowances in the UK lacks any coherent rationale. Table 10.1 illustrates the allowances available to a number of different types of family unit. A single person receives an annual tax free allowance of £2,605, which can be used to offset any form of income, either earned or unearned. A 'traditional' married single earner couple, where only the husband works, receives an allowance, the married man's allowance, of £4,095, 1.57 times as large as that of the single person. A married two-earner couple receives a total of £6, 700, comprised of the married man's allowance (MMA) of £4,095 and the wife's earned income allowance (WEA) of £2,605, the same level as the single allowance. An unmarried couple where only one of the couple works receives merely one single allowance of £3,605. A two earner unmarried couple receives total allowances of £5,210, since each receives a single allowance.

There have been a number of criticisms of this structure of allowances. Perhaps the most frequently cited is the generous treatment of married two earner couples as compared with that of married single earner couples. A single earner couple receives only 1.57 times the single allowance, while a two earner couple receives 2.57 times the single allowance. The point is made that many families are least well off when the wife gives up work to look after children, since at that time one income is lost, while necessary expenditure rises. The tax system becomes less generous at precisely the point when the family may be least able to cope.

Table 10.1 Income tax allowances under current system

	£ pa	ratio to single
Single person	2605	1
Single earner couple married	4095	1.57
Two earner couple married	6700	2.57
Single earner couple unmarried	2605	1
Two earner couple unmarried	5210	2

Source: *The reform of personal taxation*, Cmnd 9756.

A second criticism is the generous treatment of marriage. Both single earner and two earner married couples receive 0.57 times the single allowance more than their unmarried counterparts. This 0.57 of a single allowance is the difference between the married man's allowance and the single allowance. Critics suggest that tax inducements to marriage are an inappropriate form of government action. This criticism is related to another: the existence of the MMA itself, and the attitudes it enshrines. Section 37 of the Income and Corporation Taxes (ICTA) 1970 states that 'A woman's income chargeable to tax shall . . . be deemed for income tax purposes to be (her husband's) income and not to be her income'. Even if it is appropriate for the state to encourage marriage it is difficult to defend the continuation of a view of women as their husband's chattels.

Although the great bulk of couples are better off married than they would be unmarried, a small minority face financial disincentives to marriage. Most of these disincentives result from the aggregation of income and of availability of tax reliefs.

Since the incomes of husband and wife are summed for tax purposes, the higher rates of income tax are more likely to affect a two income married couple than a similar unmarried couple. In 1988/89 the basic rate band stretches from taxable income of zero to £19,200. Thus very few single people pay tax at higher rates, while the joint income of two people is much more likely to exceed this limit. If this is the case, the couple can elect to be taxed separately, in which case they forego the MMA, with the husband receiving a single allowance and the wife a WEA, and both able to have £19,200 of taxable income before being subject to higher rates of tax. This is only of assistance if the wife has earned income, since all investment income is treated as the husband's regardless of whether the couple opts for separate taxation. The automatic aggregation of investment income avoids the possibility of tax bills being reduced by reallocation of the ownership of income bearing assets, but penalises couples where the woman had investment income of her own before marriage, against which she could set her single allowance, but which is, after marriage, taxed at her husband's marginal income tax rate.

Further potential disincentives to marriage are caused by the capital gains tax regime and the treatment of mortgage interest. The capital gains of a married couple are aggregated in the same way as investment income, and only one CGT allowance, of £5,000 given. If the couple were unmarried, each would be entitled to a £5,000 allowance for CGT. The disincentive to marriage from mortgage interest relief largely disappeared in August 1988. Until then a married couple was allowed mortgage interest relief on a single mortgage of up to £30,000, while each of an unmarried couple was allowed relief on such a mortgage. From August 1988, relief will be limited to one £30,000 mortgage per property. Thus the only disincentive will occur for couples with two properties; unmarried couples will still be able to claim relief on a £30,000 mortgage each while married couples will be restricted to only one such slice of relief.

Table 10.2 Personal allowances in other countries

	Single: single earner couple	Single: two earner couple
United Kingdom	1:1.57	1:2.57
Australia	1:1.72	1:2
Canada	1:1.87	1:2
Denmark	1:2	1:2
France	1:2	1:2
Germany	1:2	1:2
Ireland	1:2	1:2
New Zealand	1:1	1:1
Sweden	1:1	1:2
USA	1:1.6	1:1.6 (2.5 max)

Source: *The reform of personal taxaxtion*, Cmnd 9765.

Before moving on to discuss possible reforms, it is perhaps worth reproducing a table from the government's 1986 Green Paper 'The reform of personal taxation'. Table 10.2 emphasises the generosity of the treatment of two earner couples relative to that of single people. It is indeed difficult to construct any argument which suggests that a two earner married couple should be treated more than twice as generously as a single person. No other country in the table does so, and the Green Paper proposed a reform which would bring the UK into line. The relative treatment of single people and single earner couples is more variable, and the UK treatment, although less favourable to the single earner couple than many lies in the middle of the range of relativities in the countries shown, rather than at the extremes.

The road to reform

Pressure for change in the method of taxing families has been mounting for more than a decade, since the Labour Government raised the issues for discussions in the mid-1970s. The first Thatcher Government produced a Green Paper *The taxation of husband and wife* (Cmnd 8093) in 1980, setting out its views on possible reform. The starting point of the 1980 Green Paper was four main criteria desirable in a tax code: simplicity, privacy, sex equality, and fairness. Unfortunately, while most people would agree that these characteristics are desirable in any tax system, or indeed any part of it, they are nowhere near sufficient to define the appropriate system of taxing husbands and wives. The problem is that these four criteria do not provide a way of choosing between the conflicting objectives of treating all people in the same way regardless of sex or marital status, and the desire to recognise the financial implications and reponsibilities of marriage. Put more simply, some wish to treat married and unmarried couples in the same way, some wish to treat single earner and two earner married couples in the same way. These two desires conflict. This tension was clear in the responses to the 1980 Green Paper, which fell broadly into two camps. One group advocated a system of wholly independent taxation, thus treating all individuals, married or unmarried, male or female, in the same way. The other group advocated transferable allowances, thus treating the couple as the tax unit, treating single and two earner married couples identically, and thus discriminating against unmarried couples. The most striking feature of the responses to the Green Paper (see Kay and Sandler, 1982) was their agreement that the current system was wrong, and in particular that the MMA should be abolished. The debate was over what should replace it. The contrast with the view expressed in the Green Paper itself, which suggests that '. . . the surprise, to most who study the matter, lies in discovering how difficult it is to find a better system than that we have today' (piii), is a significant one.

As noted above, this sentiment was not shared by most who responded to the Green Paper, although there was disagreement as to whether the new system should be one of transferable allowances or of completely independent taxation.

Transferable allowances

The principle of tax allowances which are transferable between husband and wife won widespread support. The idea is that every adult would receive the same allowance, be they married or single, male or female. If a married person was unable to use all of his or her allowance, any unused part could be transferred to his or her spouse. A system of transferable allowances treats husband and wife as essentially a single unit for tax purposes. Table 10.3 illustrates the impact such a scheme would have on the distribution of tax allowances. Single people would be unaffected, since they continue to recieve a single allowance.

Table 10.3 Alternative reforms relative to single allowance

	Current	Transferable	Independent
Single person	1	1	1
Single earner couple married	1.6	2	1
Two earner couple married	2.6	2	2
Single earner couple unmarried	1	1	1
Two earner couple unmarried	2	2	2

The principal beneficiaries of such a scheme are single earner married couples. Although the MMA has been replaced by a uniform single allowance, this is more than compensated for by the ability of the non-earning spouse to transfer his or her allowance to the earner. Thus the total allowances of a single earner and two earner married couple are the same. One result of this is that two earner married couples lose, since the loss of the excess of the MMA over the single allowance is not compensated for by any other change. Unmarried couples are unaffected by such a reform, since transferability would only be allowed within marriage. Such a scheme would be roughly revenue neutral, since the gains to single earner married couples are offset by losses to two earner married couples.

A number of criticisms can be made of the idea of transferable allowances. First such a system provides a disincentive for married women to work. At present, a woman who has been out of the labour force, perhaps looking after children, can re-enter the labour market and earn up to the WEA of £2,605 pa without paying any income tax. Under a system of transferable allowances, while out of the labour market her allowance would have been transferred to her husband. On returning to work, she could claim her allowance, thus reducing her husbands net income by some £650, or pay tax on every pound she earns (see Symons and Walker, 1986).

A second criticism is that such a scheme, while supporting families where one adult is forced to stay at home to look after children, also supports couples, one member of which stays at home through choice rather than any caring responsibilities. This characteristic of the reform is thus not very well targetted on those most in need.

A third potential problem is the administration of such a scheme. Keeping track of the current 'ownership' of transferred allowances would present a substantial challenge given the now frequent entry to and exit from the labour market of married women. The Green Paper commented that full transferability would be administratively costly and would have 'serious administrative implications . . . requiring thousands of extra staff' (para. 74).

Finally, some opposed the suggestion of transferable allowances on the basis that such a system continues to be based on marriage as the social norm, an assumption which such critics argue is no longer warranted.

Independent taxation and increased benefits

Although touched on only briefly by the 1980 Green Paper, independent taxation, augmented by inceases in benefit levels for such benefits as child benefit was put forward by the majority of respondents as the correct structural reform. Each adult would receive the same tax allowance, just as under a system of transferable allowances. However, the individual would not be allowed to transfer any unused element of his or her allowance to any other person. The consequences of such a scheme are illustrated in the third column of Table 10.3. As now, the single person receives a single allowance. A single earner couple likewise only a single allowance, since the allowance of the non-earner is worthless. Two earner couples receive two allowances. Unmarried couples receive precisely the same treatment as married couples. No type of family has gained, and married couples have lost the excess of the MMA over the SA. This would save the Government some £4 to £5 billion. Those in favour of this route suggested that this money should be spent on increasing benefits for carers, such as child benefit and attendance/disability benefits. This would have the effect of providing support for families with dependants via the benefit system rather than the tax system. Single earner couples, be they married or unmarried would thus gain if they were entitled to the increased benefits and lose if they were not.

Opponents of such a change objected that while it was possible to increase the obvious benefits such as child benfit and attendance allowance, the diversity of need was in fact very large and unlikely to be covered adequately by the benefit system. Transferable allowances, by giving support to all single earner married couples would give support regardless of the precise nature of care exercised by the non-earning member of the couple.

A second perceived problem with this scheme was that the perceived level of both taxation and public expenditure would rise, since tax allowances would be lower and benefit levels higher than with a system of transferable allowances. This 'problem' is generated by the difference in treatment of tax expenditures in the form of tax allowances, and direct expenditures in the form of benefits. The former are 'good' because they reduce the burden of taxation, the latter are 'bad' because they increase it. Such at least was the criticism.

A final criticism was that a system of individual taxation would fail to recognise marriage at all. Although some commentators saw this as an advantage, others suggested that the tax system should encourage marriage, particularly as a stable environment in which to bring up children.

Two more general problems were common to both suggested reforms. The first was concerned with the appropriate treatment of investment income. Any treatment based on aggregation of investment income will penalise marriage for those with investment income. Any treatment based on individual taxation will be expensive, since many women whose investment income is at present taxed as their husband's income would be able to offset their allowance against it. Estimates of around £500 million have been made of the potential cost. In addition, individual taxation would provide an incentive for tax avoidance through the reallocation of income bearing assets within the couple to the member with the lowest marginal tax rate. Any such reallocation would increase the revenue cost of such a scheme.

The second problem area is the tax treatment of the elderly. At present there are age allowances for those 65 years and over, both married and single. If one member of a couple is 65 years at present the married age allowance is given to the 'head'. Under either the transferable or independent taxation proposals the obvious treatment would be to give an enhanced allowance only to those actually 65 years or over themselves. This would imply losses for a number of households. Perhaps more seriously, under the independent taxation with increased benefits route, the cost of compensating pensioners for the abolition of the MMA would be very substantial. The problems associated with both investments, income and the elderly are serious, but not such as to render change impossible. The point this brief discussion aimed to make is that these issues cannot be ignored.

Although the debate continued outside government after the publication of the 1980 Green Paper, there was no sign of further activity within government for some years. The lack of any sort of consensus in response to the Green Paper seemed to have taken the momentum out of the drive to reform. All this changed on Budget Day 1985 when Mr Lawson, the then Chancellor of the Exchequer, announced in his Budget speech that he proposed 'to issue a Green Paper later this year on the reform of personal income tax'. In fact, the Green Paper was published in March 1986, on the following Budget Day; clearly Mr Lawson thinks in financial rather than calendar year. The general content of the Green Paper (Cmnd 9756) was no surprise, since Mr Lawson described in his 1985 Budget speech a system of transferable allowances, which he said would be set out in detail in the Green Paper. The complete lack of serious consideration of alternatives was more surprising.

Mr Lawson's hope had been that 'it would be possible to legislate in 1987 and have a system on those lines in place by the end of the decade' (1985 Budget speech). That was not to be. The Green Paper received an unfriendly reception from a wide range of groups, including some of the government's traditional supporters. The problems outlined above of disincentives to work for wives, administrative cost, and non-neutrality to marriage were all underlined. An additional difficulty, that of cost, also arose. The government was not prepared to impose losses on any major group. Since at present two earner couples receive a total of 2.6 times the single allowance, this meant setting the new transferable single allowance at 1.3 times the current single allowance. This protects two earner married couples, but means an increase from 1 to 1.3 SAs for single people, and 1.6 to 2.6 SAs for single earner married couples. The cost of these gains was some £4.5 billion, a sum of money which many suggested could be better spent elsewhere.

The response to the Green Paper was sufficient to discourage the Government from proceeding with their outlined reform, so nothing happened in the 1987 Budget, or indeed during 1987. Nonetheless, the public debate continued, and the government began to look for a 'half-way house'. The obvious candidate for such a half-way house was a system of partially transferable allowances (see Stark, 1988). Under such a system each adult would continue to receive the same allowance, and some fraction of it would be transferable to a spouse if unused by the original recipient. This type of scheme had a number of advantages over one of full transferability. First, it could be cheaper. One such scheme would set the single allowance at 1.3 times the current SA, and allow 0.3 to be transferred. Single people would gain, single earner couples would be unaffected, and two earner couples would be unaffected. A second advantage was administrative. Since all married women would retain a part of their allowance, the tax system would not need to know about any low paid part-time work. This advantage related to a third, that problems of incentives would be less severe, given that married women would be able to earn up to the level of the non-transferable part of their allowance without paying any tax. Finally, such a scheme would be flexible. By setting the whole of the allowance to be transferable, full transferability could be achieved, by setting the transferable element to zero, independent taxation is achieved. The main objection to such a reform was that it failed to do anything to help single earner married couples, precisely the group the Chancellor was most concerned about, while giving money to single people. It seemed a half-way house with little to recommend it except that it was a way of doing something.

The 1988 Budget proposals

The Chancellor announced in the 1988 Budget speech a reform of the system of taxing married couples which will be legislated for this year, and introduced in the tax year 1990/91. Perhaps predictably, the measures announced were unlike anything which had previously received much attention. The most important element in the package was the introduction of a system of independent taxation of all income, including that from investments. Every adult will receive the same allowance and be taxed separately on his or her total income. This sounds rather like the independent taxation option outlined above. But the Chancellor did not stop there. The second vital element is a new allowance, called the married couples allowance (MCA). The MCA is the first allowance to be given to or for something other than an individual. The MCA has been set equal to the difference between the MMA and the SA. In the first instance, the MCA will be given to the husband, but where the husband cannot make full use of it, it can be transferred to his wife. The most significant fact about the reform is that for almost everybody the practical effect will be nil. Table 10.4 compares the structure of allowances under the present system with that proposed. Single people are unaffected, since they receive a single allowance before and after. Single earner married couples are unaffected, since the loss of the excess of the MMA over the SA is compensated for by the addition of the MCA. The same is true for two earner married couples. Unmarried couples are unaffected since they receive neither the MMA nor the MCA.

Table 10.4 The current and proposed systems compared: allowances relative to SA

	Current	Transferable
Single person	1(SA)	1 (SA)
Single earner couple married	1.6 (MMA)	1.6 (SA + MCA)
Two earner couple married	2.6 (MMA + WEA)	2.6 (SA + SA + MCA)
Single earner couple unmarried	1 (SA)	1 (SA)
Two earner couple unmarried	2 (SA + SA)	2 (SA + SA)

In addition to the changes in the structure of allowances the Chancellor announced futher changes aimed at removing tax penalties to marriage. From 1st August 1988 mortgage interest relief will be limited to £30,000 per dwelling rather than per person. This change brings the tax treatment of housing for cohabiting into line with that for married couples. Also before the budget, a cohabiting couple with two or more children could each claim the additional personal allowance intended for single parents. This will not be the case from April 1989. Finally, capital gains tax becomes individual based in 1990, with each individual having a CGT allowance of £5,000 pa.

Distributional consequences

The reform has been designed to remove as much as possible of the sexual discrimination and discrimination against marriage inherent in the current system, while changing as little as possible. Nonetheless, three groups seem likely to gain, and two to lose.

The first group to gain are those couples in which the wife has some unearned income, which is at present taxed automatically at her husband's marginal tax rate. Under the new system, the wife will be able to use her own allowance against this income, and thus the couple may pay less tax.

A second group to gain are relatively well paid two earner married couples currently liable for higher tax rate. At present such couples can opt to be taxed separately on their earnings, thus reducing higher rate tax liability, but forego the excess of the MMA over the SA when they do so. Under the new system *all* married couples will be taxed separately *and* receive the MCA. In the first instance the MCA will go to the husband.

A third group of gainers are pensioner couples, because the rules surrounding the age allowance are to be more generous. While at present a married pensioner couple receives the married age allowance, in future both husband and wife will receive the equivalent of a single person's age allowance. The husband also receives a higher MCA equal to the difference between this and the old married age allowance.

The main losers are cohabiting couples and others who will no longer be able to pool their entitlements to £30,000 of tax relieved mortgage borrowing to buy a share in a single property. They are not losers in the usual sense, in that those who are sharing or who made arrangements to buy a shared property before August 1988, will continue to enjoy full interest relief. But from August it will be harder for first-time buyers to enter the housing market, although in due course the reduction in tax relief should lead to some relative reduction in the price of houses at the bottom end of the market.

A second group of losers, in the long term at least, are those couples where the wife is the principal or only earner. At present these 'bread-winner wives' receive both the MMA (because it is automatically set against the couple's total income) and the WEA (because she is a qualified working wife). By contrast a couple in which the husband is the only earner receives only the MMA. From 1990 the wife would receive an SA plus the MCA just as any other single earner couple. Transitional arrangements are promised to protect this group from cash losses.

Assessment of the reforms

The removal of most sexual discrimination from the system, and the ending of a number of minor disincentives to marriage are consistent with the objectives Mr Lawson set himself. But these were not the only or even perhaps the most important problems with the pre-1988 system. A more likely candidate for the greatest problem was and is the relative size of personal allowance given to different units. Table 10.2, taken from the 1986 Green Paper shows that the UK tax system was unique among the main developed countries in the favourable treatment it gave to two earner couples. It also contained a passage that is worth reproducing in full:

> The present structure of allowances, giving two-earner couples 2.6 times the single allowance, originated in the circumstances of war in 1942, when there was a need to give specific encouragement to married women to go out to work. Today, for most married women, it is the rule rather than the exception to be in paid employment and the system needs to be changed to remove discrimination against couples where only the husband is in paid employment. The present tax system bears hardest on couples at precisely the point when most of them can least afford it.

Certainly, the main criticism of the 1988 proposals is that they fail to tackle the relatively generous treatment of two earner couples. The 1986 Green Paper saw the relative treatment of single and two earner couples as the main problem. Although this may be true, since the point at which the first child is born is often a trough in life cycle income for a family, there are respectable arguments for treating a single earner couple less favourably than a two earner couple. At a given level of money income, a single earner couple will generally enjoy a higher standard of living because of the non-earning spouse's unpaid (and untaxed) work in the home.

However, it is very difficult to justify a system in which two earner married couples receive more allowances than two single people. Allowances are often justified in terms of the existence of dependants such as children or a non-working spouse. But many two earner couples, like many single people, have no dependants. In fact, there are strong arguments for providing two earner couples with lower allowances than two single people, because of the economies of scale in housing, heating, food, and so on, which are available to couples. Such an argument may be impractical, but emphasises the peculiarity of the current *and proposed* treatment of this group.

As well as failing to do anything about the generous treatment of two earner couples, the reform completely ignores the argument of those who were in favour of both transferable allowances and independent taxation with higher benefits, that those with dependants, especially single earner couples, need more support. These arguments were put particularly strongly in the Government's 1986 Green Paper. The reform as set out gives no extra support to single earner couples, the group specifically identified by the Government as needing help.

The proposals are little more than a minimum change method of removing the bulk of the sexual discrimination and (rare) tax disincentives to marriage of the old system. The new allowance, the MCA, is really the MMA under a new name. The MCA is just as favourable to marriage as the old MMA, but sounds less sexist.

Although the MCA has more attractive sounding name, and can be transferred between husband and wife, some element of discrimination between husband and wife remains. The default will be that the MCA goes to the husband. The argument for this is an administrative one put forward by the Inland Revenue. Given the Government's apparent view that married couples can be and should be seen as a single unit for most purposes, it is natural that the extra cost of a more flexible approach to allocating the MCA should be enough to deter them from such a route.

Nonetheless, this does mean that some elements of sexual discrimination remain.

Finally, it is worth commenting briefly on the change in arrangements for mortgage interest relief. That an unmarried couple could benefit from twice as much mortgage interest relief as an otherwise identical married couple was an obvious offence against horizontal equity. Mortgage interest relief is an undesirable element in tax system, and to a large extent simply increases the price of housing. However, it is important to note that it is not just unmarried couples who will be affected by the withdrawal of multiple mortgage interest relief. Many young single people join together to purchase property, especially in the south east of the country, since this is their only possible route into owner occupation.

Conclusions

Mr Lawson's 1989 reform proposals had two stated objectives: 'First to give married women the same privacy and independence in their tax affairs as everyone else. And second to bring to an end the ways in which the tax system can penalise marriage'. Given these objectives, it would be churlish to do other than congratulate Mr Lawson on a job pretty well done in the face of considerable difficulties.

However, as shown earlier in this article, these objectives do not correspond in full to the problems identified with the pre-1988 system, by Mr Lawson himself among others. The distribution of allowances between different units was, and still will be, anomalous in the UK, and the 1988 proposals will do little to improve this.

Notes

1 The phrase is originally Norman Lamont's, Financial Secretary to the Treasury (Lamont, 1987).

References

Kay, J A and Sandler, C (1982) The taxation of husband and wife: a view of the debate in the Green Paper. *Fiscal Studies* **3**(3).

Lamont, N (1987) Personal tax reforms postponed. *Financial Times* 19 March: 48.

Stark, G K (1988) Partially-transferable allowances *Fiscal Studies* **9** (4).

Symons, E and Walker, I (1986) The reform of personal taxation: a brief analysis. *Fiscal Studies* **7** (2)

11 Policing developments in the 1980s: An Overview

Michael Levi

Introduction

Law and order, particulary in the domain of 'public order' (or rather, dis-order!), has long been a significant theme in media and political debate (see, for example, Hall *et al*, 1978; Pearson, 1983; Norton, 1984; Vincent-Jones, 1986). Yet there is so much crime and so little success in its control that the goal of eliminating *all* crime risks rebounding upon those who advocate it, for there is a limit to the extent to which one can blame others for one's problems. Given the finite nature of policing recources in any society, there is thus a tension between a generalised 'authoritarian populism' which condemns all 'deviance' and a more pragmatic approach which sees prioritisation as inevitable. In this political (though not necessarily *party* political) process, appeals to 'public opinion' assume great significance. 'Public opinion' (and note the collective noun) is used to justify particular policing policies and manpower distributions; prosecution policies; and sentencing levels.

But what crimes are serious and how is this determined? All governments tend to lament the passage of some mythical golden age, and the Thatcher era has seen a consistent concern about 'crime in general' and successive waves of concern about particular crimes: 'soccer hooliganism', 'violent picketing', and 'violence on the streets' (but not wife-beating): 'the drugs menace': and, most recently, 'fraud in the City', 'child sexual abuse', and 'rural violence'. The Augean stables apparently occupy a rather large volume of space and although the great majority of recorded crimes (as well as those reported to but unrecorded by the police) are reported by victims or witnesses who employ their own initial seriousness sift, the police – with increasing Home Office central pressure (Weatheritt, 1986) – enjoy considerable autonomy in determining the relative priority attached to dealing with different forms of crime (and their other functions such as ' public order'). This indeed has been one point of criticism by those who argue that policing is *in*sufficiently tough on the perpetrators of racial attacks and violence against women (Maguire and Pointing, 1988).

Two generalisations may be made about this drift into the authoritarian populism of a law and order society:

1. With the possible exception of fraud in the City and child sexual abuse – which are hard to diagnose accurately without infringing respectively 'the right to do business' and 'parent's rights' – there seems to be no question of publicly tolerating any of these 'abuses' to any extent whatsoever.
2. The blame for 'crime' is located firmly in 'the permissive society', most particularly in 'the decline of the family', in pornography, and in the enterprise-sapping effects of the welfare state. All suggestions that unemployment and social despair may have anything to do with crime are firmly rebutted with the argument that in the 1930s there was plenty of unemployment, but very little crime.

   The apotheosis of this approach to criminogenesis is the 1985 Disraeli lecture given by the former Conservative party chair, Norman Tebbit. These views are shared to a considerable extent by the general public, though more strongly by the police; (see Jones and Levi, 1987). Sociologists and the Labour Party are blamed for shifting responsibility from self or the family to the state, thereby undermining moral fibre with their welfarism.

So much for criminogenesis. What about crimino-exodus? The Conservative solution to the crime problem is simple but broad ranging: on the one hand, we must give the police the tools they need to do the job and, despite the enormous cost, build more prisons to accommodate the results of the improvements in policing; on the other, we must transform social behaviour and social attitudes by enhancing discipline and social surveillance within the family and 'the community', to encourage that sense of worth that results only from reliance on self rather than on the state. The Conservatives appear to have digested Foucault (1977) on the importance of creating the disciplinary society. Criminal policy, then, is only a sub-set of social policies, and is designed to cope with the failures that inevitably must occur during the interregnum before self-regulation is established in all sectors of society.

What measures have been employed in this major transformational project? First, there have been major changes in legislation on police powers, whose ideological significance and projected practical effect are the subject of major controversy, particularly on the Left: compare Reiner (1985) and Jefferson (1986) with Baldwin (1985) and Scraton (1985, 1987). Second, there have been increases in police staffing levels and Home Office sponsored managerialist attempts to improve police use of (increasingly expensive) resources. Third, there has been ideological pressure on families to demonstrate greater responsibility for the conduct of their offspring. And fourth, there has been greater stress on crime prevention, both individual and collective, for 'the public' have to be encouraged to mobilise themselves (with police assistance) in the fight against crime.

This article maps out some of the important changes that have occurred in policing during the 1980s. It does not attempt to be comprehensive in coverage, for, given constraints of space, this would leave no room for commentary. However, one of the central questions in seeking to account for fluctuations in crime control policy is whether policy changes are driven (a) by changes in 'the crime rate' – numbers and/or seriousness of particular crimes (or of that more dangerous and heterogeneous notion 'crime') – and/or (b) by wider political imperatives such as the need to manage what seventeenth century English politicians referred to as 'the ungovernable people'. By contrast with more pragmatic focus on issues of police effectiveness characteristic of Home Office and 'Left realist' research (Kinsey, et al., 1986), much of the marxist (or perhaps more accurately, marxisant) task has been to 'demystify' criminal policy by revealing, or claiming to reveal, the hidden *motives* that lie behind the manipulation of the crime problem. (See for example, the classic study of social reaction to 'mugging' by Hall et al., 1978; the study of the artificial construction of crime statistics in Merseyside by Gill, 1987; and more general arguments about the proper way to view policing in Scraton, 1987.)

It is generally agreed that policing is one means by which modern capitalist states achieve control over the working class and *Lumpenproletariat,* though as Sparks (1980) has noted, its importance can be overstated compared with contract law. However, there remain heated debates over 'where the police are at' and where, if anywhere, policing should go, arising partly from differences in the political objectives of the academic antagonists (see Sim et al., 1987), and partly from their focusing on different aspects of what the police do. Many on the far Left concentrate their attentions on the policing of 'public order' and of political dissidents, including the gathering of what is claimed to be political intelligence (Campbell and Connor, 1986; Scraton, 1987); while others, including 'Left realists' associated with the Labour Party, neglect the policing of public order, stress in their work the reactive element of police responding to calls for assistance from the public and public concern about particular crimes, and criticise the police for not reflecting public sentiments adequately in the prioritisation of their tasks. Clearly, the police do both 'political' and 'ordinary' policing – assuming that there is any distinction – and although parts of 'the police' do collate information and carry out 'dirty tricks' against particular political target groups such as miners (Scraton and Thomas, 1985) and Irish Catholics believed to be associated with Republican paramilitaries (Stalker, 1987), much time is spent relatively aimlessly on general duties. Thus, a recent study of uniformed patrol work concludes:

> Those officers who were not assigned at parades to 'essential' postings . . . were by and large simply distributed to provide a uniformed presence over as many beats as possible. Guidance was seldom given about specific tasks to tackle . . . the majority of the instructions . . . during a shift arose from calls for service . . . time is presently available for directed patrol work . . . but ways and means of identifying productive activities for patrol officers lag far behind (Burrows and Lewis, 1988, pp37-45).

However, despite empirical data about police (in)effectiveness, there is some area of irreducible subjective interpretation in addressing questions about 'ordinary policing' such as whether (a) police action against 'muggers' is motivated 'principally' by a desire to justify repression against blacks or by a desire to help the victims of street robbery, and (b) police involvement in neighbourhood watch schemes is an attempt to reduce crime or a method of undercutting working-class self-help and self-determination. The answers depend upon whose accounts we wish to take as our explanatory baseline.

This article will largely side-step the theoretical argument about whether criminal policy is crime-driven or, 'in the last instance', 'capitalist need' driven. However in my view, except for those cases where one can actually show how issues were manipulated (Gill, 1987), a danger in the line taken by Hall et al. (1987) that the creation of a law and order society is a necessary adjunct to the crisis of capitalism is that it risks degenerating into mere *ex post facto* functionalism, in which the alleged benefits of particular policing practices for order maintenance are used to explain why those policies were adopted. There are three sorts of objection to this: first, it may be difficult to identify what 'capitalist interests' or even 'average capitalist interests' are; second, the link between 'capitalist interests' (however defined) and the relatively autonomous law enforcement agencies may be rather tenuous; and third, as self-styled 'Left realists' argue, the focus on the demystification of repression is politically bankrupt, and whatever the motivation of the powerful may be in promoting 'law'n order', the lives of 'ordinary people' and the class struggle are better off with soft than with hard repression and with less property and violent crime, for it is the poor who are the primary victims of crime (Lea and Young, 1984; Kinsey, Lea, and Young, 1986; Levi, 1987, ch 4; *Contemporary Crises,* 1987).

Changes in the law-in-books and the law-in-action relevant to this article may be divided into two basic sections:

1 changes in substantive and procedural legislation; and
2 changes in policing.

There will not be space to discuss all the developments in detail, but before outlining the trends, some data relevant to consideration of policing since 1979 are presented:

1 There has been an increase in recorded offences, from 2,377,000 in 1979 to 3,982,200 offences in 1987: a 68 % increase. Of these notifiable offences, 94 % were crimes against property and by volume (though not by value), over half recorded offences were theft, paticularly theft involving motor vehicles. Part of this rise is an artefact of police recording practices and of public reporting practices: the Home Office (1988) notes that in the period 1980 to 1985, household survey-measured burglaries rose by 5 % annually, whereas police-recorded burglaries rose by 11 % annually. (However, the discrepancy may mean that there has been a greater rise in serious and/or insured burglaries than in the uninsured ones which are less likely to be reported: Lewis and Mo, 1986.) There has also been a rise in recorded sexual offences, recent substantial increases in which have been attributed by the police and the Home Office – on what hard evidence is uncertain – not to real rises in assaults but to improvements in police recording and victim treatment practices, particularly in London (Metropolitan Police, 1987; Home Office, 1988). But whatever the decline in the 'dark figure' of unreported crime, it seems plausible that an increasing number of people (or the same number of people committing more offences) have turned to crime since 1979. This would be consistent with an economic marginalisation thesis that has become increasingly popular in explanations of female crime, male lower class crime, and even corporate crime (Box, 1983, 1987).

2 There has been an increase in the number of offences cleared up by the police (or stated by them to have been cleared up! see Gill, 1987), from 981,000 in 1979 to 1,229,427 in 1987: a more modest increase of 25 %. However, since 1979, the

clear-up rate (i.e. recorded crimes divided by numbers cleared up) has dropped from 41 % to 33 %, and this is often taken by critics to indicate that police effectiveness has gone down (Lea, Matthews, and Young, 1987).

3 Between May 1979 and March 1988, the number of police officers increased from 111,493 to 124,080: a rise of 11 %. The number of civillian staff also went up from 34, 630 to 41,800: a rise of 12 %. However, because of improvements in police pay, roughly linking it to inflation, the costs of policing have risen dramatically compared with these personnel increases. Police salaries went from £983 million in 1979 to £2,378 million in 1986–7: a rise of 47 % in real terms. In the same period, total expenditure on the police – including operational expenditure, buildings, equipment, etcetera – rose from £1,178 million to £3,163 million: an increase of 64 % in real terms. Between 1979 and 1987, Government spending on law and order has gone up dramatically, both in absolute terms and in relation to most other areas of Government spending.

The development of police powers

The 1980s have witnessed some major changes in legislation related to the powers of the police. Whereas the Left universally have treated the Police and Criminal Evidence Act 1984 (PACE) as part of a trend towards policing by coercion, the Home Office (1984, p15) claims that the Act balances powers and safeguards, and has the 'objective of encouraging effective policing with the consent and co-operation of society at large'. Under the Act, the police can require people to give their names and addresses (and detain them until they are satisfied that these are correct); stop-and-search powers were extended nationally to include the search for 'stolen or prohibited articles', levelling out disparate local provisions to permit everywhere the extreme powers prevailing formerly in London; powers of entry, search, and seizure are extended; powers of arrest, with or without warrant, were extended; arrested persons may be questioned for up to 96 hours before they are charged (though a magistrate's permission is required after 36 hours!); and fingerprints and intimate body samples may be taken from detained persons without their consent.

The Public Order Act 1986 strengthened the law against incitement to racial hatred, but also strengthened police powers to move pickets, mass assemblies, and marches to different routes, and organisers of marches now have to give six days' notice and a detailed route map. Powers of search outside fooball grounds were increased and, in response to The Convoy – 'hippies' seeking to participate in the summer solstice at Stonehenge – the police were given power to break up convoys of vehicles and to require trespassers to leave private property (Vincent-Jones, 1986). Moreover, the police were given the right to intervene where there was a risk of 'serious disruption to the life of a community', another ambiguous term giving them broad discretion. Further inroads into civil liberties may be pending, including the right to comment *adversely* to jurors if defendants exercise their right to silence, which is alleged to benefit principally sophisticated criminal defendants (McKenzie and Irving, 1988). Strong governmental pressure has been exerted in favour of 'members only' schemes for entry to football matches, and support given for local initiatives to require young people who wish to drink in pubs to carry proof of their age. Despite the political risks, it is even being contemplated that to assist the war on crime, all members of the public should be required to carry identity cards. (Checks could then be made on whether those stopped were registered for the community charge, producing a financial bonus, albeit by risking costly riots.)

On the other hand, certain aspects of police accountability have been increased. The Police and Criminal Evidence Act 1984 is accompanied by Codes of Practice which grant specific rights to citizens, violations of which are police disciplinary offences. The Codes require each stop and search to be recorded and to be justified by particular suspicion rather than by statistical probability judgments such as that young blacks are likely to be criminals. A specified police officer in each police station is designated as a custody officer, and is personally responsible for supervising prisoners and for adherence to rules governing interrogation, whatever the pressures from senior CID officers (Roddie, 1988). It is now rare for the police to deny access to a solicitor and PACE does appear to have changed police behaviour towards suspects (Maguire, 1988). Tape-recording of interviews is being introduced into police stations, to cut down on allegations of 'verbals' (i.e. manufactured unsigned admissions) and to save court time (and public expenditure on legal aid, which has escalated as the number of defendants brought to court has increased) when the defence disputes them. Field trials suggest that these objectives have been realised without inhibiting police greatly (Willis, Macleod, and Naish, 1988), though some might argue that any such increases in procedural 'fairness' are themselves objectionable since they serve to legitimate the rule of class law.

Empirical research is under way to examine the impact of these changes, but it has been argued elsewhere (Levi, 1985) that the majority who are not viewed as 'criminal types' by the police are likely to remain unaffected by them. As for those traditionally more at risk of police harassment – ethnic minorities, gay people,'political deviants', the young generally – the Police and Criminal Evidence Act 1984 and the Public Order Act 1986 may not make a great deal of difference, since the police used the informal ways and means act to deal with them before. This is a criticism of the Left perspective that these powers were needed to deal with the crisis of capitalism (Bridges and Bunyan, 1983; Scraton, 1985). Percy-Smith and Hillyard (1985) have noted that section 5 of the Public Order Act 1936 was used extensively to charge 62 % of the miners arrested during the 1984-5 miner's strike: 'what constituted "threatening, abusive, or insulting words and behaviour" appeared to be wholly a matter for discretion for the police who happened to be on duty at a particular picket line'. If the police were allowed to get away with their abuses before, why was new legislation needed? Certainly, it marks a symbolic change, and the statutes are framed in terms of police powers rather than citizen rights! But an unintended consequence is that the bureaucratic procedures and paperwork involved in implementing the legislation are a major drain on police manpower, and this alone may reduce the amount of aggravation given to groups seen by the police as a threat to their authority.

One major cosmetic change has been the requirement under section 106 of the Police and Criminal Evidence Act 1984 (PACE) to institute local consultation between police and 'community'. However, the nature and pace of local communication has been slow: police largely determine who the community representatives are and what is discussed at the meetings. Except where they use the occasion to defuse situations by 'happy talk', these are not (and were not intended to be) genuine accountability in the sense of control over the police (Morgan, 1988). Rather, they were a response to Lord Scarman's criticism that the cause of the Brixton riots of 1981 lay partly in police distancing themselves overmuch from 'the community' (Scarman, 1981). The Government has resisted all attempts to enhance the *local* accountability of the police, seeing this (not without justification) as a left-wing device for capturing control over policing policies. Thus, the Metropolitan Police report only to the Home Secretary, and not to any local political reepresentatives. In force areas outside London, where local politicians and magistrates form 'police committees', successive Home Secretaries have upheld the autonomy of the 43 chief constables to determine without interference from the committees 'operational matters', defined so widely as to include the refusal of the Chief Constable of Greater Manchester to abandon his police band – some of the highest-paid musicians in Britain! – despite local political protests that dealing with the burgeoning crime rate was a more important task for the police.

The attacks upon the efforts of police authorities to dictate aspects of policing in their areas have been upheld by the courts, who generally have supported the independence of chief constables (Uglow, 1988, pp 121-2). A case of particular interest here is *R v. Secretary of State for the Home Department, ex parte Northumbria Police Authority* (1988) 2 WLR 590. The Court of Appeal upheld the right of the Home Secretary to make available plastic 'baton rounds' (aka bullets) and CS gas to local police, even without the approval of the police authority, provided that HM Inspector of Constabulary – appointed by the Home Secretary – endorsed the chief constable's view that the materials were needed. The court held that power of police authorities 'to provide . . . such . . . equipment as may be required for police purposes of the area' did not override the power of the Secretary of State to 'provide . . . such . . . organisations and service as he considers necessary and expedient for promoting the efficiency of the police.' It held also that the Crown has a prerogative power to do what is necessary to maintain the peace of the realm against both actual and threatened disturbances: an open-ended form of power that is far from clear in its scope.

Although Labour Home Secretaries might be more reluctant to ask the courts to intervene against local police authorities, it would be a mistake to view the decisions of the courts as *party* political, for they would almost certainly have been the same whichever party was in power. In short, it appears that local accountability and, to a lesser extent, the existence of local police forces, are merely a device for evading the accountability of the Home Secretary for police actions, so that the police occupy a 'no person's land' where they can always claim that they are answerable to some other body (or to 'the Law'), although neither Home Secretaries nor the courts seem anxious to do anything to constrain police powers in the war on crime.

Complaints against the police

Another area of police accountability is the handling of complaints. As part of the famous overall package of criminal justice in PACE, and partly in response to Scarman's criticisms, the system of handling complaints against the police was overhauled in a way that many at the time thought cosmetic, replacing the Police Complaints Board by the Police Complaints Authority (PCA), with extra powers such as the supervision of police investigations into complaints, and the *duty* to supervise all complaints which include an allegation that the conduct complained of resulted in the death of, or serious injury to, some other person. The powers are set out in PACE 1984 and in statutory instruments such as the Police (Complaints) (Mandatory Referrals) Regulations 1985. The problems encountered by the PCA are set out in their annual reports which, when decoded, are a litany of obstructionism. One problem is that unlike civil proceedings in court, police disciplinary proceedings are at a criminal burden of proof. (Though, as at Lloyd's, The Securities Association, Stock Exchange, and other self-regulatory organisations established under the Financial Services Act 1986, adjudication is not before an inexperienced jury but before insiders who can more discerningly examine truth claims if they want to do so.) This is one reason why it is very difficult to get rid of police officers, for once they pass probation, they can only be sacked if they are found guilty of a dismissable disciplinary or criminal offence: tenure lives in the police!

The PCA also has the ability to use cases to suggest improvements to police practices. Its comments led, it believes, to a number of changes including, in the light of the notorious Holloway Road beatings by members of the Metropolitan Police, the clear marking of police vans so that they can be identified from a distance. (Whether these changes would have occurred anyway is a matter for judgment.)

The Annual Reports show that irrespective of the outcome of the hearings, the rate of 'disciplinary prosecution' was very low. But this only tells us part of the story. What about the reasons for no charges being brought? It is plain from the statistics that the primary reason is a conflict of evidence or insufficiency of evidence. Overall, this amounted to 86.9 % in 1985; 88 % in 1986; and 88 % in 1987. One wonders what the acquittal rate in magistrates' courts would be if magistrates took a similarly agnostic view where there was a conflict of evidence (or what would happen to the prosecution figures if the Crown Prosecution Service did so before undertaking a prosecution!)

The Police Complaints Authority has done nothing to alter the basic fact that the 'bad character' of many complainants serves as an underlying rationale for the discreditation of their allegations (Russell, 1976). It is plain from the statistics that the PCA has occasionally insisted on the bringing of disciplinary charges against the wishes of the chief constable. But these are largely symbolic. The general advice/exhortation role probably does some good, though the PCA has expressed major concerns about poor response of the Metropolitan Police, from which a quarter of its caseload originates (for 10 % of the national officers). My feedback from sources is that at the minimum, the Police Complaints Authority has generated greater concern within the police for rapid and thorough investigation than did its predecessor. However, this alleged 'general deterrent' and monitoring effect may not show up in complaint substantiation rates, and investigations conducted by outside bodies (as in Canada) might be more satisfactory to the public, though the 'conviction rate' might even be lower.

Given broadly shared attitudes about the desirability of an orderly disciplined society on the part of the Home Secretary and senior police officers, the question of who controls the police remains a matter of dispute. On the one hand, the sheer social effect of forming a political lobby has tended to weld the Association of Chief Police Officers into a formidable group (Reiner, 1985), albeit not a united one and one consisting of many *personal* rivals. On the other hand, it may be argued that the Home Office (when supported by the Prime Minister) has come to dominate the police. It determines police pay and the short list for appointments at senior police level, and its 1983 circular on effectiveness and efficiency has been used by Her Majesty's Inspectorate of Constabulary (appointed by the Home Secretary) to promote greater police accountability to government views. In the controversial area of industrial disputes – most prominently the miner's strike of 1984/5 – the police National Reporting Centre served to co-ordinate (or, with few exceptions, to direct) police tactics. It is hard to accept that these were autonomous policing initiatives which lacked positive expressions of governmental support (McCabe and Wallington, 1988; Uglow, 1988).

As for structuralist arguments that there was a 'capitalist need' for the Police and Criminal Evidence Act 1984 or for the Public Order Act 1986, the evidence is unconvincing: in civil and criminal cases alike, the magistrates normally upheld police actions, though riot and affray charges were almost invariably unsuccessful before juries (peremptory objections to whom have been abolished in the Criminal Justice Act 1988). (For a detailed radical analysis, see Scraton and Thomas, 1985; Scraton, 1987; and McCabe and Wallington, 1988.) So irrespective of specific legislative changes, the determination to win the war against disorder has been high, and this has been called into action increasingly, as the effects of the Government's social and economic policies have begun to bite. Hillyard (1987) has alleged that Northern Ireland is being used self-consciously as a training ground for police and army tactics on the mainland. There is some force in this argument over the range of police activities to which it refers. However, without going so far as to argue that any policing can be 'non-political', it should be acknowledged that (a) most parts of mainland Britain create fewer problems for the maintenance of capitalist hegemony than do Belfast, Derry, and South Armagh; and (b) perhaps as a consequence of (a), most police spend most of their time either doing paperwork or on the 'low policing' of banal incidents or modest property crime largely ignored in radical critiques of 'the police'. (For a good review, see Brogden, Jefferson, and Walklate, 1988.)

Police powers in the business world

A more recent arena of struggle over police powers has been in relation to commercial fraud and the laundering of money by organised crime groups (though none of the recent books on policing devote any attention whatever to this fact). Even prior to the wave of scandal that swept the United States and Britain, involving Levine, Boesky, and the Guinness company, the powers to investigate fraud were to be enhanced by the Police and Criminal Evidence Act 1984, the Financial Services Act 1986, the Criminal Justice Act 1987, and the Criminal Justice Act 1988. The political context of this was the need to show that with the proposed deregulation of our prime export earner – the insurance, money, and securities markets – the British had the power to root out financial fraud (see Levi, 1987, chapters 4 and 5 for an extensive discussion). In the period 1981–6, employment in financial services increased by almost one-fifth and income by nearly one-third. By comparison, since 1979, employment in manufacturing and construction has declined by nearly one-quarter, and wages have risen by one-seventh. Further impetus was given by the growing realisation that the only way to deal with narcotics trafficking was to focus upon how money was legitimised through banks, securities transactions, and corporate ownership.

Prior to the Police and Criminal Evidence Act 1984 (PACE), the police had no powers to search for evidence prior to charging a suspect (see Leigh, 1982; Levi, 1981). PACE 1984 made it possible for the police to approach a circuit judge to obtain access to bank accounts and other documentary evidence prior to charge, either – when the bank or other party concerned is expected to co-operate – *inter partes* (both parties represented) or – when those conditions are absent and the offence is a serious arrestable one, this being defined in s 116 as an offence which has led, or is intended or likely to lead, to substantial financial gain or loss to any person – *ex parte* (without defence representation) (see, generally, Stone, 1988).

No warrant may be issued by anyone to search for evidence which is legally privileged. Section 10(2) of PACE states that no privilege is attached to items held with the intention of furthering a criminal purpose, but this may be hard to establish without having access to the items first! However, in a recent case involving a solicitor, the courts have held that the criminal purpose exemption applies to the solicitor's client and may include the criminal purpose of a third party if the solicitor's client is the innocent beneficiary of the criminal purpose. This was a case where the police believed that a drug trafficker provided substantial sums to members of his family to buy property, and the solicitor was acting innocently for one such relative: see *R* v *Central Criminal Court ex parte Francis and Francis* [1988] 1 All ER 677. Cases that smack of drug-trafficking are more likely than those in which, say, tax evasion is suspected to be allowed to override legal privilege and commercial privacy.

The courts have not given the police a totally free hand in gathering evidence related to alleged fraud. In *R* v *Central Criminal Court ex parte Adegbesan and others* [1986] 3 All ER 113, involving allegations of corruption in the administration of funds by a trustee of the Youth Association on the riot-hit Broadwater Farm Estate in London, the Divisional Court quashed the 'special procedure' order made by the judge to allow the accountant's documents to be inspected, stating that the police had to set out a description of all the material that was to be produced. Failure to do so could result in the recipient of the notice unwittingly destroying the material, since it was impossible for him to know whether or not it was covered by the order. The police did provide further particulars, but the defendants appealed that the particulars were still inadequate. This is a characteristic problem in police investigations: the police may not know precisely where they may be able to find documents which they suspect exist without inspecting them, but they cannot get an order requiring production until they know where the information can be found! The Adegbesan case, which has now gone to the House of Lords on appeal, shows that the privacy of professionals is protected by law, even where the ultimate objective of the investigation relates to 'troublesome blacks' rather than to members of commercial elites.

So we see a major difference between these cases and the courts' views about the rights of individuals operating in 'public space'. Moreover, the police are far more circumspect in applying for warrants to inspect bank accounts than they are in the routine rubber stamping of warrants by magistrates. Even where fraud is suspected, the caution exercised by the Inland Revenue (Levi, 1987, 163–70) may be contrasted with the enthusiasm displayed by DHSS in its handling of benefit claimants (Cook, forthcoming). The use of powers by different agencies is broadly responsive to the level of tolerance they expect from politicians and the media. For those official agencies who take a long view, the use of powers is influenced also by its potential impact on future relations with those sectors of the public who are affected or who see themselves as being affected. Generally, except where collective bargaining by riot is feared, agencies dealing with business elites are more prone than those dealing with the poor to employ a co-operative mode.

The powers of the Department of Trade and Industry

The police, however, are by no means the only 'policy' agency dealing with major fraud. The Department of Trade and Industry (DTI) has power under the Companies Act 1985 and the Financial Services Act 1986 to require people to answer questions even if it may incriminate them. The extensiveness of the requirement to disclose is indicated by the judgment of the House of Lords in the case of Jeremy Warner, the journalist who refused to disclose his source of leaked takeover information to the Department of Trade Inspectors. The court took the robust view that if the information is necessary for the prevention of crime – taken in the most general sense – there is no reasonable excuse for withholding it. Lord Griffiths observed that ' "necessary" has a meaning that lies somewhere between 'indispensable", on the one hand, and "useful" or "expedient" on the other . . . The nearest paraphrase I can suggest is "really needed" ' (*Re an Inquiry under the Company Securities (Insider Dealing) Act 1985* [1988] 1 All ER 203). Journalists are less popular than 'professionals' with the judiciary, but if the courts can override so readily the normal presumption of journalistic privilege in s 10 of the Contempt of Court Act 1981, professional people (including bankers) may expect little tolerance either.

The Serious Fraud Office

The Director of the Serious Fraud Office, a new body established by the Criminal Justice Act 1987 under the Attorney General, also has extensive powers of inquisition, similar to those of the DTI in insider dealing enquiries except that information obtained under compulsion is not admissible against an accused unless he or she makes statements in court inconsistent with it.

Drug Trafficking Offences Act 1986

Section 24 of the Act both creates an offence of assisting drug trafficking and provides immunity from being sued for breach of contract where (ss 3):

> a person discloses to a Constable a suspicion or belief that any funds or investments are derived from, or used in connection with, drug trafficking or any matter on which such a suspicion or belief is based . . .

(Section 27 provides for the obtaining of Production Orders *ex parte* from a circuit judge (similar to schedule 1 of PACE 1984).)

These provisions caused great alarm in banking circles, even though it is a defence (ss 4) to prove inter alia that one did not know or suspect that the arrangement related to any person's proceeds of drug trafficking. They could, for example, have been the more acceptable laundering of the proceeds of tax evasion! Less draconian provisions to deal with fraud were introduced in the Criminal Justice Act 1988, including waiving any civil liabilities if banks inform suspicions of fraud in good faith.

Taken together, all the recent changes in legislation reveal that the state is extending its intelligence-gathering capabilities into the upperworld as well as into the underworld and the *lumpenproletariat*. Jeremy Bentham's notion of the panopticon from which all society can be viewed is coming closer to reality.

Changes in policing practice

Examination of developments in 'black-letter' law indicates that civil liberties in England and Wales have declined substantially in the 1980s (though the police might respond that the rights of potential crime victims may thereby be enhanced). However, given the limitations necessarily imposed by personnel restrictions – quality and quantity – has this affected the *practice* of policing? This is a difficult question, not least because our information about policing is patchy: the realities of everyday policing outside the inner city remain considerably more banal than those headlined either in the media or in the accounts of radical criminologists and police representatives.

One area where there has been a dramatic change is in the prosecution of some high-profile cases of commercial fraud by senior figures at Morgan Grenfell merchant bank, Johnson Matthey Bankers, Guinness, Lloyd's, and, most recently Barlow Clowes. Policing resources are still modest in relation to the scale of business criminality and to the resources allocated to other areas of crime and public order, but the degree of symbolic change should not be understated. On the other hand, resources in other, normally less financially and politically sensitive, areas of 'white-collar crime' such as health and safety at work have been run down, despite disasters such as the Zeebrugge ferry and the Piper Alpha North Sea oil field. Indeed, it is plausible that the diminution of regulation was a necessary though not sufficient cause of those disasters.

The tough approach to public order policing, urged on by the Government, is combined with a renewed stress on crime prevention: the theme, after all, of Sir Robert Peel when he founded the Metropolitan Police despite opposition from the rural Conservatives who feared the encroachment of the state upon the liberties of Englishmen (Reiner, 1985; Brogden, Jefferson, and Walklate, 1988). Thus, there are better locks and bolts on homes and cars – accompanied by a discount on domestic insurance policies for those who (can afford to) install them, following a public lashing from the Prime Minister to insurance companies for failing to give crime prevention incentives. Just as importantly, *social* prevention, via neighbourhood watch schemes, has been stepped up, as the police seek to divert blame for their failure to enhance the clear-up rate despite vast pay and manpower increases since 1979, and to improve their local intelligence by encouraging links with the local community. Again, appeals to the recreation of 'community' – which has been broken down by housing and economic policies of Labour and Conservative governments since the 1950s – are central to this, as 'partnership policing' (on police terms) is the keynote. However, whilst committed to this at a public rhetorical level, most police officers, from PC to chief constable, remain sceptical about the changes of 'soft policing' ideas obtaining the consent of the 'rough working class', and their alienation from working class communities has been increased by their own drift to the suburbs, itself the consequence of their high pay levels and freedom not to live in police accommodation.

So the focus of policing has shifted slightly towards crime prevention and 'partnership' or 'multi-agency' policing. Symbolically, this shift may be observed in the Metropolitan Police annual report for 1985 (Metropolitan Police, 1986), which moved from the dry, plain-blue covered annual report of the Commissioner of the Metropolis of previous years to *A police for the people* sporting a glossy cover showing a squatting 'light black' male and sitting white female officer talking to two young white women accompanied by one child each, sitting on a park seat (rather than crossing a nightmare huge open space in a dismal housing estate). This trend has continued: the report for 1987 is headed 'We can improve the quality of life' and mixes images of hi-tech with sympathy for female – possibly rape – victims and police–black child schools liaison!

The trouble with notions such as crime prevention, support for victims, and emphasis on police service rather than on police force, is that apart from being in many ways antithetical to the Starsky and Hutch self-image of many police officers, their product is difficult to measure by inexpensive, routine feedback (Reiner, 1988). With enhanced emphasis upon performance indicators in all the public services, the easiest measures of police effectiveness are crime-related, and the organisation provides little explicit positive reinforcement for crime prevention (or for regulatory roles such as that of custody officer). Furthermore, some crimes are intrinsically easier to clear up than others: there is a continuum from motoring offences and (largely unprosecuted) family violence at the 'easy' extreme to pickpocketing, street robbery by strangers, and burglary at the 'hard' one. So unless specified carefully, crime-related performance indicators can lead to concentration on offences not viewed as serious by 'the public' (whoever they are). Moreover, many evaluations of social prevention schemes – though hard to disentangle into evaluations of specifically police performance within them – produce negative results. The most hotly contested example of this was the pessimistic evaluation of neighbourhood watch in two areas of London (Bennett, 1987), but the Home Office survey by Hosain (1988) is muted in its praise also, and questions police use of their expensive resources on such projects. Nevertheless, the rhetorical attractiveness of the idea of 'community' means that neighbourhood watch continues to receive governmental support.

Concluding thoughts on policing in the 1980s

The net effects of policing (and of Crown Prosecution Service and magisterial, judge and jury actions) are set out in Table 11.1. It is clear from these figures that although the financial effects of upperworld crime are greater, the impact of policing and of prosecution are felt most heavily by the lower socio-economic groups (or rather, since the great majority of convictions relate to juveniles and young adults, to the children of persons in those groups). It has been argued elsewhere (Levi, 1987) that these results are not explicable simply as class bias, and in numerical terms, the increased arrests of leading City figures is likely to change little.

More generally, despite the increases in police powers, the centralisation and concentration of power by the Home Office and the Association of Chief Police Officers, and the acrimony involved in the policing of industrial disputes, it would be an exaggeration to describe mainland Britain as a police state in the sense used by Chapman (1970). There is more dissent among senior police and within government than the generally authoritarian trend discussed here would suggest, though fearful self-interest often produces surface conformity which, for all practical intents and purposes, may be what matters. Most police are aware that public disorder occurs more outside football grounds than inside them, and that unless we travel the Luton path of banning away supporters, the mere requirement to be an 'authorised supporter' to gain entrance may have little effect on soccer violence. Many police actually like football and are unhappy about 'member-only' schemes leading to team closures because gates are too low to pay players' salaries. (Or is this just a subtle method of wage control?) Similarly, much disorder in pubs and clubs arises when people are refused entrance or drinks, and this makes 'entry control' there problematic. Many opponents have noted the contradictions involved between liberalising opening hours/allowing advertisements for drink on television on the one hand, and condemning the foreseeable results on the other. So the view that crime and social disorder can be handled by simple repression is not shared in governmental and policing circles, though the government can usually get its way in drafting the rules.

Table 11.1 The costs of crimes and numbers dealt with for them, England and Wales, 1986

Type of Crime	Costs of crime (£)	No. of convicted or cautioned	
Burglary in dwelling	356,538,000	23,307	(i)
Burglary other than dwelling	180,137,000	43,143	(i)
Robbery	29,650,000	4,397	
Autotheft	607,073,000	32,079	
Shoplifting	11,591,000	128,044	
Theft by employees	14,861,000	5,954	
Police-recorded frauds (1985)	2,163,000,000	27,574	(ii)
Income tax evasion (1986–7)	1,678,000,000	319	(iii)
VAT Evasion (1986–7)	17,267,551	196	(iv)

Notes: (i) Includes aggravated burglaries.
(ii) The majority of fraudsters convicted and cautioned have committed offences whose cost is not included in the above Fraud Squad total, since they are dealt with by divisional CID officers.
(iii) The cost figures for income tax evasion are estimates of the yield of the compliance activities of the Inland Revenue, not statements of the amount of recorded or unrecorded fraud. The Inland Revenue figures include 274 convictions for sub-contractor frauds – 'the lump' – which are not 'elite crimes'.
(iv) The VAT evasion costs relate only to those persons prosecuted. The number prosecuted excludes 382 cases that were settled at a criminal burden of proof by compounding fines.

Source: Criminal Statistics and author's research

Theorists of 'the police' also have to confront the reality of a police force in which line management efforts have been resolutely and consistently subverted by junior ranks (PSI, 1983; Punch, 1983; Bradley, Walker, and Wilkie, 1986). So the underlying assumption and conclusion of the 1962 Royal Commission on the Police – that the problem of police accountability was essentially the problem of controlling the chief constable – may have been a failure of theory, for making *chief* constables accountable (de facto, to the Home Office) may have relatively little effect on policing on the ground. Public order policing, which is highly visible, tends to be the exception to this, though it is a crucial exception. So one message that emerges from the sociology of the police is that organisational deviance rules, OK?

Whatever one's empirical beliefs about who actually *does* decide police behaviour, it is wishful thinking to believe that policing as described here is lacking in support from the majority of the public – including working class adults – and that the greater police accountability advocated by 'Left realists' will lead to more genteel policing. Unless they rely upon police authorities not reflecting public sentiments, i.e. upon distorted political accountability, greater responsiveness to majority views about crime and dealing with crime might lead to even more hard-line policing and sentencing than we have seen in the past. It is only by transforming the hegemony of current crime control ideology that progress in civil liberties will be made, and the means by which that transformation is likely to be achieved remain as obscure now as they have ever done. Perhaps, following the lead of the Roman Legions, school-leavers on their way to the dole queue might be encouraged to bow in front of their local police station and intone proudly *Incarcerandi te salutant*. So long as they do so without obstructing the highway!

References

Baldwin, R (1985) Taking rules to excess: police powers and the Police and Criminal Evidence Bill 1984. In Brenton, M and Jones, C (eds) *Yearbook of Social Policy in Britain, 1984–5*. Routledge and Kegan Paul.

Bennett, T (1988) An assessment of the design, implementation and effectiveness of Neighbourhood Watch in London. *Havard Journal of Criminal Justice* **27**(4): 241–55.

Box, S (1983) *Power, crime, and mystification*. Tavistock.

Box, S (1987) *Recession, crime, and punishment*. Macmillan.

Bradley, N, Walker, N and Wilkie, R (1986) *Managing the police*. Wheatsheaf.

Bridges, L and Bunyan, T (1983) Britain's new urban policing strategy – the police and criminal evidence bill in context. *Journal of Law and Society* **10**(1): 85–108.

Brogden, M, Jefferson, T and Walklate, S (1988) *Introducing Police Work*. Allen and Unwin.

Burrows J and Lewis, H (1988) *Directing patrol work; a study of uniformed policing*. Home Office research study 99. HMSO.

Campbell, D and Connor, S (1986) *On the Record*. Michael Joseph.

Chapman, B (1970) *Police State*. Macmillan.

Contemporary Crises (1987) Special issue on Left realism, **4**.

Cook, D (forthcoming) *Rich law, poor law:* Open University Press.

Foucault, M (1977) *Discipline and punish: the birth of the prison*. Allen Lane.

Gill, P (1987) Clearing up crime: the big con. *Journal of Law and Society* **14**(2): 254–65.

Hall, S, Critcher, C, Jefferson, T, Clarke, J, and Roberts, B (1978) *Policing the Crisis*. Macmillan.

Hillyard, P (1987) The normalisation of special powers: from Northern Ireland to Britain. In Scraton, P (ed) *Law, order and the authoritarian state*. Open University Press.

Home Office (1984) *Criminal justice: a working paper*. Home Office.

Home Office (1988) *Bulletin on criminal statistics in England and Wales, 1987*. Home Office.

Hosain, S (1988) *Neighbourhood watch in England and Wales*. Crime prevention paper 12. Home Office.

Jefferson, T (1986) Policing the miners: law, politics, and accountability. In Brenton, M and Ungerson, C (eds) *The Yearbook of Social Policy in Britain, 1985–6*. Routledge and Kegan Paul.

Jones, S and Levi, M (1987) Law and order and the causes of crime: some police and public perspectives. *The Howard Journal of Criminal Justice* **26**(1): 1–14.

Kinsey, R, Lea, J and Young, J (1986) *Losing the fight against crime*. Basil Blackwell.

Lea, J and Young, J (1984) *What is to be done about law and order?* Penguin.

Lea, J, Matthews, R and Young, J (1987) *Law and order: five years on*. Middlesex Polytechnic.

Leigh, L (1982) *The control of commercial fraud*. Gower (originally: Heinemann).

Levi, M (1981) *The phantom capitalists: the organisation and control of long-firm fraud*. Gower (originally Heinemann).

Levi, M (1985) Police powers and police-public relationships. In Alves, E and Shapland, J (eds) *Legislation for policing today: the police and criminal evidence act*. British Psychological Society.

Levi, M (1987) *Regulating fraud: white-collar crime and the criminal process*. Tavistock, New York: Methuen.

Lewis, H and Mo, J (1986) Burglary insurance: findings from the British Crime Survey. *Home Office Research and Planning Unit Research Bulletin* **22**; 33–6.

Maguire, M (1988) The effects of PACE powers on detention and questioning: some preliminary findings. *British Journal of Criminology* **28**(1): 19–43.

Maguire, M and Pointing, J (eds) (1988) *Victims of crime: a new deal?*. Open University Press.
McCabe, S and Wallington, P (1988) *The police, public order and civil liberties*. Routledge.
McKenzie, I and Irving B (1988) The right to silence. *Policing*. **4**(2); 88–105.
Metropolitan Police (1986) *A police for the people: Annual Report of the Commissioner of the Metropolis, 1985*. HMSO
Metropolitan Police (1987) *Annual Report, 1986*. HMSO.
Metropolitan Police (1988) *Annual Report, 1987*. HMSO.
Morgan, R (1988) Policing by consent: legitimating the doctrine, paper presented at the Police Foundation Conference on Policing Research, University of Oxford.
Norton, P (ed) (1984) *Law and order and British policies*. Gower.
Pearson, G (1983) *Hooligan*. Macmillan.
Percy-Smith, J and Hillyard, P (1985) Miners in the arms of the law: a statistical analysis. *Journal of Law and Society* **12**(3): 345–54.
PSI (1983) *The police and people in London*. Policy Studies Institute.
Punch, M (ed) (1983) *Control in the police organisation*. MIT Press.
Reiner, R (1985) *The politics of the police*. Wheatsheaf.
Reiner, R (1988) Keeping the Home Office happy. *Policing* **4**(1): 28–36.
Roddie, J (1988) The undervalued custody officer. *Policing* **4**(1): 4–27.
Russell, K (1976) *Complaints against the police: a sociological view*. Milltak.
Scarman, Lord (1981) *The Scarman Report; Brixton disorders*. HMSO.
Scraton, P (1985) *The state of the police*. Pluto.
Scraton, P (ed) (1987) *Law, order, and the authoritarian state*. Open University Press.
Scraton, P and Thomas, P (eds) (1985) The State v. The People: Lessons from the coal dispute. *Journal of Law and Society Special Issues* **12**(2).
Sim, J, Scraton, P and Gordon, P (1987) Introduction: crime, the state, and critical analysis. In Scraton P, *Law, order, and the authoritarian state*. Open University Press.
Sparks, R (1980) Marxism and criminology. In Tonry, M and Morris, N (eds) *Crime and Justice* **1**. Chicago: University of Chicago Press.
Stalker, J (1987) *Stalker*. Harrap.
Stone, R (1988) PACE: special procedures and legal privilege. *Criminal Law Review* 498–507.
Uglow, S (1988) *Policing liberal society*. Oxford University Press.
Vincent-Jones, P (1986) The hippy convoy and criminal trespass. *Journal of Law and Society* **13**(3): 343–70.
Weatheritt, M (1986) *Innovations in policing*. Croom Helm.
Willis, C, Macleod, J and Naish, P (1988) *The tape-recording of police interviews with suspects: a second interim report*. Home Office Research Study 97. HMSO.

12 The Church of England and social policy in the 1980s

Graham Bowpitt

Introduction

For centuries the Church of England has been branded with an assumed political identity. In recent years, however, the 'Tory Party at prayer' has been associated with a number of highly critical pronouncements on the policies of the present Tory Government, culminating in the Bishop of Durham's judgment of its tax and social security policy as 'verging on the wicked'. Two questions are thrown up by these developments. First, has the Church really changed its political outlook, or are we looking at the same Church responding to a totally new set of political circumstances? Second, what are the implications for the Church of this political involvement? The Church has been subjected to repeated attacks from within its own ranks not only for what it has said and done, but for 'meddling in politics' at all. Do its political comments mean that it has simply transferred its political loyalties in a narrow partisan sense, and if so is its traditional role as the church for all the people, regardless of political outlook, thereby threatened? Three factors will be examined for their impact on the Church's role in social policy: its social constituency, its social and political theology, and its constitutional position. Church involvement in the reform of social security will then be presented as a case study, before concluding by examining the implications for Church–State relations.

The Tory Party at prayer

The traditional affinity of the Church of England with the Tory Party must be treated with caution. Anglican loyalty to Conservative party-political interests reached its hey-day in the last quarter of the nineteenth century, and began to wane after the first world war. (Wald, 1983; Gilbert, 1980, pp 86–7). However, it is the identification of the Church with a particular 'Tory' social and political outlook which has longer historical roots. The reasons for this might give us a clue as to whether the Church's current stance towards the social policy initiatives of the present Conservative Government constitutes a genuine departure.

The first reason was the Church of England's constitutional position. Since the seventeenth century, this has bestowed upon the Church privileges and responsibilities, and subjected it to constraints, all of which have given it a vested interest in defending the Establishment. These privileges included episcopal representation in the House of Lords (amounting to 15 % of members in the eighteenth century), and the restriction of public offices, the professions, the universities and virtually all positions of social and political power to Anglicans. In exchange, the control of higher Church appointments and Church affairs was vested in parliament, while appointments to clerical livings rested on the patronage of lay landowners (Armstrong, 1973, pt I; Reader, 1966, chap 1). The erosion of ecclesiastical privileges in the nineteenth century, if anything, further forced the Church into the hands of the Tory Party as the defender of its interests in parliament. Though the importance of this relationship has diminished, ancient loyalties have persisted. In the 1930s, the General Assembly's House of Laity could boast twelve Tory MPs among its membership, while more recently still, the Macmillan Cabinet contained eight practising Anglicans (Hastings, 1986, pp 252, 425).

The Church's economic interests constituted a second reason for past political loyalties. Historically, the wealth and income of the Church derived very largely from land, and this inevitably inclined it towards the defence of landed interests. It was not only that it was itself a large landowner, but also that it was dependent on the good will of lay proprietors who, through the payment of tithes and Church rates, guaranteed the Church's income (Gilbert, 1976, p 5). Though these forms of revenue are things of the past, it is only recently that we have seen the decline of the role of property as a source of income, via the stewardship of the Church Commissioners, and the Church become largely reliant for its income upon the voluntary contributions of its own members (Welsby, 1985, pp 63–6).

A third and more important reason derived from the social implications of the Church's constitutional position. The Church was expected to uphold the social order, and to be the primary instrument of social cohesion. It fulfilled its responsibilities in several ways, the best known being ideological. Again, care must be taken to understand precisely what this involved. The Church did not ally itself unreservedly with the ruling class, and preach the unremitting subservience of the poor. If anything, its theology came into conflict with its economic and political interests on social questions. True, it retained a belief in a hierarchical social order, with sharp gradations of rank and wealth. But such a society could only be upheld if the privileged fully met their obligations to the poor. This belief in interdependence has been a basic axiom of the Church's social theology to the present day. In the nineteenth century, it was limited to a dislike among many clergy for the teachings of political economy, and a sustained ambivalence towards the New Poor Law (Norman, 1976, pp 41–2; Soloway, 1969, pp 93–*4; Kitson-Clarke, 1973, pp 149*–163). In the twentieth century, it has assumed more radical overtones in the teachings of R H Tawney and William Temple, and in the Church's support for the institutions of the Welfare State, yet not because of a sudden conversion to socialism, but because they represented the triumph of interdependence over the conflicts engendered by capitalism (Hastings, 1986, pp 398, 422–4; Norman, 1976, pp 221, 314, 370).

The Church also upheld the social order through the parochial system, and the role of the clergy in it. Before the 1830s, the Church effectively sanctified the aristocratic control of local affairs. The landed background of most of the clergy, combined with the Church's control over education, charity and other significant parochial institutions, made it an ideal instrument of social control (Perkin, 1969, p 205; Gilbert, 1976, pp 74–81; 1980, pp 70–75). However, with the onset of urbanisation and the breakdown of the parochial system in the new industrial towns came a population effectively beyond the Church's immediate reach, and for whose allegiance it would have to compete with other churches, and with entirely secular attractions (Gilbert, 1980, pp 80–82).

The fourth and most decisive factor was the changing social character of the Church's membership which, in the nineteenth century, virtually turned the Church of England from a church for all the people into an exclusive denomination for the rich. With the advent of industrialisation, Anglican support was profoundly influenced by two ecclesiastical 'ladders' (Perkin, 1969, pp 33–37, 196–205). The first was a status ladder by which rising social status was marked firstly by a move towards Nonconformity, and then back to the Church of England as the church of the elite. The second was a descending ladder taken by the poor from rural Anglicanism through Methodism to the unbelief which increasingly characterised the urban working class (Inglis, 1963; Mudie-Smith, 1904; Norman, 1976, pp 123–7; Chadwick, 1970, chap 4). It was thus that the revival of the Church of England which took place in the second half of the nineteenth century was largely confined to the suburban middle and upper-middle classes (Gilbert, 1976, pp 137–8). Care must be taken in interpreting the evidence on this point. The parochial system has always enabled the Church to retain a presence in working class areas, but the principal expansion took place elsewhere. The Church of England became the church of the wealthy and powerful, and this was especially reflected in the social background of its leadership (Soloway, 1969, pp 14–17; Hastings, 1986, pp 55–8).

The Church's social constituency

Analyses of how far the Church has changed demographically and politically are immediately thwarted by a shortage of recent evidence. The Archbishop of Canterbury's Commission on Urban Priority Areas (ACUPA) provides us with the most recent evidence on social class (1985, p 35). In 'urban priority areas', with 85 % of the population on average designated as 'working class', only 59 % of Church congregations and 45 % of members of Parochial Church Councils (PCC) were working class. In other areas, where on average 21 % of the population were working class, only 12 % of the congregations and 8 % of PCC members were working class. Moving further up the Church hierarchy, Leech (1982, p 17) suggested that, at the time of writing, as little as 1 % of the members of the General Synod were working class. With regard to the clergy, despite claims regarding their declining social status (Gilbert, 1980, p 116), Towler and Coxon (1979, p 212) discovered that, in the early 1960s, 19 % of ordinands still came from social class I, compared with 4 % from the population generally. They also noted (ibid, p 213) that nearly 37 % had attended a public or independent secondary school, compared with 3.5 % of the population generally. Moreover, Paul (1964, p 283) found that, of the diocesan bishops consecrated during the period 1940–59, 42 % had been educated at the ten leading public schools, and that this had scarcely changed from the 44 % for the period 1860–79.

With regard to party political loyalties, Miller and Raab (1977) concluded that by 1963 denominational allegiance was exerting a significant but declining influence on voting behaviour, in contrast to the period before 1918 when it had been the prime determinant. However, Medhurst and Moyser (1978, p 92) have offered only qualified support to this conclusion. Surveying political loyalties at the time of the 1966 General Election, they found that, whereas 40 % of the general population identified themselves as 'Tories', 55 % of active Anglicans and 58 % of General Synod members did so. However, if only the middle class population is considered, 67 % of the general public identified themselves as Tories, as did

77 % of active Anglicans, but only 57 % of General Synod members. They also discerned more liberal attitudes among Synod members, in contrast to both their social class and other Anglicans, on such contemporary issues as immigration and capital punishment (ibid, p 94), and this is reinforced by Leech's more recent findings (1982, p 17).

Thus, even this limited evidence would call into question the arguments which maintain that nothing has changed concerning the political attitudes of the Church and its leaders. For instance, Parkin (1968, pp 21–5) has sought to demonstrate the persistence of the established Church as one of the key institutional orders essential to the maintenance of dominant values. This implies that Church members, and especially their leaders, would tend to support those values, and the political party most committed to upholding them. Secondly, Norman (1976, pp 8–10) has argued that Church leaders have always reflected the social and political attitudes of the social class from which they are largely drawn. While the Church still primarily draws its active members, and especially its leaders, from the higher socio-economic classes, Medhurst and Moyser's research casts some doubt on Parkin's and Norman's hypotheses. As Medhurst and Moyser conclude, 'religious beliefs may still have an autonomous role to play' (1978, p 95).

Changing theological perspectives

One of the main contributions which the Church has made to social policy in the 1980s has taken the form of published reports of inquiries into social, moral and economic questions conducted mainly by the General Synod's Board for Social Responsibility, although the most widely known, *Faith in the city* (ACUPA, 1985), was the result of the work of a special Archbishop's Commission. All display theological insights which suggest that, to a degree at least, the Church's apparent new social radicalism arises from the tapping of fresh theological currents.

There is nothing new about the Church taking a critical stance towards government policy. The social radicalism which dominated the Church throughout the first half of the century has already been noted. This radicalism was founded upon the Catholic tradition of Church theology, and dates back to F D Maurice and the Christian Socialists of the nineteenth century (Jones, 1968, pp 86–92). Emphasis is placed upon the universal Fatherhood of God, and upon the Incarnation through which the whole of humanity has been bound together as the family and mystical body of Christ. There is thus an impetus to make this unit a reality in society as a whole, and not just in the Church, and to infuse the entire social and economic order with Christian principles. The Reformation is played down as the ideological source of competitive individualism, and the Church's continuity with its mediaeval past is stressed, with pre-eminence being attached to the economic teachings of the Church Fathers (Temple, 1950, pp 19, 38). Though the dominance of this tradition has waned considerably since the death of William Temple, it has undoubtedly survived to influence the social thought of the Church today (Sleeman, 1985, pp 257–261).

However, the Church's social involvement has been considerably strengthened in recent years by the revival of the Evangelical social conscience. The impact of Evangelicalism upon Victorian society through philanthropy and social reform is proverbial (Heasman, 1962; Bready, 1928). However, in the years following the first world war the Evangelical social commitment waned, partly because of the growing belief that the world is irredeemably evil, the Christian's prime task being to call out of the world small groups of believers through evangelism (Stott, 1984, pp 6–10). The tide began to turn in the 1960s, culminating in the International Congress on World Evangelisation held in Lausanne, Switzerland, in 1974, which issued a Covenant, an important element of which were statements concerning the Christian's social responsibility.

A stream of publications since then have sought to develop an Evangelical social perspective. Considerable emphasis has been placed upon the Old Testament, and especially the principles of social and economic justice which underpinned Israelite society, and the constant castigation of God's people delivered by the prophets for their oppression of the poor, the widow, the orphan and the stranger (Wright, 1977). Evangelicals have further pointed to the implications for social involvement of the key doctrines of the Bible (Stott, 1984, pp 13–25; Gladwin, 1979). The idea of Creation implies that God is concerned for the whole world, and especially human beings, who were created in His own image. The tragedy of 'the Fall' is that evil has permeated not only individual lives, but the structure of society (Carey, 1977). However, the coming of salvation has meant the establishment of Christ's sovereignty, at least in principle, over the whole of life, and not simply the life of the Church. Finally, the Christian's hope lies in working for the establishment of the Kingdom of God as a present as well as a future reality (Sugden, 1977). However, what has given the revival of the Evangelical social conscience a radical twist has been the attention which has been drawn to the alleged 'bias to the poor' which God has shown in His dealings with humanity throughout history (Sider, 1977; Sheppard, 1983). God has shown a special concern for the poor, has frequently used them as instruments in His purposes, and is establishing a kingdom in which the materialist values of this world are reversed. The new Evangelical social theology has thrown down a challenge to the Church towards a radical political involvement.

The third and most controversial theological influence takes the language of 'bias' one stage further. Out of the shanty towns of Latin America has come Liberation Theology, an attempt to build a political theology around a Marxist revolutionary consciousness stripped of its atheistic implications. Liberation theologians have taken a Marxist philosophy of history, and have infused it with theological meaning. Central to this is a new way of doing theology, less by deduction from authoritative texts and theological system-building by academics than by 'praxis', a critical reflection on the social world as it is experienced, with a view to transforming it (Gutierrez, 1974, pp 11–15). A second theme is a view of salvation as political liberation, with a call on Christians to be involved in the struggle for a just society as part of the salvation process (ibid, pp 158–177). A third theme is the call towards total solidarity with poor and oppressed people, inspired by Christ's identification with suffering and despair on the cross (Moltmann, 1974, pp 326–9). Finally, the poor as makers of salvation history are to be 'the protagonists of their own liberation' (Gutierrez, 1974, p 307).

Liberation theology has been controversial in the Church because of its influence on some of its better known figures such as the Bishop of Durham (Jenkins, 1985), and on some of its recent publications. For instance its use in underpinning a theology for the inner city (ACUPA, 1985, pp 63–5) was enough to provoke one Government Minister allegedly to reject the ACUPA report as 'pure Marxist theology' (*Guardian* 2 December 1985). Again, its use as a basis for the development of a black theology has led to some far-reaching proposals for countering institutional racism in the Church (Wilson, 1986).

Lastly, it has contributed to the birth of feminist theology which has had an impact at two levels. First, it has compelled the Church of England to address challenges within its own community about the ordination of women to the priesthood, and about the role of women generally in worship, pastoral work and church leadership. It has begun slowly to realise that its decision-making bodies at all levels, and its working parties, must reflect the experience of women, and must allow women to play a full part (Dodds and Webster, 1988). Feminist theology, with its critique of the patriarchal aspects of Christianity, its affirmation of the value of women's experience, and its willingness to look at questions of spirituality, sexuality and power, has equipped many men and women in a new way. Groups like the Movement for the Ordination of Women, and Women in Theology, have become places where women and men can explore some of these issues. Second, the Church has been moved to look at gender issues in wider society. Its main response has been a study of women and work, the results of which were debated by General Synod in 1987, and its main recommendations enthusiastically endorsed, especially its commitment to pursuing more just patterns of employment for women, and to improving the Church's own attitude to women in society, and its practice as an employer (General Synod BSR, 1986a).

Social principles and social policies

As the above analysis indicates, modern theology has important implications for social policy. Yet Church reports are rarely written from a single theological perspective, because of the desire to produce documents which will attract the support of Anglicans generally, and even appeal to the non-Christian public. The Church has therefore developed the 'middle axiom' view of social involvement, of which William Temple was so fond (1950, pp 24–5), which urges the Church to avoid the three extremes of vacuous generalities, partisan political and theological positions, and commitment to ephemeral policy programmes, restricting itself to principles which are sufficiently precise to be practical and recognisably Christian, but impregnable to the winds of political fashion (Preston, 1979; Forrester, 1985, pp 88–92). An attempt will be made to identify the 'middle axioms' implicit in a number of recent Church reports (ACUPA, 1985; General Synod BSR, 1982; 1986b; 1987a), and their theological roots. However, in an increasingly secular and pluralist society, it is doubtful whether this approach is either tenable or desirable, as we shall see later (Plant, 1985, pp 320–2).

The first principle is a recognition of the value of persons, derived from their being created in God's image, and the objects of Christ's redemptive love. The Church should therefore support policies which facilitate personal fulfilment, including freedom, creativity and inter-relatedness, and policies which recognise human equality, but which also value diversity (General Synod BSR, 1987a, paras 57, 58; 1986b, para 2.8). It should oppose policies which divide the world into givers and receivers, and which deny the contribution which the weaker members of society can make to the common good (General Synod BSR, 1986b, para 2.13; ACUPA, 1985, para 3.6).

Secondly, the traditional value of interdependence should be maintained. The ACUPA report (para 1.45) identified polarisation as one of the primary evils besetting modern Britain. The Church's commitment to interdependence is a direct response to the Government's insistence on independence. Interdependence reinforces 'the moral obligation carried by the community as a whole for the well-being and liberty of each individual member' (General Synod BSR, 1986b, para 2.16), thus creating the context in which both independence and dependence find their place. People were created for each other and for God, and cannot find fulfilment in isolation (ibid, para 2.6). This implies a commitment to related values, such as community or *koinonia* (fellowship) (General Synod BSR, 1987a, para 61–65). The ACUPA report (para 3.16) attacked the modern consumer economy both for its idolatrous materialism, and for the way it undermines community life by increasing the alienation and powerlessness of those too poor to participate. The Church should especially promote policies which foster community by identifying the neighbourhood as the primary locus for the giving and receiving of services, and in this the Church itself has an important role to play (ibid, paras 3.19–3.23).

However, alienation requires more than community work to overcome it. The third principle is a commitment to social justice (ibid, para 3.4). This must involve the creation of structures which limit the growth of social and economic inequalities. More than this, wealth must be created justly and distributed fairly, and the Church should oppose policies which are concerned primarily with the promotion of economic efficiency, regardless of the social costs (ibid, paras 3.11–4.14; General Synod BSR, 1986b, paras 2.23–2.39). Instead, the Church should promote policies which demand that the better-off fulfil their social obligations according to the extent of their wealth, and to do so in a manner which preserves the dignity of the poor. In these respects, a particular concern has been expressed for the fields of taxation, social security and the finance of housing (ACUPA, 1985, para 3.17; General Synod BSR, 1982, paras 134–6). To sum up in the words of the Archbishop's Commission,

> Ultimately it is only an absolute commitment to our solidarity one with another, a recognition of the importance of all forms of collective action for the common good, and a passionate concern for the rights and well-being of those least able to help themselves, which can redress the balance of the excessive individualism which has crept into both public and private life today (ACUPA, 1985, para 3.17).

In recent years however, the Church has made a significant departure from the middle axiom view, and has demonstrated a clear willingness to embody its social principles in precise social policy proposals. Nowhere is this better illustrated than in the report of the Archbishop's Commission on Urban Priority Areas. The report begins with an analysis of the inner city, the Church's position in it, and some theological reflections on it. The report then moves on to set out a programme for putting the Church's own house in order, and to make its ministry more relevant to the needs of deprived urban areas.

However, by far the largest part of the report is addressed to the Nation in general, and the Government in particular. A wide-ranging manifesto is developed which covers virtually every aspect of domestic policy, including housing and urban policy, poverty and employment, health care, social and community work, education and youth work, and law and order. But the key theme that runs throughout is the insistence that social policies should be more consistently sensitive to the needs of urban priority areas (UPAs), because only by so doing could they embody the social principles outlined above. A sample of the main proposals will serve to illustrate this. Thus revenue support by central government to local authorities should be increased, with the increase earmarked for UPAs. The Urban and Community Programmes should be expanded. Public sector housing should be greatly expanded and improved, especially in UPAs. It is recognised that the health of deprived people can only be improved if their whole quality of life is enhanced. Care in the community only makes sense in UPAs if properly supported by adequately funded public services. Finally, the civil rights of inner city inhabitants can only be properly upheld through a network of publicly funded law centres (ACUPA, 1985, paras 8.55, 8.67, 9.80, 10.77, 11.20, 12.26, 14.53).

What is distinctive about this report is not the originality of these proposals, but what they signify. For many, this was the report of the Royal Commission which the Government declined to set up in the aftermath of the 1981 riots. It was no party political manifesto, but the product of detailed analysis by members of an institution, representing a vast array of political opinions and life experiences, who rooted their arguments not in party dogma but in timeless spiritual values. Yet in this report the Church identified itself with a clear set of policies, virtually none of which could be found in the Conservative Party's election manifesto of 1987.

Commentators are divided over whether or not all this constitutes conclusive proof of a move to the left in the Church's political outlook. Kenneth Leech's discussion of this question was inconclusive, recognising some movement, but nothing like the degree feared by the *Daily Express*! Moyser, on the other hand, has insisted that 'the Church of England as a whole, and its corporate leadership in particular, has indisputably shifted its centre of political gravity to the left . . .' (Moyser, 1985, p 22). More recent evidence is provided by the Church's critical response to the Prime

Minister's recent attempt to defend her individualism theologically before the General Assembly of the Church of Scotland. In a penetrating theological critique of her whole political philosophy, the Bishop of Gloucester maintained that:

> governments . . . have clear social and moral obligations . . . to pursue policies which create and encourage that sense of community and mutuality which are the hallmarks of a complete human life . . . . It cannot be the case that we should encourage generosity by individuals at one and the same time as government works on a policy of giving only the barest minimum (Yates and Gladwin, 1988, pp 1,2).

One Tory MP was reported to have dismissed the Bishop's comments as 'outrageous' (*Guardian* 1 June 1988). But is the Church really saying and doing anything which amounts to a radical departure from its traditional paternalism, which only seems radical when set against the current Tory orthodoxy? A final answer depends on how far the Church is able to translate its radical thought into radical practice.

The Church's constitutional position

When entering the political arena, the Church, up to a point, has access to the same opportunities as any pressure group. It can lobby Parliament; it can use the media; it can respond to government proposals. Yet its historic status within the British Establishment gives the Church privileges, and subjects it to constraints, which make its role within the political process quite unique. Though these constraints and privileges have been systematically whittled away over the last two hundred years (Cornwell, 1985), they are still significant. The remaining privileges include the restriction of certain offices to Anglican clergymen, the role of the Archbishop of Canterbury as a national religious figurehead, the episcopal presence in the House of Lords, and the role of the parochial clergy in the performance of religious duties for the whole population. The main constitutional constraints are the Crown appointment of bishops, and the vesting of ultimate authority over Church affairs in Parliament (Welsby, 1985, pp 45–9). However, as we shall see, a more general constraint derives from the Church's privileged position as the National Church. Each of the main channels of Church influence on social policy will now be considered to see how that influence is affected by the Church's constitutional position.

The days when the combined strength of the episcopal bench could thwart the progress of the Great Reform Bill in 1831 are over. The two Archbishops and 24 senior diocesan bishops constitute a far smaller proportion of members of the House of Lords than they did 150 years ago. The bishops no longer have the status nor the numerical strength to set themselves up as a Christian caucus within Parliament, or to engage in sustained campaigns (General Synod BSR, 1981, para 102). Furthermore, they are selected to represent theological diversity rather than political unity, and they speak and vote in the House of Lords as individuals, albeit guided by the recommendations of General Synod and its advisory bodies. More importantly, the role of the bishops has changed so as to place far greater emphasis on the performance of pastoral than parliamentary duties (Medhurst and Moyser, 1986, pp 77–87).

Notwithstanding these caveats, the bishops have demonstrated an ability to exert a more informal kind of influence to some effect. Through their parliamentary speeches, they can influence the tone of debate through the presentation of the general principles identified above, in an arena which is widely reported on the media. Moreover, the support of the General Synod advisory bodies gives the bishops a more informed back-up than is available to most members of the Upper House. Furthermore, like any other member, they can propose amendments to legislation, and have successfully done so in significant ways. The Bishop of London's amendments to the Education Reform Bill to secure the mainly Christian character of religious education provide the best recent examples. In most cases, however, their influence is exerted through the support they give to amendments tabled by others. Finally, their seats in the House of Lords give them access to the corridors of power which provides further opportunities for informal influence. Taken together, these factors have given the bishops an influence which has been considerable, and generally critical of Government policy, to the dismay of the Prime Minister who, it seems, felt obliged to exercise her right to refuse the Church's preference in at least one recent appointment to the episcopal bench, and to invite a group of bishops to Chequers in an attempt to harness that influence in a more favourable direction.

The main source of opinion on social policy is the General Synod which, since the Chadwick Commission in 1970, has been the main legislative body, subject to the Parliamentary right of veto (Hastings, 1986, pp 546–7; Welsby, 1985, pp 50–56). The three Houses of Bishops, Clergy and Laity, with a current total of 575 members, meet three times a year to legislate for the Church, to determine forms of worship, to finance the central administration, and deliberate on issues of national, international, ecclesiastical, or ecumenical importance. Its debates on key issues of social policy provide a platform for the dissemination of Church opinion on the media. Its deliberations are informed by four advisory bodies on the Church's ministry, education, mission, and social responsibility. It is the Board for Social Responsibility (BSR), through its Standing Committees on Industrial and Economic Affairs, International Affairs, Social Policy, and Race and Community Relations, which is expected, in the words of the General Synod's constitution, 'to promote and co-ordinate the thought and action of the Church in matters affecting the lives of men and women in society' (cf Ecclestone, 1985, pp 110–2). To this end, the BSR produces reports, submits evidence in response to Government proposals, and is consulted by ministers when the views of the Church are being sought. When engaging in this activity, the BSR acts with a fair degree of autonomy, yet carries the authority of the Church behind it, though without binding anyone to the views it expresses (General Synod BSR, 1981, paras 15, 16, 88). If this role is ambivalent, it is because the Church's position as a pressure group within the Establishment is ambivalent. Insofar as Synodical government has given the Church the freedom to exercise a prophetic role in society in the light of its own theological reflection, then it has forfeited its right to speak as the conscience of the Nation (ibid, paras 103–5, 118). Yet the Church is listened to precisely because it is seen to be more than a mere pressure group promoting particular interests or causes. But to speak on behalf of the Nation in an age of secular pluralism is no longer to speak with a distinctively Christian voice (Habgood, 1983, chap 2). Herein lies the central dilemma for the Church in social policy.

From moral welfare to community action

This dilemma is mirrored at the level of the parochial ministry. The role of the parish church as a source of social welfare is of almost timeless origin, but achieved particular prominence in the mid-Victorian age of the residual state (Kitson-Clarke, 1973, chap 6). The incumbent has always held a general responsibility for the social, moral and spiritual welfare of all the inhabitants of his parish, and this survived the advent of religious pluralism. As the state assumed responsibility for social welfare, the Church retained a general commitment to 'moral welfare' through family casework especially with unmarried mothers (Hall and Howes, 1965).

However, all this appears to be changing. To begin with, traditional extra-parochial Church organisations such as the Children's Society and the Mothers' Union are increasingly engaging in pressure group activities, as well as diversifying their traditional services. However, it is at the level of the parish that change has been most marked. The BSR's directory of resources (General Synod BSR, 1987b) reveals that was well as maintaining established forms of Church social work – family welfare, support for the elderly, mental welfare, marital and bereavement counselling – most dioceses are now committed to new responses to social need – community work, race relations, and projects on poverty, unemployment and homelessness. Not only is the nature of Church social provision changing, but so also is its style, with a rejection of the paternalism of the past, and a recognition of 'the need to listen to a neighbourhood and help residents to participate in the management of their own locality' (Ballinger, 1988, p 19). This thrust towards church-based community work has been given a further impetus in recent Church reports (General Synod BSR, 1981, paras 83–6; ACUPA, 1985, paras 12.27–12.54; General Synod BSR, 1988).

Yet it is not without its problems. A minister who wishes to defend the rights of minority groups against an unyielding state bureaucracy is forced to take sides, as some have discovered by personal experience (Wheale, 1985, pp 161–3). But is this what a Christian minister is supposed to do? Many would argue that his or her primary duty is to the spiritual welfare of the flock, while others emphasise the responsibility of Anglican clergy in upholding 'folk religion' by providing those ancient 'rites of passage' and other services which are invulnerable to changes in political fashion, and which bind communities together in a common heritage (Habgood, 1983, pp 96–7). But the advocates of community politics remind us of the prophetic role of the Christian ministry, and of the origins of the church among the poor and the oppressed. In the end, the stand which the Church takes in the field of social policy, at local and national level, will depend upon its understanding of its relationship with the state in a secular pluralist society.

The reform of social security

The Church's involvement in the reform of social security over the last four years illustrates both its theological preoccupations, and the constitutional dilemmas thrown up by its political involvement. In 1984, the BSR sent evidence to the review committees set up by the Secretary of State, and during the following year made a formal response to the Green Paper. The document explained the Church's intervention in theological terms which echo the social principles identified above.

> We reaffirm the Christian belief derived from the Old Testament that every person is made in the image of God, and so all should be equally respected and valued. Christians therefore should always be concerned

> about practices and attitudes which tend to devalue people. We also affirm that interdependence which comes from our common humanity. We believe that poverty can undermine this, by making some permanently dependent on the state or on the benevolence of others. Welfare policies should seek to remove the fear of such poverty and to meet the genuine needs of those who are poor. They should aim to help every person to have the opportunity to develop and grow as individuals, leading a full and dignified life and contributing to the well-being of the whole community (General Synod BSR, 1985, para 4).

The document further justified the Church's right to speak in terms of its tradition of Christian service, its proximity to those in need, and its responsibility to speak out on behalf of the vulnerable.

> The Church has always included people who are experiencing hardship: down the centuries men and women have been motivated by their Christian faith to offer help to those in need, and to challenge those social policies which keep the poor dependent as a result of disability, sickness, low pay or unemployment. Our history shows that many Christians in the past addressed themselves to the acute human needs they saw around them, and took enormous risks in the struggle for justice. The Church also has a recognised responsibility to meet people at times of change and stress: the birth of a child, marriage, the funeral of a spouse or a parent. Through our networks of Social Responsibility Officers, social workers and community workers in the dioceses, as well as voluntary church bodies, we are aware of the hardship experienced by many who are dependent on benefits for their subsistence. In addition, clergy may well be the only professional workers to live in disadvantaged areas. They are very well placed to speak of the problems of those who live on the margins of poverty (ibid, para 5).

The response then went on to assess the proposed changes in public policy with three questions in mind: 'what are the implications for the poorest and most vulnerable members of our society; in the allocation of resources available, will the proposals achieve a just and fair distribution; are the proposals likely to increase the divisions in our society?' (ibid, para 6).

Under each of these headings, the BSR found cause for concern. While welcoming some of the DHSS's proposals, many were viewed with alarm. On levels of income support, the BSR was glad to note the Green Paper's assurance that 'the changes in the main structure of supplementary benefits are not intended to reduce the overall help provided', but commented: 'We are concerned that removal of special allowances may not be matched by sufficient increase in basic payments .... We fear that some elderly people may experience hardship as a result of the removal of heating and special dietary allowances' (ibid, para 7a). On the proposals about young people, the submission observed that 'aspects of the Green Paper seem to rely on unrealistic assumptions about the nature of family life. We do not think there is any justification for paying a lower rate of income support to young people under 25, particularly in the case of married couples with children .... Overall, it is hard to see how the proposals concerning young people will enable them to achieve proper responsibility and independence' (ibid, para 7c). On the social fund, the BSR commented that 'cash limits will introduce an arbitrary factor in its operation .... It will mean that one claimant may qualify for assistance at the beginning of the financial year, but another, in exactly the same circumstances, fail at the end, simply because the money has run out. This seems to us a potentially unjust system which will create hostility and incomprehension' (ibid, para 9a).

When the Social Security Bill was passing through the House of Lords in 1986, a number of bishops supported small but important amendments, mainly those proposed by Baroness Faithfull and Lady Jane Ewart-Biggs, including for example the requirement to pay family credit directly to the primary carer rather than through the pay packet, and the attempt to prevent the abolition of local authorities' duties to provide free school meals for children living in low income families. Their contribution emphasised the need to reform some aspects of the social security system, but argued that the Bill as it stood could weaken the already precarious economic position of many living on benefit or on low pay. However, in the end, few major changes to the Bill were achieved.

In the same year, the BSR Report, *Not just for the poor*, was published, which concluded that a firm framework of public welfare services was essential, and affirmed 'much of the vision, if not the detail of the post-war settlement, which was fundamentally sound' (General Synod BSR, 1986b, para 7.50). In relation to social security, it declared that

> ... we cannot approve a system which allows a large minority of our population to live at a level of income which sinks lower and lower in comparison with the wage-earning majority .... Christians must be wary of trends which divide the nation into those who draw on social security and those who do not .... Welfare provision should not just be about directing benefits to the very poor. It should be concerned with justice for all citizens and any tendency to allow the development of a disenfranchised sub-class of those receiving benefit is unacceptable (ibid, paras 7.56, 7.57).

This report was debated by General Synod in 1987, and its conclusions about how services should be provided were firmly backed.

What does this involvement of a Church of England advisory body amount to? Impact can be measured in several ways. Firstly, the comments were part of a wider debate within the Church about poverty and disadvantage. In the discussion which has followed the publication of *Faith in the city* in particular, many congregations and individual Christians have found themselves having to think about wealth and poverty in a new way. Indeed, during the passage of the Social Security Bill, local churches of different denominations joined together to sign petitions expressing their concern. Secondly, many people outside the Church have realised that it has a role beyond encouraging individual spirituality or maintaining its own institutions. Many local authorities and secular voluntary organisations have seen an urgency and importance in the themes of *Faith in the city*. Thirdly, the Church's involvement has reminded politicians of the need to spell out the moral basis of political judgments hitherto dominated by economic arguments.

The Church and State in conflict?

The Church has not been without its critics. The fact that they have all come from the right is probably the most conclusive evidence of the Church's leftward drift. Critics from the political right have generally attacked the substance of Church pronouncements on social issues. Many of these criticisms merely echo the dogmas of monetarist economics (Anderson, 1984, chaps 1, 7, 9), but some have attempted a theological analysis. Griffiths (1984, pp 105–115), for instance, has argued that wealth creation is a creation ordinance, that capitalism is the only system which takes proper account of sin by ensuring that power is diffused, and that excessive reliance on state benefits undermines human creativity. Moreover, Oddie (1984, pp 123–133) has attacked the scriptural evidence which has been cited to demonstrate a divine bias to the poor.

A more widespread criticism has come from Conservative elements within the Church, and has focussed on the very desirability of Church involvement in political affairs. In addition to the better known critiques of politicians like John Gummer and Enoch Powell, the historian Edward Norman has attacked the politicisation of Christianity, 'the evaporation of any sense that religious tradition conveys a unique understanding of human life' (Norman, 1979, p 11) and its replacement by the uncritical acceptance by Church leaders of the ephemeral values of secular liberalism. Moreover, the Bishop of London has argued that the Church has lost its nerve, and has capitulated to the fashion for schemes of social reform, ignoring 'the dimension of eternity' by which means alone genuine personal regeneration can take place (Ionescu, 1982, pp 351–361). Lastly, the sociologist David Martin (1984, pp 134–142) has lamented the consequences of politicisation, arguing that the Church is increasingly behaving like a pressure group, a private association or a sect, instead of the *corpus Christianorum*, committed to timeless spiritual values, and rooted in Nation and history.

The criticisms especially of Church traditionalists have sparked off an unresolved debate on the political role of the Church. With increasing ideological pluralism in the welfare field, the 'middle axioms' of William Temple may no longer command a consensus either in society as a whole, or in the Church. A number of models of Church-State relations have been put forward, but all have their weaknesses (Plant, 1985, pp 313–336). The Christendom model, by which the Church develops an all-embracing political theology into which the state and all other institutions are fully absorbed, may have made sense in the Middle Ages, but has to find some way of coping with the Church's minority status in modern society. The pluralist view, that the Church has no authority beyond its own members, and the Conservative view, that the Church's duties reside solely in the spheres of individual salvation and personal morality, both offer little basis for public morality and the direction of public affairs. The Archbishop of York has argued that the Church's role might lay in the upholding of the values and institutions without which a pluralist society would disintegrate, though he admits that shared values are the fruits of consensus, not the basis of it (Habgood, 1983, p 33). Finally, the secularist view that the Church's role lies in underpinning political principles of secular origin ultimately founders on the spectre of the Church's role in Nazi Germany.

Where does this leave the Church of England at the end of the 1980s? We have seen that there are clear impediments to its effective involvement in the social policy arena. It represents a constituency which, until recently, was dwindling and still predominantly middle class. Moreover, its constitutional position maintains a set of public expectations about the Church's behaviour which do not include radical political involvement. Yet we have also seen how the Church has been able to exploit its position to become an effective critical commentator on Government policy, precisely because of its non-partisan character. Thus the parochial system still gives some clergy an intimate acquaintance with the lives of the poor, and this is enhanced by a Synodical structure which enables parts of the Church to develop a valuable expertise in social issues. Moreover, its constitutional position gives the

Church an access to, and an involvement in, the process of government which is denied to most pressure groups.

Finally, we have begun to examine the dilemma in which political involvement has placed the Church. The effectiveness of the Church's voice depends upon the breadth of the constituency which it can claim to represent. Yet the power of the Church's message depends upon the extent to which it is prepared to take a stand. The increasingly critical stance which it has taken towards Government policy, paralleled by an equally critical reception of its pronouncements by the Government and its supporters, both point to the demise of Christian consensus both in society at large, and in governments even of a Tory political persuasion. The Church can no longer rely on consensus, even in its own ranks, before it resolves to speak out on social issues, and act in the political arena. Its justification for so doing is coming less from its constitutional position, and more from the kind of theological inspiration described so forcefully by the BSR's current General Secretary, Prebendary John Gladwin.

> It is because this is God's world and he cared for it to the point of incarnation and crucifixion that we are inevitably committed to work for God's justice in the face of oppression, for God's truth in the face of lies and deceits, for service in the face of the abuse of power, for love in the face of selfishness, for co-operation in the face of destructive antagonism, and for reconciliation in the face of division and hostility. The motivating power is the love of Christ which has gripped our hearts and consciences (Gladwin, 1979, p 125).

The challenge for the Church lies first in how far it is prepared to follow through the implications of its own theology in laying aside the privileges of political respectability in favour of a radical identification with the poor and alienated, and secondly in the extent to which it can carry its own membership with it.

Notes

1 Though it is recognised that many other Christian denominations have become politically active in recent years, there are issues peculiar to the Church of England which derive from its unique position in the establishment, and which deserve special consideration. The scope of the article is limited accordingly.

2 I would like to give my warmest thanks to Alison Webster of the Church of England Board for Social Responsibility for all the help which she has given me in the production of this article.

References

Anderson, D (ed) (1984) *The kindness that kills.* SPCK,

Archbishop of Canterbury's Commission on Urban Priority Areas (ACUPA) (1985) *Faith in the city: a call for action by Church and Nation.* Church House Publishing.

Armstrong, A (1973) *The Church of England, the Methodists and Society.* University of London Press.

Ballinger, F (1988) Congregating care. *Community Care* 4 February. 18–19.

Bready, JW (1928) *Lord Shaftesbury and social-industrial progress.* Allen and Unwin.

Carey, G (1977) Falling structures. *Third Way* **1**(17) 13–15.

Chadwick, O (1966) (1970) *The Victorian Church.* 2 vols. Adam and Charles Black.

Cornwell P (1985) The Church of England and the State: changing constitutional links in historical perspective. In Moyser, G (ed) (1985) *Church and politics today: essays on the role of the Church of England.* T and T Clark.

Dodds, E and Webster, A (1988) Ministering angels. *Community Care* 26 May.

Ecclestone, G (1985) The General Synod and politics. In Moyser, G (ed) (1985) *Church and politics today: essays on the role of the Church of England.* T and T clark.

Forrester, DB (1985) *Christianity and the Future of Welfare.* Epworth Press.

General Synod Board for Social Responsibility (BSR) (1981) *The Church of England and politics.* CIO Publishing.

General Synod BSR (1982) *Housing and homelessness.* CIO Publishing.

General Synod BSR (1985) *Reform of social security.* BSR.

General Synod BSR (1986a) *And all that is unseen: a new look at women and work.* Church House Publishing.

General Synod BSR (1986b) *Not just for the poor: Christian perspectives on the welfare state.* Church House Publishing.

General Synod BSR (1987a) *Changing Britain: social diversity and moral unity.* Church House Publishing.

General Synod BSR (1987b) *A directory of resources in the Church of England.* BSR.

General Synod BSR (1988) *Church and community work.* BSR.

Gilbert, AD (1976) *Religion and society in industrial England.* Longman.

Gilbert, AD (1980) *The making of post-Christian Britain.* Longman.

Gladwin, J (1979) *God's people in God's world.* Inter-Varsity Press.

Griffiths, B (1984) Christianity and capitalism. In Anderson, D (ed) (1984) *The kindness that kills.* SPCK.

Gutierrez G (1974) *A theology of liberation.* SCM Press.

Habgood, J (1983) *Church and nation in a secular age.* Darton, Longman and Todd.

Hall, M P and Howes, I V (1965) *The Church in social work.* Routledge and Kegan Paul.

Hastings, A (1986) *A history of English Christianity, 1920–1985.* Collins.

Heasman, K (1962) *Evangelicals in action*. Geoffrey Bles.
Inglis, K S (1963) *Churches and the working class in Victorian England*. Routledge and Kegan Paul.
Ionescu, G (1982) Speaking notes with the Bishop of London on how and why the Church might be losing its nerve and its role in the modern society. *Government and Opposition* **17**, (3): 351–61.
Jenkins, D (1985) A theology for the liberation of tomorrow's Britian. *Guardian* 15 April.
Jones, P d'A (1968) *The Christian Socialist revival, 1877–1914*. Princeton, Princeton University Press.
Kitson-Clarke, G (1973) *Churchmen and the condition of England, 1832–1885*. Methuen.
Leech, K (1982) Is the Church of England really moving to the left? *Marxism Today* October. 16–9.
Martin, D (1984) The Church of England: from established Church to secular lobby. In Anderson, D (ed) (1984) Political participation and attitudes in the Church of England. *Government and Opposition*. **13** (1): 81–93.
Medhurst, K and Moyser, G (1985) Lambeth Palace, the bishops and politics. In Moyser, G (ed) (1985) *Church and politics today: essays on the role of the Church of England in contemporary politics*. T and T Clark.
Miller, W L and Raab, G (1977) The religious alignment at English elections between 1918 and 1970. *Political Studies* **25** (2): 227–51.
Moltmann, J (1974) *The crucified God*. SCM Press.
Moyser, G (ed) (1985) *Church and politics today: essays on the role of the Church of England in contemporary politics*. T and T Clark.
Moyser, G (1985) The Church of England and politics: patterns and trends. In Moyser, G (ed) (1985) *Church and politics today: essays on the role of the Church of England in contemporary politics*. T and T Clark.
Mudie-Smith, R (ed) (1904) *The religious life of London*. Hodder and Stoughton.
Norman E (1976) *Church and society in England, 1770–1970*. The Clarendon Press.
Norman E (1979) *Christianity and the world order*. Oxford University Press.
Oddie, W (1984) Christian Socialism: an old heresy? In Anderson, D (ed) (1984) *The kindness that kills*. SPCK.
Parkin, F (1968) *Middle class radicalism*. Manchester University Press.
Paul, L (1964) *The development and payment of the clergy*. Church Information Office.
Perkin, H (1969) *The origins of modern English society, 1780–1880*. Routledge and Kegan Paul.
Plant, R (1985) The Anglican Church and the secular state. In Moyser, G (ed) (1985) *Church and politics today: essays on the role of the Church of England in contemporary politics*. T and T Clark.
Preston, R H (1979) *Religion and the persistence of capitalism*. SCM Press.
Reader, W J (1966) *Professional men: the rise of the professional class in nineteenth century England*. Weidenfeld and Nicolson.

Sheppard, D (1983) *Bias to the Poor*. Hodder and Stoughton.

Sider, R J (1977) *Rich Christians in an age of hunger*. Hodder and Stoughton.

Sleeman, J (1985) The Church and economic policy. In Moyser, G (ed) (1985) *Church and politics today: essays on the role of the Church of England in contemporary politics*. T and T Clark.

Soloway, R A (1969) *Prelates and people*. Routledge and Kegan Paul.

Stott, J (1984) *Issues facing Christians today*. Marshall, Morgan and Scott.

Sugden, G (1977) The Kingdom and the kingdom. *Third Way* **1** (13). 6–9; (14): 3–6.

Temple, W (1950) *Christianity and social order*. 3rd edn, SCM Press.

Towler, R and Coxon, A P M (1979) *The fate of the Anglican clergy: a sociological study*. Methuen.

Wald, K D (1983) *Crosses on the ballot: patterns of British voter alignment since 1885*. Princeton: Princeton University Press.

Welsby, P (1985) *How the Church of England works*. Church Information Office.

Wheale, G (1985) *The parish and politics*. In Moyser, G (ed) (1985) *Church and politics today: essays on the role of the Church of England in contemporary politics*. T and T Clark.

Wilson, S A (1986) Towards a black theology of liberation. In *Anglicans and Racism*. BSR.

Wright D (1977) Ethics and the Old Testament: the jubilee. *Third Way* **1** (11): 3–5.

Yates, J and Gladwin, J (1988) Open letter to the Prime Minister, 27 May 1988. BSR.